LEADERSHIP DEFINED

INSIGHT PUBLISHING
SEVIERVILLE, TENNESSEE

LEADERSHIP DEFINED

Published by Insight Publishing Company
P.O. Box 4189
Sevierville, Tennessee 37864

10 9 8 7 6 5 4 3 2

Printed in Canada

ISBN: 1-932863-10-9

Table Of Contents

A Message From The Publisher

Our world is becoming more and more technical every day. Almost every task associated with business activity involves multiple layers of technology. Millions of dollars are spent annually by businesses in an effort to improve bottom line results through the use of technology. Does it help? Of course. Can we live without it? Absolutely not. Are we missing something along the way? You bet!

One of the most critical issues related to business and personal success has nothing to do with technology. It involves the human brain and the human heart. It's *leadership*. And without solid leadership, all the technological advances in the world won't save a struggling organization.

Leadership has been the topic of thousands of books, but it is still a subject worth studying. We don't teach leadership skills in our public schools so children don't grow up with an awareness of what it means to be a good, or bad, leader. Men and women enter the work force without any real understanding of how leadership impacts their personal lives or the health of their company. Because of this, organizations around the world lose billions of dollars annually, not because their products won't sell, but because their leaders won't lead.

And so it is with great pride that we offer you *Leadership Defined*. In these pages, you will meet men and women who know what it means to lead and can offer you and your organization ideas and strategies to help you develop great leaders in the future. We hope you'll read every chapter with a highlighter in your hand—take notes, share your book with colleagues and with your management and ownership team. You'll find real treasure here.

Interviews conducted by:

David E. Wright
President, International Speakers Network

Chapter 1

ALEXANDER M. HAIG, JR.

THE INTERVIEW

David E. Wright (Wright)

General Haig really needs no introduction as he is among the most decorated military and civilian figures of our times. In addition to his military accomplishments, General Haig has held a number of key positions in political and business leadership and presently serves as Chairman of Worldwide Associates, Inc., an international advisory firm based in Washington, D.C. He is a senior advisor to United Technologies Corporation, a corporation for which he served as President and Chief Operating Officer, 1979-1981. In addition, he is the host of the weekly television program, "World Business Review." General Haig is perhaps best known as United States Secretary of State under President Ronald Reagan, appointed by the President-elect and confirmed by the United States Senate. However, many are familiar with General Haig's reputation as a paragon of statesmanship with the mental and tactical genius befitting a four-star general, and the consummate diplomacy of a master negotiator at the highest levels of the public and private sectors. General Haig, welcome to *Leadership Defined*.

Alexander M. Haig, Jr. (Haig)

Thank you very much. It's great to be with you David.

Wright

Before we get into some of the questions that I have prepared, knowing how you worked for President Reagan, his funeral was very difficult for the nation. How did you view that whole funeral that the United States people got to share in?

Haig

In hindsight now that the emotional side of the funeral is fading, I think one of the event's greatest satisfactions to me is that the President was so widely recognized for his accomplishments as a leader of our nation. That recognition was universal regardless of party. Some of the positive tone in the liberal press was unfortunately a product of their recognizing that critical or unacceptable analyses would not be welcomed by the majority of American readers. That's true of the networks as well. So they were on their good behavior after a few forays in the opposite direction. Having said that, I think really it gave us all an opportunity to reflect on the great accomplishments of this wonderful leader and the superb achievements he realized during his brief eight-year incumbency.

Wright

You know I felt really good about the entire funeral process. I thought honoring him that way was something that I think the American people really, really wanted to do. But I did read two or three columns that kind of offended me that so soon after his passing they would write negative articles about the President.

Haig

I had one interrogation on CNN where the interrogator said, in effect, "You left the President, so you obviously had differences. Would you tell us what his shortcomings were?" And I replied, "If I thought he had shortcomings, which I didn't, you'd be the last person I'd give them to. Furthermore, at this time, the question is very inappropriate in any event."

Wright

Well, great!

Haig

And so he got rather apologetic. I was naughty on that occasion.

Wright

Well, you deserved to be. Most men and women of my generation are familiar with your career, General. We watched you advance in the military and go onto play a vital role in the Vietnam ceasefire and the return of the U.S. prisoners of war. We remember that part you played in President Nixon's historic opening to China. We've watched you on the world stage as Secretary of State under Ronald Reagan, after your distinguished service as NATO Commander. There may be, however, a segment of our population that does not understand the depth of your contribution to the United States and the world for that matter. Before we move into a discussion focused on the topic of leadership, would you look back over your career and tell us how you feel about the life you've lived? In other words, what aspect of your life gives you the most satisfaction?

Haig

I think, basically, I look back with gratitude to the Almighty for having exposed me to the great array of historic events that I participated in, and that is from the first day of my military service, with my close exposure to Douglas MacArthur in Tokyo and later during the Korean War including the landing in Inchon and finally evacuation on a stretcher in late 1951 following the Chinese Intervention. In addition to the Korean War, I witnessed every major historic event up until quite recently. I participated in the Cuban missile crisis at the highest level in the Pentagon and in Vietnam where I commanded a battalion of infantry and a brigade of infantry of the First Infantry Division in '66 and '67 at the height of the war. Beyond that, of course, serving as President Reagan's first Secretary of State, as well as my time with Presidents Nixon, Ford and Carter.

But I think I really look back mostly at my beginnings, and that was to be part of a family unit in which we had strong Christian convictions under a father who was a high Episcopalian and a very ardent one, and a mother who was a devout Roman Catholic. They say, "never the twain shall meet." But in this case it did! As a result, my father became a Catholic and was really the most devout of any member of the family. He instilled strong Christian convictions in our entire family. My mother lived by them, as well, showing great respect and love for her husband who died when she was in her thirties.

I was only nine years old. He was also an extremely successful lawyer in Philadelphia, so our life's expectations suddenly changed dramatically. At that time my mother didn't even know how to keep a checkbook. She had to take over a family that had more debt than assets because my father had been such a generous provider. Nevertheless, she educated her only daughter, in the law, graduating from the University of Pennsylvania. My sister became a very successful lawyer. My younger brother became a Jesuit Priest, a highly regarded educator, a nuclear and astronautical physicist. He also was the President of two Jesuit universities and he is still teaching at Loyola University in Baltimore.

Of course my greatest joy these days is anchored to my wonderful wife, Patricia, who like my mother had to fill in for me because of my frequent absences and the outrageous hours I keep. She did a superb job and today I have three wonderful children and eight grandchildren. My oldest son is like my father and sister, a lawyer. He is working with me in my many varied business activities. My second son is a best selling author who has just completed his fifth novel that will be released by Warner Books early next year. He was a West Point trained infantry officer and was one of the Army's top strategic planners. Finally, my daughter, Barbara, is a senior executive in the National Endowment for Democracy located in our nation's Capital. She has dedicated her life to the promotion of democratic values worldwide.

Wright

Hmmm, that's a varied career.

Haig

As a youth as World War II was approaching, I saw the military as my best hope for the future. From my early years, I also had a very keen interest in national security and foreign affairs. Then, as today, our service academies provided great opportunities for young men and today for women including those who come from less than affluent backgrounds. I was admitted to West Point and graduated in 1947. I look back on those experiences with the utmost satisfaction.

I am, of course, also thankful for the opportunity to be a witness in such a span of history, working for Presidents Kennedy, Johnson, Nixon, Ford, Carter, and Reagan. That's six presidents, four of whom called me by my first name. I think few Americans have had more rewarding experiences.

Wright

You know of all of the accomplishments, I'm certainly impressed with one that I hadn't realized before. You were actually on General MacArthur's staff, were you not?

Haig

Indeed I was. I worked with his Chief of Staff, Lt. General "Ned" Almond and worked almost daily with General MacArthur himself. I frequently carried papers back and forth from his office and briefed him on the battlefield situation each evening during the early weeks of the Korean War. I saw firsthand an individual who I consider to be one of the finest leaders I have ever known.

Wright

Yes,

Haig

Few people appreciate the lessons that one learns from close contact with such men. I sat just outside the conference room door, during the meeting between Douglas MacArthur and the Joint Chiefs of Staff, who had been sent by President Truman to Tokyo to tell MacArthur he should not execute the Inchon Landing. During this meeting each service chief one way or another said that they couldn't support the operation. The one that was the least negative was Admiral Sherman, the Chief of Naval Operations. MacArthur sat there silently during each of their presentations. When they finished he stood up, carefully put his pipe in the ashtray before him, looked directly at the assembled leaders, and said, "Gentlemen, I will land at Inchon on the 15th of September or you will have a new commander in the Far East." He then slowly walked out of the room. The opposition completely collapsed under what I would describe as the towering character of a rare individual who would rather be right than simply keep his job.

Wright

Right!

Haig

And that's a very important principle of leadership forgotten so often by many of our contemporary leaders.

Wright

We're discussing leadership principles from a variety of perspectives today. I'd be very interested in hearing your thoughts on the <u>character of a leader</u>. Do you think people are born hardwired to be good leaders or can it be taught?

Haig

This is a classic and very relevant question. I've thought about it many times. My answer would be <u>both</u>. Some are gifted with strong leadership traits and certainly MacArthur and Ronald Reagan fit that mold in every respect. Some, however, have acquired their talents through study and diligence. They recognize that they can learn and develop leadership principles if they study and analyze those traits demonstrated by the more gifted. Both the gifted and the less gifted can always improve their leadership skills and seek to do so by constant attention to building sound leadership traits. This is what our service academies attempt to accomplish. It is also what all of our schools should teach and emphasize especially in professions where leadership is essential.

Wright

You know with the recent corporate scandals still fresh in our memories, a million people today think that we're experiencing a leadership crisis in America. I've been thinking about how different America was in past generations. Fathers led their families with a firm discipline and many men attended military school as youngsters. Our national leaders presented a model that most men and women admired. Even the wars we fought in the past fostered great leaders. Things are very different now. General Haig, do you have any thoughts or theories about the status of leadership in America today?

Haig

I think, David, we've all thought about this as we watched some of the modern tendencies emerge. There are many complex contributors to this in my view. One, above all, would be the breakdown of the family unit in America. Sometimes that's not the choice of the parents involved but the product of necessity in modern society. In these cases frequently it results in failure to instill traditional family values and principles. But there are other factors. One, of course, is today's educational process. History has become a lost art. Political theory is seldom taught. The study of political theory refines for its students the proven universal principles of human conduct and behavior. Take for example some of our liberal education today. It seems to focus less on teaching classical values highlighted in the study of political theory, and emphasizes what works at the moment in a purely pragmatic sense. That approach emphasizes what's of contemporary utility rather than what's right. The second major contributor, I think, is the explosion in information sciences and its impact, some of which is good, but some of which has had a deleterious impact on modern society. It has created the "modern populist" in government, in business, in education, and in other leadership positions around America. Populism has produced the fellow who gets up every morning, puts his finger to the wind, and says, "What's going to make me popular today?" He then rushes to deliver. Too many leaders today are populists, especially among contemporary political leaders. This style also affects their subordinates. It has produced a character who tends to tell the boss what he thinks the boss wishes to hear rather than what he should hear. We see a lot of that in government today. And that's why presidents who become isolated by the sycophants within their staffs, risk not knowing what's really going on in the country.

Wright

I recently had an opportunity to go into the attic and I found my old University of Tennessee catalog that I got when I started in 1957, and I looked at the course outlines for the four years in my college education. And I compared it with the ones today. And I mean badminton and ping pong just doesn't seem to make it, you know. You get credits for the strangest things in our universities today and you don't have to take as many hours.

Haig

I agree with you. You know I think back to Winston Churchill who was asked by a group of students after the end of World War II, "Mr. Prime Minister, how did you learn statecraft?" And he replied, "Read history, young man. Read history, because only through a knowledge of history can you begin to open the secrets of statecraft." We have forgotten that in today's educational system.

Wright

If you don't mind, I'd like to go back to your time on active duty in Vietnam. Were there significant events that took place while you were overseas fighting for America that shaped you as a leader or influenced your effectiveness as a political statesman for example?

Haig

Unquestionably. There is nothing more intense than having responsibility for the lives of young men and women in battle. I think one of the characteristics resulting from that experience was the <u>requirement to communicate</u>. And I mean the need to communicate continuously, time permitting. If you do that as a military leader especially, but also as a corporate leader or a political leader, then those who you are responsible for will tend to follow you when time doesn't permit you to communicate. They will recognize that were time available you would explain everything because they learned to count on you to do that.

Another principle is to remember that <u>a flawed policy adopted on time is better than a perfect policy decided too late</u>. Perhaps most importantly you must be able to separate the problems from the facts. Take for example those who have been critical of what they think is the policy of globalism. The truth is that globalism <u>is not a policy</u>. Rather, <u>it's a fact</u>. Today we live in a world that is increasingly interdependent, politically, and economically and in every other sense of the word, even in moral and security terms. In sum, you must learn to accept and to work with <u>facts</u> while you must solve problems with appropriate policies. So, what our leaders must do is learn to work with "globalism" and to do so in a way that best suits the interests of our people. These are the things that combat experience taught me. But they also come from government and business experience.

Finally, too frequently among some of the six presidents I've served at close range, loyalty seemed to be a question of "what did you do for me today?" The real obligation of loyalty is to remember that it goes down more importantly than it goes up. And oddly enough, and you'll be surprised at this, the President that I knew well that was most heavily imbued with the principle of loyalty was Richard Nixon. There was never a day that I spoke to that man—and I did every day—that he didn't inquire about my family, or apologize for placing me in the position he did during the height of Watergate. In general he was the most solicitous of all of the presidents I served. It is very important that leaders remember that <u>loyalty must go down as well as go up.</u>

Wright

You mentioned Nixon. If I could and if he were alive, I'd vote for him again today. I think he was a great president. Many Americans have become fans of the hit television show, *The West Wing.*

Haig

Oh, boy!

Wright

I find the behind the scenes aspect of the show fascinating. You spent many years in the White House serving Presidents Nixon, Ford and Reagan. Your role as Chief of Staff in 1973 is particularly relevant to today's discussion on leadership. Are there lessons that you learned serving with the top decision makers in the free world that our readers can apply to their role as business leaders?

Haig

I think frequently it is important to avoid what I call the exclusive preoccupation with expediency. You can't always look for something that will chase the wolf away today. You also must think about the long-term interests of the corporation or any institution. And sometimes that requires you to do things that are very unpopular. Take Mr. Reagan's Presidency, where he had to start out and create the impression of a two-gun cowboy. He knew that our hostages in Iran had inflicted a mortal blow on American credibility throughout the Middle East and he was determined that he was going to obtain their release. During the transition then-Secretary of State Ed Muskey came to me and asked if the Democrats could get the President-elect's okay to continue the negotiations with Tehran for another six months. And I said, "Well, I haven't had a chance to talk to President Reagan and I'll do so immediately, but, if you need your answer now, you can tell the Iranians that the President-elect has made it clear to me that with the first moment of his Presidency, if those prisoners have not been released, it will be an entirely new ballgame." I then rushed over to the Blair House to talk to the President to be sure he was comfortable with what I had said. He looked at me, smiled and said, "Al, I think you were a little bit <u>too soft</u>." You'll recall that those prisoners were released minutes before he commenced his Inaugural Address.

That began a process of re-establishing American credibility. Our attacks on Libya, Panama, Grenada, and the other actions that he took early on created a whole new and greatly needed respect for his foreign policies. Before his inauguration, we had discussed the fact that the Soviets were in an advanced state of decay. Unfortunately, they also believed America was soft and wouldn't fight if need be. The credibility that President Reagan established in those early days of his presidency enabled us years later to witness the collapse of the Soviet system and the liberation of Eastern Europe without a shot being fired. This is the same challenge we as a nation face in the struggle with global terrorism today. We simply must re-establish America's credibility in the struggle with Islamic extremism.

Wright

I can remember when the prisoners were freed, and I remember the pride that I had just as a citizen. And I remember that I laid all of that right at the feet of Ronald Reagan. I gave him the mental credit for that.

Haig

You were absolutely right. And another characteristic that he showed at that time was not to rush over to Europe and take full credit for it, but to ask former President Carter to go to Europe and receive our prisoners in Germany. So he wasn't thirsting for the credit.

Wright

Are you at liberty to share one or two specific historical examples of when you and those around you in the White House were forced to exercise extreme leadership qualities under pressure?

Haig

One always is subjective on such matters. And the first thing I'd like to touch upon was the day President Reagan was shot. The Cabinet and staff members were assembled in the White House Situation Room. All knew the President was seriously wounded, but after checking with the Chief of Staff who was at the hospital, we decided not to invoke the 25th Amendment and not to consider designating the Vice President as Acting President. This was a unanimous Cabinet group decision. (Later confirmed by the Vice President). Subsequently, we learned the Secretary of Defense had altered our nuclear alert status from a normal "DEFCON" to a higher level of alert, which could easily be picked up by both the press, and the Soviets.

We also observed on national television the acting press secretary telling the press assembled in the White House that he didn't know if we had changed our alert status or who was administering the government with the President wounded and Vice President in the air and out of town. I then rushed to the pressroom with the National Security Advisor to be sure friend and foe knew we had a functioning government, especially since the Secretary of Defense had changed our nuclear alert, which was probably known to the Soviets with very dangerous potential consequences. During the press conference I told the press (and friends and foe) that our government was being administered by a Cabinet Group under me as the Senior Cabinet Member and that we were on our normal alert status. Just afterwards, Dan Rather on CBS attacked me on CBS television claiming I thought I was next in line to be President. This had been triggered by a senior member of the White House Staff and has been the subject of a recent totally inaccurate TV film. Recently, I have learned that before that fateful press conference, Soviet nuclear forces were at their highest state of alert, but returned to normal just after my presentation. I still get lambasted for that pressroom appearance. Believe me, under similar circumstances, I would do it again. As I've gone around the world, leaders in many capitols have said to me, "Thank God you did what you did."

Wright
Well, that was my take on it. Of course, I've heard it a thousand times since you said it, but I took a different view. I thought, "Thank God he's in charge."

Haig
Dan Rather had a cute way of editing what I said then bringing in two professors from colleges in New York City to confirm that I didn't know the line of succession.

Wright
They were giving us a civics lesson.

Haig
But as usual you always have to remember that the press sometimes is rather evil in its own right. But more often than not, is triggered by some insidious character right in the president's own family—leakers with other axes to grind. Now the second incident

worth noting was the Christmas bombing during the Vietnam War. You recall it was very controversial, and that we had bombed Hanoi and Haiphong, using B-52s and against massive opposition from the Congress. Before long, they were threatening impeachment and removal of the President. Even the President's most ardent supporters within his staff finally caved in and said to the President, "You've got to cease." At the same time the North Vietnamese blinked and said they wanted to resume the talks in Paris. I was opposed and urged the President to continue to bomb until we had an agreement that Hanoi would totally withdraw from South Vietnam. Unfortunately, the political pressure was overwhelming, and the President was forced to halt the bombing and resume negotiations. And I have said to other Presidents since then, "Mr. President better you be impeached for doing what is right for our people." So I hope that people will understand that the pressures the United States is under today in the Iraq War are not unprecedented. There are those that are now suggesting that we get out of Iraq. They should remember we didn't win a battle in World War II until over a year after we entered it. We lost an armored division at Kasserine Pass and Anzio was a disaster. There were many other failures as well, but we didn't have the American press nor political opponents condemning the President, calling him a liar, and a cheat, and a dissembler. I am confident we are doing the right thing in the war on terrorism, and history will confirm that. Of course we have done some of it in a flawed way, which is not uncommon. We have to be more patient. But what is now at stake is the belief among many Americans, aided and abetted by the liberal press in America, that because there were flaws in the way we did the right thing, <u>we shouldn't have done the right thing in the first place</u>. And that's the great danger that we are now confronting.

Wright

Because many of the old international walls have come down in the past 20 years, some Americans don't remember how extraordinary it was when President Nixon visited China in February of 1972. You were instrumental in making this trip a success, which leads me to the topic of negotiating, strategy, and détente in relationship to leadership. What lessons can you share with American business professionals based on your experience in world politics?

Haig

A very important lesson is patience. We spent almost two years with the great skills of Henry Kissinger and all of the National Security Council team sending signals back and forth to China, some of whch were rebuffed. Now, we all know, Ronald Reagan was indispensable to the victory in the Cold War, but he didn't win that war single handedly. That was a process that was inevitable over time because of the internal contradictions and flawed character of Marxist Leninism. Everybody who has studied history knew that, and certainly Ronald Reagan above all knew that. When I first discussed the Soviet Union with him, he said he also agreed with me that the Soviets were failing. He also noted as history confirms that when totalitarian regimes are in an advanced state of decay, they are the most dangerous because they lash out seeking to divert the peoples' attention. And so he said, "First, Al, we have to re-establish American credibility," which had been so damaged by the previous administration due to the hostage crisis and other mistakes. This as I said dominated his handling of the hostage crisis with Iran. We also had Libya. We had Panama. We had Grenada. As a result, Mr. Gorbechev realized that he was not only confronting failure, but a resolute new America that was willing to fight for its values. Ronald Reagan did this by his firm policies and clearheaded decision-making. He brought about the end of the Cold War without firing a shot. We should be careful that we don't claim more than we've earned and that we keep that victory in focus because in the process of over simplifying, we don't make the late-President look nearly as thoughtful as he really was.

Wright

So this was a matter of teamwork over many years?

Haig

Many years, and it was contributed to by almost every American president. Some did it successfully like President Reagan; some did it less than successfully. But by staying together and by using détente as a shield in the nuclear age, together with the recognition that communism would ultimately fail of its own internal contradictions. Reagan also realized that negotiations were far better than a nuclear war. Happily our leaders managed to stand together with those who shared our values especially in Europe and NATO, to unify and create the coalition of deterrence that brought about a victory for all.

Wright

General Haig, can you tell us how you're using your leadership experience during this exciting phase of your career? I understand you advise a number of corporate leaders. What kind of impact do you have in the private sector?

Haig

Like most human endeavors sometimes I'm successful, sometimes I'm not heard, and sometimes it's good I'm not. I think the two most important things I can reflect on would be that I believed years ago that the world is changing and we must work with these facts or changes. The world was becoming more interdependent, or as we call it today, more global, and that the future of the corporations and American businesses require expanding our horizons into international trade and commerce. Again, that this was a fact and not a policy choice to be made or rejected.

Wright

I noted that you have had significant influence in academic circles having served in a variety of leadership roles for schools such as Princeton, Tulane, and Yale, and such think tanks as the Foreign Policy Research Institute in Philadelphia. You also lecture at colleges and universities across America. Do you believe our universities are doing an acceptable job preparing men and women to lead?

Haig

First let me say this in general. We have great standards especially in higher education. America is the best in the world by far, and that's why foreign students are streaming to our shores despite political differences. But again I would say there is not a sufficient amount of attention to the wisdom of the ages, which only comes through an intimate knowledge of political theory. All our quests for knowledge are quests for the truth, and the truth is very hard to arrive at in a universal sense because of the constantly changing environment in which these values mature. So we've got to get back to a point where we don't just teach what the professors might think is currently successful by looking at the world as a snapshot in time. That to me is the most serious educational flaw that we face today in both lower and higher education. All of the other things that we've talked about—family, values, and principles—are, of course, an intimate part of this need. So I guess I'm a little old fashioned and I believe in the lessons of yesterday.

Wright

You know I talked to one of your associates earlier this week and quite frankly just asked him, "Is it going to be easy to get along with General Haig? Am I going to be smart enough to talk to this man? And he laughed. He said, "Yes." He said, "What kind of questions are you going to ask him?" I told him a few, and he said, "You really need to ask him about his nine commandments of leadership," which I had no knowledge of. So I hope I'm not taking you by surprise, but I would love for you to share these nine commandments of leadership for our readers.

Haig

All right. Well, David, I'll keep these short because I've given you some of the examples already in what we've said. So the first, of course, would be integrity, and that is a leader must mean what he says and say what he means. I suppose the second rule would be what we've already discussed rather ad nauseam and that's loyalty. Good leaders know it goes down as well as up. Rule three I talked about, communication. I won't say any more rather than the fact that if you communicate, you lead. If you just order in martinet fashion, it's very hard to do that except by fear, and that's not the way traditional American leadership excels. Rule four is follow and demonstrate the courage of your convictions like MacArthur did when he said, "I either land in Inchon because I know the theater better than you fellows, and it's the right thing to do. If you disagree, get yourself another leader." I have resigned from three presidencies on principle, and I would do it again. The fifth is to welcome dissent. I usually, whether it was in business or in the military, bring in the implementers including those that are at the cutting edge of implementation. That usually involves going down to the younger people. If you listen only to the older or more senior executives you risk talking to the sycophants. So always try to get down on to the floor at the cutting edge of your business whether it's a shop floor or whether it's a marketing structure where the guys are in the trenches, so to speak. Talk to them regularly, listen to them, and shape your policies in accordance with their hands-on experience. Rule six is work hard. There's nothing for nothing in this world. But also remember that old adage of "All work and no play make Jack a dull boy." So be sure your people understand that and pursue policies that provide exercise and recreation. I've talked about rule seven—decide carefully but in a timely fashion. I've belabored that already too much, but it's very important. And of course, rule eight I've talked about already and that's avoid populism. Don't be a finger in the wind leader. And finally rule nine is professionalism. We haven't talked about that, but it's critically important for whatever discipline you work in that you know your business and that comes from constant reading, constant study, constant interface with other experts in the field, to be sure you know the latest thinking, the latest developments, as well as the principles that guide the discipline you're involved with.

Wright

Boy, those are great. Our readers and I thank you. General Haig, our time together has really been a sincere pleasure for me. Before we let you go, do you have any closing remarks for our readers?

Haig

I think the most important is to be very leery of instantaneous press reporting in the modern world. We've seen it in instance after instance. The most recent was that there was no connection whatsoever between Saddam Hussein and al Qaeda when the facts are really to the contrary as the 9/11 Commission concluded. Every scholarly assessment that I've read, including the most recent, *The Secret History of the Iraq War*, by Yossef Bodansky, presents a remarkable confirmation of the interrelationship of all terrorist activities. The father of terrorism was none other than the Marxist-Leninist Soviet Russia. They're the ones that taught all of the techniques and principles that the terrorists are adhering to today. So these are the things that I think are the most important. Also, stay behind our leaders and have the vision to recognize these dangers. This is a global conflict. It's going to go on for a long, long time. There are going to be setbacks as well as victories. But ultimately this great nation, if we work in concert with our allies abroad, those who share our values, we are going to triumph and the world will be the beneficiary.

Wright

As I stated in the beginning, it has been an honor to welcome you, General Alexander Haig, to *Leadership Defined*. You just don't know how much I appreciate the time that you've spent with me here today, and I'm sure that our readers are going to get a tremendous amount of information from this. Thank you so much, sir.

Haig

Thank you very much.

General Haig is a voice of authority and experience, having served as White House Chief of Staff for President Nixon, NATO Commander (1974-79), Secretary of State (1981-82), corporate leader, scholar, teacher, diplomat and military leader. He is host of his own weekly television program, World Business Review, and is a regular commentator on the war on terrorism, Iraq and North Korea, having been seen recently on programs such as Hardball and Hannity and Colmes.

General Haig is the author of two books: *Caveat: Realism, Reagan and Foreign Policy (1984)*, and his autobiography, *Inner Circles: How America Changed the World A Memoir (1992)*. He is married to the former Patricia Fox. The Haigs are the parents of three children and have eight grandchildren.

Chapter 2

DR. JOHN MYERS

THE INTERVIEW

David E. Wright (Wright)
Today we are talking to John Myers. John Myers is a leader. This is proven time and time again throughout his life. His earliest leadership roles and development took shape when he led the student bodies of both his junior and senior high schools. It continues today as he provides leadership for clients both in the for-profit and not-for-profit worlds. Dr. Myers' experience and training is primarily in the humanities—values, character, media, interpersonal communications, business ethics, and personal motivation. He holds degrees from Purdue University (Mass Communications), Duke University (Theology and Psychology), and United Theological Seminary (International Relations). John's company, Greater Things Enterprises, provides motivational keynotes, seminars, products, and services across America in the areas of vision, leadership, networking, marketing, and strategic planning. He is also the Founder and Executive Director of the Greater Things Institute. John is a motivational expert. His life experiences and signature stories illustrate with entertaining energy the principles of how to be a leader that affects positive change. Dr. Myers is a solicitor for the Wealth Management

Corporation of Newport Beach, California. Dr. Myers, welcome to *Leadership Defined*!

Dr. John Myers (Myers)

Thank you very much, David. I appreciate it.

Wright

John, you have it seems always been a leader. Could you tell our readers about your earliest leadership lessons, and how that has affected your leadership practices today?

Myers

Well, some people are born leaders, but all leaders have to be shaped by experience and mentors. My early experiences, such as in junior high when I was elected as the president of the Student Body, help illustrate being given the power of office without the necessary training to hold office with excellence. In fact, I was totally clueless about what it was to be a leader. I was honored that my peers thought I could lead. I was given a lot of authority. The principal gave me a key to my own office. I thought I was pretty hot stuff. I could even write my own hall passes.

The *leadership lesson* that I learned was that to be a leader you've got to have, you must have, integrity. No one sees what you are doing half the time, so you have to be disciplined and straight on in order to lead with excellence. I learned the hard way because I abused some of my leadership privileges. I'd write hall passes when I didn't need to be out of class. I'd go to my office and just sit around and think I was doing some pretty interesting things, but then I realized how empty it felt not to have integrity. And I learned at that point that to be a really good leader, you can't behave that way. You've got to have integrity.

Later on in high school, I decided to run for the president of the Student Body for the senior class. We had about 1,000 students in my class, and my campaign theme was "Elect John R. Myers. The R stands for Reliable." Corny, I know, but it worked. There were six candidates vying for a position in a class of nearly a 1,000 students. I was elated when I was elected, and I'll never forget telling my father. It was one of the proudest moments of my life when I met him on the golf course in 1974 and told him the good news. He was so proud. And of course, that made me extremely happy as his son.

The *Leadership Lesson* that I learned as the Senior High Class President was the significant art of building a strong team and the art of delegation. The vice principal of the school taught me this lesson. I've been able to utilize that ever since. It was probably the most important leadership lesson that I could learn at that time in my life and easy to apply.

Wright

So your father was an entrepreneur and businessman in Marion, Indiana, where you were brought up. What did you learn working in the business from your father, Bill?

Myers

Working in our family business was a great experience. Dad owned five restaurants, a car wash, and a dairy bar! He was a great entrepreneur and manager. In fact, in the early 1960s, he invented something that is now in use in every fast food restaurant across America—The Drive-Through Window.

Wright

Ah, you're kidding!

Myers

Nope, it's a fact. One day dad noticed that there were two cars sitting in the parking lot of the Thrifty-Chef. This was our restaurant with the drive through window. He went outside to ask what the men in the two cars were doing. One driver said, "Oh, I work for McDonald's. I've been assigned to study how much business you do using that window." The other driver said, "Oh, I work for Burger Chef. I've been assigned to see how much business you do using that drive through window." And the rest is literally restaurant history. Dad told me the story several years later. I asked him, "Did you patent the window?" He said, "I didn't know it would be that popular."

The *Leadership Lesson* that I learned from my father was "be a visionary, be inventive, find a need and fill it, and patent inventive ideas." Another *Leadership Lesson* that I learned was that no task is too small. Dad taught me this when I was age 12. I wanted to go to work so I could earn some spending money. I thought I'd start out by cooking in the kitchen. Not quite! Dad started me out with a stick that had a nail at the end of it. The mission was to pick up trash every morning throughout the property and mow the grass once a week. The lesson was if you don't pick up the trash properly, you shred the leftover trash with the mower and have to pick the shredded trash up by hand. Or, you do the job right the first time and you won't waste time cleaning up after yourself. I graduated from trash man and lawn mower to the soda fountain at age 14, then fry cook at age 16, assistant manager at 18, and then I went to college.

The *Leadership Lessons* learned from my dad really was that 1) no job is too small, 2) every job is important, 3) every person doing a job is important, 4) being the boss's son means that you work extra hard to earn respect because everyone thinks you already have it easy, 5) and thank God for a good family and for the fun of being in business.

So those were the lessons that I learned, but I also learned something about managing people. My father taught me these things. Over the years I've recognized these lessons as I've reflected on how to treat people in his employment. The first one is never judge anyone. The second one is always respect everyone. Third, find the intrinsic good in each person. Fourth, celebrate their worth and value. Fifth, help them discover greater things in their lives. Sixth, encourage them to move upward and onward to do greater things for others as well as themselves.

Wright

You know Purdue University recognized your leadership skills and awarded you a full scholarship for leadership and vocal performance. You were a tenor soloist with the Purdue Varsity Glee Club, the official ambassadors of the university. You won several awards and were placed in several key leadership roles during your tenure at Purdue. So tell me, what are some of the key leadership lessons that you learned during these formative years?

Myers

One was that you really must lead by example. You've got to walk the talk. Another one is that you lead with talent. If you've got talent, you should use it. Don't hide it under a bushel. The third one is always lead with compassion. Care about the people that you're working with or leading. And another one is to develop and define the network. I learned so much about how to network with people while I was at Purdue University. In fact, that's probably one of the greatest lessons that I learned, and to learn how to connect the dots, to get to know people, and be of service to them, care about them, and then find out how to leverage all that networking to accomplish something greater. Another leadership lesson is to be kind to everybody. The other thing that I learned was to keep an open mind. People are different. But just because someone is a little different doesn't mean that they're bad or not good. Keeping an open mind and learning from people's differences is extremely important. Another lesson is to lead with humility. Never get too caught up on the fact that you're a leader. Lead with humility and gentleness as much as possible. Another thing that I learned at Purdue was follow the vision of the organization and represent it with excellence in all that you do and all that you are. The reality is when you are a leader in an organization, you're not only representing yourself, you are also representing the organization. In this case, it was the Purdue Varsity Glee Club and Purdue University. Then finally, the most important leadership skill I probably acquired at Purdue was to have fun. Enjoy being a leader. Enjoy being a part of the organization. We had a motto at Purdue in the Varsity Glee Club—there's no fun without music and there's no music without fun. I love that one.

Wright

You've worked extensively across the disciplines of education, business, entertainment, politics, and religion. Your doctoral work focused on networking in the global village. What did you learn about the significance of building networks of people?

Myers

I spent a huge amount of time in Russia and networked with people both in America and Russia. I learned something. I learned that the principle or the theory of the six degrees of separation is in fact true. In my work and travels across the nation and around the world, I'm amazed at how simple it is to develop and cultivate a network that can truly help open doors to accomplish greater things in our lives, our organizations, our communities, our business, and our world.

Wright

So what do you mean? Can you give me an illustration or two?

Myers

Yeah, I can. But before I do, let me paint the backdrop for my illustrations. One of my favorite authors is Napoleon Hill. His book, *Think and Grow Rich*, illustrates beautifully how leaders who cultivate a sixth sense (called autosuggestion) become magnates with others who also have this trait. Greater things always seem to be coming to them. Connections are made that would not normally be made. Deals are developed and struck that cannot be made without a highly cultivated leadership skill and mindset. And the benefits are amazing. Hill lists several characteristics of leaders that I find helpful. I came across these while I was on a cruise to the Bahamas in 1993, and they affirmed that which I have been learning much of my life. In fact, the person that pointed me to Napoleon Hill's work, a great leader named Dr. Arthur Decruyter of Chicago, asked if I had read the book. He and I were having lunch one day, and I said, "No, I haven't read that book." He said, "I can't believe it. You live your life as if you've read the book." I said, "Well, then I better read the book." I purchased the book and took it on the cruise in 1993. Here are some of the highlights that I find amazing. In fact, they're programmed in my computer. They're on my palm pilot for regular reflection. I think you'll find them useful too.

Think and Grow Rich by Napoleon Hill. These are great statements that can motivate us to be great leaders!

A quitter never wins and a winner never quits. Not bad. He's got 11 secrets of leadership. One, unwavering courage; two, self control; three, a keen sense of justice; four, definiteness of decision; five, definiteness of plans; six, the habit of doing more than paid for; seven, a pleasing personality; eight, sympathy and understanding; nine, mastery of detail; ten, willingness to assume full responsibility; and eleven, cooperation. And then he tags a twelfth one. He calls it QQS, quality, quantity, service with spirit. So I find those to be helpful. Another couple of other quotes that he has that I just find so significant, the days of the go-getter have passed. He or she has been supplanted by the go-giver. Another really good maxim is this. Tell the world what you intend to do, but first show it. And then these three gems of wisdom: listen, don't talk, accumulate knowledge, don't divulge information. The second one is acquire facts or secure information quietly without disclosing your purpose. And the third one is sad but true. People who envy you will attempt to defeat you. And then, a couple of others. Genuine wisdom is usually conspicuous through modesty and silence. Keep a closed mouth and open ears. And then, this one I like quite well. Every powerful man has himself within his own power, and of course, this was written decades ago. We'd also have to say every powerful woman has herself within her own power.

Some others from this wonderful book: success requires no explanations, failure permits no alibis. And then why leaders fail: unwillingness to render humble service and temperance, emphasis of authority of leadership, and emphasis of title. His point is there's no room for egomaniac behavior if you're a leader. Hill also describes 31 ways to fail in life as well as seven major positive emotions. And the positive emotions are wonderful: desire, faith, love, sex, enthusiasm, romance, and hope. Hill describes a sixth sense that guides people to excellence in living and relationships and businesses. He says, "Most people wish for riches, but few people provide the definite plan and the burning desire to pave the road to wealth." And he gives us three principles for thought and accomplishment: one, subconscious mind; two, creative imagination; and three, that which I have already mentioned, autosuggestion or a sixth sense. He says, "A sixth sense is the apex of his philosophy. It can be assimilated, understood, applied only by first mastering the other twelve principles, and the sixth sense is the creative imagination through which ideas and plans and insights flash into the mind. The flashes are sometimes called hunches or inspiration, and through the aid of the sixth sense, you'll be warned of impending dangers in time to avoid them, notified of opportunities in time to embrace them. And the sixth sense is the guardian angel who opens the door at times to the temple of wisdom."

Another thing that he says is that the ladder of success is never crowded at the top. And then, of course, as a leader we have to understand fear. And understand that there are six ghosts of fear: poverty, criticism, ill health, lost love, old age, and death. And a seventh one is the susceptibility to negative influences. Then finally, I love this quote: "A fearless person thrives on far horizons." Napoleon Hill's work encourages people to expect greater things in their lives by thinking and growing rich relationally, financially, and spiritually.

Wright

Wow! That is awesome. So how have you seen the sixth sense be a magnet for you in your life?

Myers

Well, you know it's operative when there's a powerful synergy in a relationship. It's almost tangible, but yet inexplicable. It can compliment your life's mission and work. You might say that both minds are so finely tuned on their mission in life's purpose that they automatically link and know that's there's a synergy worth exploring. Why did theses things happen? So that you and the other person, or organization, are able to mutually benefit each other and do greater things together for the larger good. It is simply a great rush when that happens. I've had several experiences where these things have kicked in.

For example, one is a story about a woman named Ida Cromer. I met her when I was a student at Purdue University, and she was 86 years old at the time. She'd graduated from Purdue in 1914 and became one of the first women principals in the state of Indiana. She was a pioneer. Ida loved to travel. In fact, she was on a trip to Europe with the Varsity Glee Club, and that's when I met her. I showed up late to a dinner one night in Paris. The only seat was next to this little old lady who would become one of my closest and dearest friends. We talked and I shared my heart and my vision and my dreams and everything with her. She told me about her life. We were on the bus and she was sitting up front. She was cold, and I said, "You look cold." And she said, "I am cold." So I got her a blanket and put it on her, and that was about all that we talked about or the only contract we had. Shortly after I came back from Europe, I got a letter from her, and it said, "Dear John, I've been looking for someone for five years who I could send any place in the world for study, and I want to send you any place you want to go. I specifically thought of the Middle East for you. Give me a call and we can talk about it." Well, Mrs. Cromer became one of my very closest friends and a great sponsor. She sent me to the Middle East. She sent me to Europe. She sent me to China. Why? So I could study history, culture, current events, scales of economy, political structure, and the like. She wanted me to become educated and to learn about the fact that people are different but basically people have the same needs—to be cared for and loved and to be inspired and to find hope and to give hope.

She became my dear friend and at age 99 she passed away. I was honored when her family invited me to speak at the celebration of her life. I performed the ceremony and gave the eulogy for Mrs. Cromer. She impacted my life in a way that not too many other people have. It was because of the sixth sense that the synergy happened!

Another story is about the time that I was able to coordinate a meeting with Mikhail Gorbechev in 1992 shortly after he stepped down from power in the USSR and Russia. I was traveling with a group of 16 leaders from across America. We were to go to Russia. Five months before the trip to Russia, I was in Southern California. I was preparing to go to a leadership training institute. While I was there, I stopped at the hotel and wanted to spend the night there.

And I inquired about how nice the rooms were, and the CEO of the Western Rim Management Corporation happened to be on the property that day. He came down the stairs and the desk clerk said, "Mr. Craddock, this is John Myers. And he's going to be here for a few days, and he'd like to see the property." And he said, "Hey, I'll show you around." Well, we started walking around and he became a fast friend and he said, "So, what are you doing?" I told him about the leadership conference, and I said, "And I'm getting very excited because part of the training is prepare for this trip to Russia." And he said, "Oh, Russia." He said, "I've done a lot of work in Russia. I've got a hotel in Russia too." And I said, "Well, I'm hoping to meet with Mikhail Gorbechev, but I'm not sure how in the world I'll get to him." And he said, "I'll tell you what. Meet me for breakfast tomorrow. I have two friends from Russia who I think might be able to open the door."

So we met for breakfast the next day and I met the head of the Finance Division for the entire country. Accompanying him was the nephew of the former leader of the KGB. And as we chatted, they talked about how acrimonious things were over there and how they wanted to create new business opportunities and relationships. Then one said that he was very good friends with Mikhail Gorbechev. So, time passed and connections were made and sure enough, on April 24, 1992, I was in a meeting with Mikhail Gorbechev for 1½ hours. He talked to us about leadership, vision and integrity, speaking to the spiritual nature of human beings. He even accepted the opportunity to join hands with him and have a closing prayer. It was an amazing experience, and I think it happened because of the power of autosuggestion and the six degrees of separation. It made a difference in my life. If you're living your life with a passion to make an impact on other peoples' lives, greater things follow you and come to you.

Wright

You do a lot of keynoting and consulting across the nation and abroad on topics of leadership, vision, networking, a commitment to excellence, strategic planning, and marketing. This is under your company, Greater Things Enterprises. What do you look for when you're engaged to work with a business, an organization, a company, or a conference group?

Myers

Well, first of all, I want to learn as much about the client as possible. Learn about their history, their management team, their strength, their points of need, their hopes for the future, and their desired outcome as a result of my leadership with them.

The second thing is to understand the culture of the client, and come prepared to be a part of the culture while engaged with them. For instance, if the corporate culture of a client is button down shirts and ties and really nice suits, well, it would really be inappropriate to show up in island wear.

Wright

Right.

Myers

On the other hand, if the culture is laid back like so much of south Florida tends to be, to show up in a coat and tie at certain meetings would be totally inappropriate. And so it's important to understand how dressing for success is to be interpreted when we're working with that kind of a culture.

The third thing though is to think outside the box and to provide new insights and challenges to the client. I mean, after all that's really part of why they're hiring me. And this starts at the leadership level and is shaped then for the broader distribution in conjunction with the leader's vision.

The fourth thing is to always work with the client in identifying the goals and objectives related to my work with them. If it's to help discern a vision, well then that requires a great deal of time with the core leadership team of the client or of the organization. On the other hand, if it's to come and do a keynote that inspires and fires up the troops, that takes a different kind of preparation. Both are important and both can be lots of fun.

The fifth thing is that I want to build a long-term relationship with the client. This way I can work with the client on a long-term basis and assist them in a strategic plan or a turn around strategy. There's a great deal of joy in this facet of my work with Greater Things Enterprises, because the relationships, long-term relationships, are really what makes life beneficial.

Wright

I understand you are also working on another book, *Greater Things*. Could you tell us about it?

Myers

Well, *Greater Things* will be the foundation book for several books in a series. The first book is laid out in three chapters. It's very simple. Chapter one is *Expect Greater Things;* Chapter two is *Grow in Greater Things*; Chapter three, *Do Greater Things*. This will be a simple book with a profound message and some how-to advice. It will carry several stories as well as insights from some wonderful minds. This book will motivate its audience to expect greater things from their lives by power training their minds through visionary thinking. It will inspire the audience to dig deeper, and will offer suggestions as to how to do so. That's *Growing in Greater Things*. And finally, it will encourage the reader to go beyond the self or their current world view to *Do Greater Things* in practical and meaningful ways. I can't wait to release this book. The second book is titled *Twelve Principles for Greater Things Living*, and it builds on the first book by providing essential keys for living a tremendously fulfilled life.

Wright

How can your current readers find the books and become familiar with how to reach for keynotes and consultations?

Myers

Well, the best way to do it is to order it directly from me or through the website or to write to me at drjohnrmyers@comcast.net. All of the information is located at the end of this chapter.

Wright

Dr. John Myers, entrepreneur, leader, businessman, author, vocalist, keynote speaker, strategic planner. So what do you do in your spare time?

Myers

Well, I'll tell you what. I love to spend time on my boat *Greater Things*. I enjoy entertaining clients, friends, and family on the boat *Greater Things*. I also do a lot of writing onboard. It's kind of a sanctuary for me. I also have a great time biking. South Florida is a wonderful place to ride a bicycle. I leave from my house, ride 2½ miles to the beach, and then ride another 10 or 15 miles north on A1A, and enjoy the beauty of the sea and the sand and the sun, all those palm trees and all those great people. And I love to go fishing, love to swim, enjoy traveling a great deal, reading, and always enjoy playing a great game of golf.

Wright

Well, John, you are by nature and by cultivation a great example of leadership defined. I really appreciate this time you spent with me today, and it's just really been a pleasure. And I've learned a tremendous amount. Thank you so much for being with us on *Leadership Defined*.

Myers

Well, thank you, David, and I'm appreciative to have been invited to be a part of this venture. I hope it's a great success for all involved.

About The Author

Ever since he was a young man, Dr. John Myers has enjoyed leading, entertaining, inspiring, making people laugh and helping people reach their full potential. These natural inclination and talents, combined with academic training and life's experience, have make it possible for Dr. Myers to travel, speak, consult and study in over twenty-one countries, as well as a large portion of the United States. His "Greater Things" philosophy encourages people to believe the best, train for the best and be the best they can be. The philosophy teaches people how to Expect Greater Things, Grow in Greater Things and Do Greater Things.

Dr. John R. Myers

Greater Things Enterprises, Inc.

Greater Things Institute, Inc.

Bank of America City Centre

401 E. Las Olas Blvd #130

Ft. Lauderdale, Florida 33301

Phone: 954.649.7905

Fax: 954.523.5257

Email: DrJohnMyers@comcast.net

www.expectgreaterthings.com

Chapter 3

PATRICK J. ATKINSON

THE INTERVIEW

David E. Wright (Wright)

Today we are talking to Patrick Atkinson. Patrick is in constant national demand as a highly inspirational speaker and is nationally sought after for presentations and conferences on health, education, and family related matters. He has been interviewed in numerous international, national and regional media outlets such as CNN, The Los Angeles Times and the Christian Science Monitor. He is a widely-regarded human rights leader, as well as the founder of Casa Alianza programs throughout Central America during the 1980's.

Patrick Atkinson is most recently known as the founder and executive director of The GOD'S CHILD Project, an international program that cares for, educates and provides health services to 12,000 poor people in Central America, Africa, and the United States. He is the creator of the Bismarck Educational System for developing nations, a model now widely used in both Central America and Africa. A native of Bismarck, North Dakota and graduate of Minnesota State University Moorhead and Regis University, Denver, Colorado. While completing a Masters at Regis University, he co-developed a service learning university course model for which he coined the term S.O.F.E.: Service Oriented Field Experience.

In 2000 and 2001, Patrick Atkinson was invited by the United Nations to develop residential, health and educational programs for rural women left widowed, and street children left orphaned, by the rampaging AIDS crisis in East and South Africa. He and The GOD'S CHILD Project continue to be active in this development and relief effort.

Patrick Atkinson recently co-founded and directs the Santa Madre Homeless Shelter of Antigua, Guatemala, and he serves on national select committees to develop human rights and justice processes in developing countries.

Patrick, welcome to Leadership Defined!

Patrick Atkinson (Atkinson)

Thank you, David. It's great to be here today.

Wright

You might have to go back and help me pronounce some of the words I just butchered while introducing you to our listeners.

Atkinson

Nothing to apologize for, David. You did a great job. Also, you just spoke words in four different languages.

Wright

Well good! Patrick, you certainly seem to have a strong character. Must a leader always have a dominant personality?

Atkinson

Not at all. In fact, for leaders to be effective, they must also be servants. While a leader must be able to motivate and inspire others, in order to compel skilled and talented people to follow, you're not going to get a loyal following if you're mean, manipulative, angry or abusive. Those are not the traits of a good leader.

Some of the strongest and most powerful people in the world have been, first and foremost, servants. They led by example. Let me give you three obvious examples and then one of someone you will have never heard of. The first obvious example is Jesus Christ. Here is a man who even though He lived 2,000 years ago, has a following today of millions. While part of this is because of His divinity, the other part comes from the leadership qualities and abilities He had to motivate and change people, communities and nations.

At the same time, Christ literally knelt on the floor and washed the feet of His disciples. He stopped to listen to the common people on the streets. He went to their homes when they needed help. In the end, He died to save them, and to save the hundreds of millions of people who follow Him today.

A second well-known example is Mahatma Gandhi. Gandhi had strength of character, personal power, an amazing intellect, and a huge and loyal following, but he also very clearly put himself in the role of servant. To millions of people in India he proved he was willing to be beaten, become ill, and even sacrifice his own life to further the cause of their freedom. Because of the depth of this commitment, Gandhi was loved and respected, even by his enemies.

A much more contemporary example and somebody we often read about in the newspapers and magazines is Mother Theresa. Mother Theresa was very smart, very clever, tremendously powerful, had strength of character, and was very wise in how to handle people. She took all of those qualities and put them into a package that moved forward with the force of a freight train.

At the same time Mother Theresa never hesitated to get down on her hands and knees to lift a lice-covered, dying person from the slimy filth of the gutter. Ultimately it was her servitude, not her ability to strategize, that enabled her to influence heads of state, bring tears to the eyes of an American president, inspire an English princess to soil her hands in a home for the dying, and found a volunteer community that has served millions of the poorest people in our world.

The fourth and final example is a young boy named Francisco. Francisco was born, deaf and unable to speak, to a terribly poor squatter family that lived on the mountainsides of Guatemala, Central America. Several years ago Francisco showed up at my door in Guatemala holding a bag filled with moldy bread and rotting meat he had begged from my neighbors. This was his only food. With no access to clean water, he stank to high heaven, but once we took him in and began the job of nourishing and educating him, once he began to trust us, he cleaned up pretty well. He then left and brought in his seven brothers and sisters and all but demanded, in a gentle but persistent way, that they too be nourished and educated. Even with his physical disabilities, he was clearly the strong leader in his family.

Today Francisco works for us in The GOD'S CHILD Project, and he still leads and inspires others through example.

Wright

What, in your opinion, are the most important qualities found in a leader?

Atkinson

The single most important quality for a leader is vision. Where do you want your cause to end up? In other words, where do you want to take the people you are leading? Suppose I was standing in the middle of a crowded room and suddenly I jumped up and said, "Let's go!" or "Follow me!" People would look at me and say, "Who is this guy and where is he going?"

In this situation, people might start laughing at me, but they definitely wouldn't run in circles with me. Yet this is exactly what is happening in corporate boardrooms across America today. Businesses and entire nations are being led by people who have no clear plan, no vision of where they are going or how they want to get there. The number one trait good leaders have is a clear vision of where they want their group to go.

The second most important quality in a leader is courage. I can guarantee you that if you are going to be a leader in today's world, you are going to be misunderstood. Some people are going to disrespect you. They and maybe others will say hurtful things about you. If you can't take that kind of ankle biting, think again about whether or not you want to lead.

Also, depending on the size of the group you are leading, there are definitely times when you are going to feel isolated and lonely. There are many things you just won't be able to talk about, and other times when people demand explanations and you can't express everything that you know.

For example, I work on a number of national and international committees that deal with human rights and justice issues, which means I sometimes know negative or compromising information about very powerful, highly visible people. Sometimes these people have sterling reputations, yet behind the scenes they might be alcoholics, or involved in the international narcotics trade, or are somehow profiting from the violence or corruption we are trying to stop. I may know about these hidden problems and this knowledge may influence my actions and decisions, but I can't say anything to anyone outside of our working group. We can't explain why we've been blocked from taking the easiest, most apparent road to success.

Leaders need to have strength, courage, and conviction to do the right thing, even when it's uncomfortable to do so.

Much of the work I do in prisons has to do with dispute mediation. The goal is to identify and stop a problem before it turns into bloodshed. About three years ago I was called to help prevent a single-location prison riot from spreading nationwide. Inmates in one of the prisons were actually beheading other inmates and playing soccer with their heads. It was a gruesome display of violence, and during the talks I heard horrendous things, not just from the prisoners but also from the guards. Still, you can't show any fear in a situation like this because if you do, you're a dead man. On their own terms, both the prisoners and the guards responded to me because I was willing to walk among them, and they knew their secrets were safe. Fortunately most of us won't have to risk our lives to make good leadership decisions, but when we're forced to make tough calls, it's important to honor our values and trust the courage of our convictions.

A third very important trait for a leader to have is the ability to persuade - to be able to communicate your thoughts and decisions. You need to be able to persuade others that your path is the right path to take even when they don't know or understand all of the dynamics that you, as their leader, had to take into account.

Unfortunately, I'm afraid the all-important skill of being able to communicate, through both the spoken and the written word, is being lost in today's world. People aren't reading as much as they should, and because they don't read, they aren't learning how to speak or write. Good leaders must be able to write convincingly. This is just as important as being able to speak convincingly. Leaders must be able to put together good, cohesive, convincing messages that others will understand and want to accept. A poorly communicated message is D.O.D.—dead on delivery.

Finally, the last needed leadership trait I'll talk about today is faith. You need to believe in what you're doing. You need to believe in the greater good of what you are seeking, of what you are asking your team to do. Otherwise how can you motivate people to action? It's impossible.

Some people say they are such great salespeople they can sell anyone anything, even something they don't believe in. Baloney. That might work once or twice, but eventually these people become spotted for what they really are: con men, schmoozers, and snake oil salesmen. Soon no one wants to buy from them so they move on to a new crowd. These aren't leaders. They're one-time game players.

In the international work we do, I ask people to put themselves at social or physical risk, to change their lives and give of themselves, to work extra-long and hard hours. It's only if you have faith and are willing to give in equal or greater portion that you can convey your message convincingly enough for people to want to leave their comfort zones and follow you.

When I talk about faith, this also includes faith in God. Quite often people have lost their faith, or they never really had it in the first place. They don't believe there's anything out there worth taking risks for, getting involved with, or going after and fighting for. These people need to develop their belief in God, because only then will they have an absolute reason to move ahead and fight for a greater, nobler cause.

When people are believers, they can accomplish amazing things. Several years ago I pulled a small abandoned boy out from under a park bench. Though he was just 7-years old, his mother had thrown him into the streets. He would wake up early every morning, crawl out from under his park bench, bath himself in a public fountain, go into the bushes and put on his one set of clean clothes, grab his books, and go to school. At noon, when classes ended, he would go back to the park and into the bushes, change from his one set of clean clothes into his one set of dirty clothes, and shine shoes for the rest of the afternoon.

At the end of the day, after the shops had closed and the tourists had gone, this small boy would take whatever coins he had earned, buy some bread, eat it, hide his shoeshine box, and then crawl back under his park bench where he would spend the rest of the night fighting off the spiders, rain, cold and perverts. He did this because he wanted to be a doctor when he grew up. He believed that one day he would get his chance, he just didn't know when.

Of course, I took this small boy into our orphanage and told him we would care for and educate him if he studied hard. When he was 12, he again said he wanted to be a doctor, and he said it yet again when he graduated from high school.

Today he's a nationally regarded pediatrician, as well as the founder of the Atkinson Family Clinics for the poor and homeless. Because he believed it, he accomplished it!

Most people who volunteer with us say they come because they want to help make the world a better place. However, if you delve more deeply, the vast majority will admit they have an even bigger motivation. They volunteer because they have faith in God and they want to find a real-world way to put their faith into action. They believe!

Wright

You know, I'm sure there are people listening to this interview or reading this book who are also contemplating the possibility of becoming a leader, but they don't want to recreate the wheel. What are the most common mistakes you find in leaders today?

Atkinson

The greatest mistake leaders can make, particularly successful leaders, is to believe their own public relations. I mean this very seriously. If people start to say wonderful things about you and you believe them, you will change. In that change, you will not only lose the people who believed in you, you will also lose your original motivations for doing the work you are doing.

Wright

Right!

Atkinson

We can probably all name different charitable, religious or national leaders who have fallen because they started to believe the good things other people said about them. My advice: say thank-you when you hear people say these things, and then forget them.

As for unsuccessful leaders, well, that's a little different. Most would-be leaders fail because they give up too soon. Their cause may be just, but they simply don't believe they can succeed. Or perhaps they have faith, but they didn't take the time to develop their technical and communication skills. Because they didn't learn how to speak or write, they aren't able to inspire others to follow them towards that greater goal, so they fail.

Wright

It's interesting you should say that. I recently read that 98% of all failure is caused by quitting.

Atkinson

That would be it. Some people give up too soon. Abraham Lincoln, on the other hand, lost this election, he lost that election, and then he lost again. Finally he was elected President of the United States and was perhaps one of America's and our world's greatest leaders ever.

When the North won the Civil War, Lincoln was in a position to do terrible things in revenge and retribution to those who fought against him in the South. But he didn't. Instead, he said, "This is a time for reconciliation. This is a time for us to come back together, as one nation, as one family under God."

Some of Lincoln's followers didn't have that faith. They didn't have that vision. They were violent, mean and vengeful men. How different life and our national development could have been if Lincoln had been one of those men.

When you're a leader, you need what I call rhinoceros skin. In other words, you have to be able to walk down the street believing in your heart and knowing in your soul that you are doing the right thing. You have to understand intellectually that you are, to the best of your ability, making the right decisions for the right reasons.

At the same time you need to accept that nobody is right 100% of the time. There are times you will make mistakes. It's a certainty you'll be misunderstood and criticized. Your competitors and the people who don't want you to succeed are going to shoot arrows into your back as you walk away from them. They will snipe at your ankles when they think you can't see them. I have no respect for people like this. They are cowards.

You'll just have to accept that in today's world people like this are going to spread rumors about you and do whatever they can to hurt or discredit you. Just like we can't believe our own positive PR, we can't let false rumors or negative gossip bring us down either.

Some people give up trying to lead others to a greater cause simply because their skin is too thin. They don't understand that in the greater scheme of things, if their actions are faith-based and their intentions pure, all of those day-in and day-out skirmishes, which nick their armor, don't mean a thing.

Wright

When I ask about the important qualities found in a leader, you said that the first is vision. How does an effective leader convey his or her vision?

Atkinson

Leaders must believe in the vision they are trying to convey to others. I can speak very passionately about the poor because I've seen them. I've worked with them, eaten with them, cried with them. I've buried their parents and helped birth their children. I believe a better life is possible for them, and I want it to happen. Because of my sincerity and depth of passion for the poor, I can make you believe in them, too.

I've already mentioned the importance of a leader developing his or her communication skills. The power of conviction is only effective if it can be well communicated.

Wright

Do you think it's possible to teach someone to be a leader? Or can you only teach leadership skills?

Atkinson

Learning leadership skills and being a natural leader are two different things. To be a natural leader is an aspect of character. It's the core of who we are. You've probably been to a party or meeting where somebody walks in the room and boom! All eyes immediately go to that person. There's your natural born leader. That's not me.

A trained leader needs to be born with some basic skills, and also acquire and develop other skills over time. It's a package deal. How we speak, dress, convey our message, and what we say to draw the troops together are all leadership skills that can be developed with time, patience, and practice. A three-year-old child might be able to take her toy trucks apart and put them back together, but that doesn't make her a mechanic. Send her to technical school, though, teach her to work hard, give her books and the right tools, and those God-given, natural skills can be developed into a successful career.

I'm much more of a trained leader than a natural-born leader. I was in the same Boy Scout troop from when I was eight years old until I became an Eagle Scout at age sixteen, yet the former Scout Masters and the other scouts in my troop barely remember me being there at all.

Wright

Oh my!

Atkinson

Seriously! A reporter once asked my former Scout Master what I was like as a scout for eight years with him, and he said, "I don't remember him, so I guess the best I can say is he didn't cause any problems." Since then, of course, I've traveled around the world many times and have helped the poor in 38 different nations. I recently gave a major workshop on street children and AIDS in Africa, and have spoken on almost every Ivy League campus in America. With study, practice and time, I am learning how to deliver my message.

People who hear me probably won't remember me for very long, but if I've done my job right, they should remember my message. They will leave these presentations with a burning desire to do more for their poorer brothers and sisters. I want to put a fire in their belly. I want them to hear sincere passion and commitment in my voice, and to see that if I'm not afraid to suffer for my belief in those who are poor, they shouldn't be afraid to either.

Wright

So if you can teach leadership, what is the difference between mentoring, role modeling and copying? And when is it appropriate for a leader to ask a subordinate for help?

Atkinson

A good teacher should first conduct an objective and then a subjective analysis of the learners' traits, abilities, strengths and weaknesses. Knowing these considerations means everything when it's time to develop the learning process.

The objective traits are the easiest to define and deal with. These are the technical skills—the "how to's" of writing, speaking, dressing, presenting, and the importance of looking someone in the eye when you talk to them, to name just a few.

The subjective traits, on the other hand, are less obvious and require more time to understand. Teaching these require the teacher to share her real-world knowledge of what was learned. The leadership mentor needs to go beyond the technical skills and take the time to share the subtle nuances that she's learned through sweat and tears and long, late-night hours. I do this best when I am walking with someone.

I call it the leadership learning practicum: the teaching by explained example. It's always more effective to show than it is to tell.

Role modeling means actually doing what you say. People can tell when you are sincere. They know when you practice what you preach. Christ was obviously a very powerful leader, a very dynamic and inspirational leader. He talked about love and acceptance, and then ate with sinners. He talked about forgiveness, and then forgave those who hurt and eventually killed him. If somebody said to him, "I am hungry," he gave that person food. He led by example. He role-modeled love and compassion, commitment and forgiveness.

What the learners decide to do with the knowledge they are given is their choice. Generally speaking, the odds are greater the learner will emulate the mentor if she believes in that person, if the mentor is worth following. People will copy us if they believe in us.

Wright

With the personal rewards that a leader can receive being as high as they are, why do leaders burn out? And what can a leader do to ensure that he doesn't burn out?

Atkinson

The number one reason leaders burn out is because they forget to take care of themselves. They get so far out in front of the group they're leading that they become isolated. Their dreams, vision, strength and courage stretch beyond their physical capabilities, or surpass their ability to handle the minutia of details they confront daily.

When leaders forget to take care of their own needs, it's like the spillway on a massive dam opening up and staying open while the water flows out. Eventually the dam empties and suddenly it's dry. In effect, the dam burned itself out because at no point did the spillway's gates close long enough so the dam could fill back up with water.

Letting the dam run dry is a trap I sometimes fall into, too. Over the years I've had countless illnesses that probably could have been avoided, or certainly would have been less severe, if I had just taken better care of myself. For example, years ago I contracted malaria while working with Amerasian street prostitutes in Vietnam. Okay, things like this happen and there's not much you can do about it if a malaria-infected mosquito decides to bite you. Since then, however, I've had horrible malaria flare ups that usually occur when I'm excessively tired.

While the bugs I pick up in the streets and slums and war zones cause many of these illnesses, I've also been laid flat by illnesses that started as simple colds. Instead of taking care of myself and getting proper rest, I just keep going and wham! A bad case of the sniffles turns into pneumonia.

I'm trying to learn to make time for myself. There's a mistaken belief that there's something glorious about giving until you're on the edge of collapse. In reality that's just plain silly; its short-term thinking that ultimately puts all of your long-term goals at risk.

Wright

I know leadership and management are two different topics. However, in both cases a lot of people say that one of the top characteristics of a good leader is the ability to listen.

Atkinson

Absolutely.

Wright

So how should leaders listen?

Atkinson

Actively. By that I don't mean just closing your mouth. That's only the start.

Listening means looking at the person you are talking to, putting aside your work and not doing e-mail, checking a letter, or reading a report. I once read that 90% of all communication is non-verbal. I can say, "We are good friends," but if I say this with angry eyes and clenched lips, are you going to believe me? Probably not.

Active listening is tough to do if you put a big old desk between you and the person you are trying to listen to. If there's a physical barrier between you, there will be a tremendous psychological barrier as well.

One of the biggest errors in communication is that people, even world leaders and corporate executives, can feel insecure while talking to others, so they work to formulate their next comment when they should really be listening. They assume they know what the other person is trying to say. In reality, though, they don't know, so their response is usually premature, inadequate, or off the mark.

Quite often people don't know how to best convey their message, so we also have to watch their body language, which will speak volumes. Years ago a little boy named Maximino was dropped off at the door of a homeless shelter I was running. He didn't say much about himself and when we asked him questions, he simply shrugged his shoulders. This went on for days.

One night, while I was working late on a very important project, Maximino crept in to my office and sat at my feet. Deciding it was better to let him stay instead of sending him back to his room, I set aside the papers I was working on, bent over so I was on his level, and asked him how he was doing. He still didn't say anything and pretended to be asleep, so I went back to work.

A few minutes later, though, Maximino climbed onto my lap, and without my saying a word, started to tell me how he had seen his village massacred by Guatemalan soldiers. He described in horrible detail how he had tried to escape by running with his grandfather into some nearby woods, but eventually the soldiers found them both. They tied Maximino to a tree and forced him to watch while they slowly killed his grandfather. The soldiers then left, leaving the little boy tied to that tree.

For three days Maximino cried and fought off wild animals by kicking at them, while at the same time watching these animals ravage his grandfather's body that lay just a few feet in front of him. Finally a passerby discovered the two and brought Maximino's badly malnourished and barely-alive body to our front door.

Only when the child reached this point in his story did he start to cry. Then he began to sob in a convulsing, heart-ripping way that brought tears to my eyes too. Mercifully for both of us, he eventually fell asleep on my lap, where he slept for about an hour before he suddenly woke up, smiled, said goodnight, and left my office for his room.

Only after Maximino told me his cathartic story did he start to heal. What would have happened to him, I wonder, if when he came into my office I had automatically said something like, "What are you doing up? It's past your bedtime. Go back to bed!" We need to listen with our instincts as much as with our ears and body.

Wright

I've even heard it said by more than one person that there's very little communication in our culture. We just take turns talking.

Atkinson

That's a great way of putting it.

Wright

Do all leaders need to be charismatic? You spoke of Christ a few minutes ago and one thing that fascinates me is to think that 2,000 years ago a man could draw 5,000 people to Him, or even 150,000 if you include the women and children who probably weren't counted. To draw those kinds of crowds, you'd have to be very charismatic. But do all leaders need to be charismatic?

Atkinson

No, they don't. Remember, leadership is a combination of different skills, and not all of them are flashy. On one hand, you can have tremendously charismatic people with no depth to them. They create a flurry of activity and a rush of exalted excitement, but it's only going to last for a few minutes, days, or weeks. Then their movement dies.

On the other hand, a leader can be technically very good, have great organizational abilities and yet be timid or shy. Take Bill Gates. He's technically very good but I understand he's not at all charismatic. Still, no individual in the history of technical development has changed the world as much as Bill Gates.

The good news for most of us is that you don't need to have a strong and forceful character to be a good leader. You can also let your work, abilities, and product do the wowing for you.

Wright

Can an organization have more than one leader and still be effective?

Atkinson

A large organization must have more than one leader, because the group's followers need constant contact, feedback, direction and structure. No one person can provide all of this, so you need your sub leaders as well.

While all of a group's leaders don't have to be singing the exact same words, they should be singing the same tune. It's important that they share the same message.

On the other hand, a smaller effort can have just one leader, even if that smaller effort is actually part of a bigger picture. Let's use a hotel as an example. If there are two chefs in the kitchen, that spells trouble. The kitchen needs a leader. The sales force needs a leader. Reception needs a leader. And, of course, all of these players need to work together under a main leader who has delegated leadership roles to those under him.

Wright

So how does a leader relinquish control and still sleep at night?

Atkinson

You need to feel confident in the people you choose, and trust how you train them. You need good systems in place, which provide positive checks and balances. Inexperienced people sometimes feel that internal checks and balances mean you don't trust them. That's incorrect. Checks and balances mean you have created a system that does not allow misunderstandings or undesired consequences. A good system actually protects the individual more than it does the system itself.

For example, if someone gets a job as a teller in a bank and decides he's going to take $500 home every night, he'll soon find he can't do it. The system won't allow that kind of theft to go undetected. Likewise, a teller can't come in and find his starting cash drawer $500 short; a good internal system won't let that happen either.

Wright

Finally, Patrick, let me ask you what should a leader's priorities be?

Atkinson

A leader's first priority should be to serve their God. I say this is because ultimately this is the only forever-and-ever dynamic in life.

A leader's second priority should be to decide if the group wants to be led. It's not unusual for a leader to stand up and say, "Let's go!" only to turn around and discover there's no one standing behind her. You have to know where you want to take your people. You can be a great leader but if you don't know where you're going, people aren't going to follow you for very far.

A third priority is to be fair and just, and never forget you are leading people and not numbers, votes or petitions. You're leading people with hopes and dreams and baggage. Quite often leaders forget this, and their people become numbers or free-labor body counts. If this happens, you're not leading anymore; you're manipulating and using others.

Finally and perhaps most important, leaders must thank their people and let them know they are sincerely appreciated. Quite often leaders don't do this because they forget, or they start to take their people for granted. In some situations leaders start to believe their own PR and begin to believe they're such great leaders people should be grateful they are their followers. Naturally this is a very big mistake that is often fatal to a leader's cause.

Wright

Well, what an interesting conversation! Today we have been talking to Patrick Atkinson, a gifted and committed individual who has clearly been living the concepts of leadership and mission for the past quarter century. Mr. Atkinson is in constant demand as a speaker and group educator, and he's nationally sought after for presentations and conferences on health, education, family and charity management-related matters. He has developed nonprofit programs, and designed health and educational systems that currently benefit the poor in several nations on four continents. Today he is best known as the founder and executive director of The GOD'S CHILD Project, an international program that cares for, educates and provides health, community-development and human-rights protection services to 12,000 poor people in Central America, Africa and the United States.

Some Final Thoughts

Using vivid real-world examples ranging from Jesus Christ to Bill Gates, Abraham Lincoln to a handicapped Guatemalan boy named Francisco, Patrick Atkinson brings together street experience and academic learning to capture the true essence of leadership.

The nature of successful leadership begins, Atkinson says, with belief and desire. From those simple roots, leadership then requires commitment, training and practice for it to bloom into the organizational and communication skill set necessary to lead causes, direct businesses, and change entire nations.

In this *Leadership Defined* interview, Atkinson insightfully refers to leadership as "the ultimate act of service." He describes the four most important qualities he sees as necessary for positive leadership: vision, courage, technical ability and faith. He discusses the need for persistence, and for the development of what he refers to as "rhinoceros skin": the ability to stand up to the black-hole negativity of critics, gossips and arrow-shooters. "Just as good leaders never believe their own positive public relations," Atkinson says in this interview, "they should also never be defeated by the negative comments they hear or read about themselves."

Atkinson encourages delegation, persistence and rest for all achieved and learning leaders, and gives a clear-cut blueprint for those who strive to inspire others to achieve their "greater, nobler cause."

About The Author

Patrick Atkinson has worked for 25 years as an international missionary and nonprofit leader. He travels worldwide as a consultant on issues involving the homeless, the orphaned, and abandoned women.

He has ranched cattle in North Dakota, bedded down with the Mossai in Kenya, held dying babies in Vietnam, been knifed in Guatemala, smuggled medicines to starving villagers in El Salvador, has his nose broken while aiding prisoners, and suffered a whole host of tropical diseases. He is frequently a national keynote speaker who addresses health, educational and family and charity management-related matters.

A single father, his greatest love, after his relationship with God, is his son Ernesto.

Patrick J. Atkinson

721 Memorial Highway

Post Office Box 1573

Bismarck, North Dakota 58502-1573

Phone: 701.255.7956

Fax: 701.222.0874

Email: omanager@godschild.org

www.GodsChild.org

www.AtkinsonConsulting.org

Chapter 4

DR. WARREN LINGER

THE INTERVIEW

David E. Wright (Wright)
Today we are talking to Dr. Warren Linger. Dr. Linger has been recognized as a leading diversity and culture trainer and speaker working to unite businesses and customers around the world. He's known for evoking action oriented responses from those attending his seminars and workshops. Being an "architect of the possibilities of human beings," Warren delivers presentations filled with high impact and useful information. Warren understands that everyone has different needs and he has devoted his life to learning, understanding, and developing ways to meet and exceed those needs. Dr. Linger, welcome to *Leadership Defined*!

Dr. Warren Linger (Linger)
Well, thank you very much.

Wright
Your company specializes in communications differences and making good companies great. What made you want to start a business in this kind of work?

Linger

In 1985, I was sitting in a leadership workshop and my life changed. I had just become the president of an organization that was failing and I was looking for anything that could save us. When the speaker came onto the stage my world and life changed, as I knew them. I don't remember the name of the speaker but I remember he was passionate and cared about the members of the audience. Most important, what he said helped me gain hope that the future is going to be better. Within a year we came from being almost bankrupt to winning an award for being a most outstanding group in the organization.

That day I created a clear vision that I wanted to help others succeed. This was the beginning of my personal (and my company) vision, which is to "help those who want to be great." I help companies plant seeds of change, and they nurture the rest of the growth of the plant. I've seen groups spend huge amounts of money and get no change because management does not take a leadership stand and create an environment of diversity for success. The best leaders encourage innovation and creativity and fight the tendency toward uniformity. The leadership of organizations is responsible for success of the organization and as the saying goes, "The bottle neck is at the top of the bottle."

At the end of our lives we are not going to remember every thing that has happened to us. We are only going to remember moments. The question is: will you remember the good you have done for your family, friends and clients, or will you remember the bad others have done to you? Caring about others and accepting others is how we really help others in this life.

Recently a mentor of mine, Randy Hunt, said to me, "Warren, if you can open up your heart you will be able to help him and many others." At the time I didn't understand exactly what he meant when he said, "If you can open up your heart." Randy was trying to tell me that I wasn't caring—truly caring—for my client. When I finally did open up my heart I saw that he was right. We can best help our clients if we truly care about them and their success. The Chinese term for the word "happy" is translated in the two words "open heart." That is what success is about. When we truly care enough about others we can make them most happy. This means that we give up prejudices and accept those who are different from us. We must care for them the way they want to be cared for, not the way we want to care for them.

What does this have to do with diversity and leadership? Well, diversity is about understanding and accepting differences. One of the biggest differences among diverse people of the world is what makes them happy. What makes me happy may anger another person. When we care enough to learn what makes others happy we can help our customers better than anyone else.

Wright

You're known as a leader in cross culture and diversity communications in business. What sparked your interest in this line of work?

Linger

To find the answer, I guess we need to go way back. I was born and raised in Colorado and there was really no diversity in the area where I grew up. My parents were pretty open and didn't teach my sister and I that we were better than anyone because we were Caucasian. Also, I was always interested in "exploring personalities" which is what I call meeting and getting to know new people.

At a very young age I often asked my parents about other people and events going on in the world and wanted to experience these different wonders. I still remember my mother's response to most of my questions; "We have to go to Denver [the nearest big city] for that." In turn, my question was, "Then why don't we LIVE in Denver?"

After finishing my BA at the University of Colorado I moved to San Francisco, an area very rich in diversity with many of different types of people from around the world. I started studying San Francisco State University where, being Caucasian, I was actually a minority. This was a great opportunity to learn about many other diverse people and cultures. At San Francisco State I was working on my master's degree in Speech Communication, which gave me an incredible chance to learn about communication, cultural differences, similarities and acceptance of others.

In fact, the majority of the students in the speech communication program were from Asia, i.e. Japan, Taiwan, Hong Kong, the Philippines and Thailand. With that introduction to looking at diversity, culture and different communication styles, I became very fascinated because there is a whole rest of the world out there and we know so little about everyone in it. I began to see that we are not that different. We just have different ways of communicating and showing care, happiness and respect. In this environment I had the opportunity to teach communications courses to the diverse student body. I learned so much from the mix in that diverse, multicultural environment that I knew that I would someday make that a part of my life.

As I continued in my studies, I went on for my doctorate at the University of San Francisco, and there I studied adult education and what helps adults learn best. Again, the University of San Francisco was a school rich in diversity. These were great backgrounds for me to study with, talk to and learn about other cultures. Then I started leading seminars and speaking around the world because I was really fascinated by the similarities and differences among cultures. What one culture will define as respect can be very different from another culture. All of those ideas made me think, "Well, you know, if I really want to experience diversity and culture, I want to go to another culture to experience it. Then I can reflect back on what people go through when they are not majority like I was in the USA."

Wright

So why did you move to Hong Kong to start a company?

Linger

I moved to Hong Kong to start a company because I felt it was a great place to experience diversity and other cultures. I wanted to learn more about others, so I looked at a world map to see where I wanted to move. I wanted a culture that was rich in diversity where I could still make money training and speaking.

Hong Kong is often described as an East meets West culture. We have a dominant Chinese culture that had a British/U.K. influence for 150 years. Mixing the two cultures creates a very rich combination and everyone seems to be getting along. In fact everyone seems to get along very well compared to what we read in the paper about tension and strife around the rest of the world. Also, much of the early research on culture and diversity came from this area. Looking at these criteria, I thought, "All right, why not go Hong Kong and check out Asia."

Wright

How has living in a different culture changed your outlook on doing business?

Linger

I would say that living in a different culture has had a profound impact on my view of doing business. Living in a different culture shows me ways diversity and differences in communication styles and cultural behaviors can influence markets. I wouldn't notice these differences if I just stayed here for a few months. This diversity greatly influences how companies do business.

Having this experience with diversity, I provide a much more rich background to help my clients and my audiences when I'm training or speaking. I take my U.S. experience, mix it with differences that I've seen in these other new cultures, and provide a better service and more value to my clients.

In addition to living in different cultures, I have worked in many different companies and industries. I have worked in professional services, construction, finance, hospitality, government and non-profit.

One day in a seminar someone teased me by asking if I worked in so many places because I couldn't keep a job. Yes, everyone laughed. I told them, "I have almost always known that I wanted to be a trainer and speaker to help good people and good companies become great. I knew if I was going to help others I needed to know what kind of problems they faced. As a result, I intentionally worked in many different professions to learn about different types of problems people faced."

Because I give my clients advice to make their companies great, they tell me that my background experience is priceless for them. The good companies which invest in their people become great. The best companies create a winning environment by adding value to their people by training and developing them.

I've seen companies spend millions on a computer system that is obsolete in a few years yet they won't spend a few thousand on their people because the company "may loose one or two." The statistics show that companies that spend the money on their people have a lower turnover rate than the rest. Actually, it is the companies that don't train and add value to their people, lose people all the time. This becomes a loss for both the company and the employees.

Wright

I remember, I went to University of Tennessee, and most of the people who were not of my nationality were from Asia. Are our schools better than the ones in Asia?

Linger

I wouldn't say that their schools aren't as good. They go to the U.S. to learn the American business methods and skills and to improve their English. The U.S. is a strong engine that drives the world economy. Many come to the U.S. to learn how to compete better or what the "big kids" (big businesses) are doing. They say, "Let's learn how they are doing it." Also, some want to improve their English so they go over to just learn in the U.S. universities and gain the English skills to work with the U.S. market. Overall, the people I have met in Asia have an insatiable appetite for learning.

With the Internet, the world is no longer just the U.S. engine running the world economy. There are so many more opportunities to build and grow and offer services to others. If a company thinks it is going to make it playing a small game, that company will see a loss in market if they offer only average products and services.

Wright

I never thought I would be operating my business internationally, but every time we publish a book that has fine color prints and that sort of thing, we always go to Hong Kong for that. It takes three more weeks to deliver them because it's got to come over by boat, but it sure is worth it. The people have always treated us with respect, and I just found them great people to deal with. What made you interested in starting a training and speaking company back in '89?

Linger

I started my training and speaking company back in 1989 because I wanted to help people communicate and get along better. Like I said before, I love to explore personalities and talk to people. Thinking back on my life I realize the most difficult times were when I wasn't getting along with others. As I got older I noticed that other people all over the world had the same experience. I wanted to help people overcome the challenge of getting along with others.

At a very young age, actually I think before I even before I got out of college, I was saying to friend's things like, "When I own my own company I want to teach people." Back in '89 I started my company part time. I just started by leading a few training workshops a year back then. I remember I didn't even get paid for leading the first few and just did it for fun. Eventually I kept on doing more and more and in the mid 1990s I started teaching and training full time while I was in graduate school.

Wright

Why did you pick speech communications instead of an MBA for your master's degree?

Linger

In 1990, I began exploring the idea of earning an MBA. A friend of mine who had just received an MBA and was struggling to find a job even though she went to Santa Clara University. My friend said, "Do something fun because the job market isn't that stable and it's important to enjoy what you do." Also, she told me, "The job market right now has many MBAs, so why don't you just study something you enjoy?" Interestingly, now I teach MBA and DBA courses in Mainland China.

I found that there are a lot of people who can run a business, but is running a business what the world needs right now, or do we need fresh new ideas? Do we need new ways to communicate? Do we need to create new opportunities? I just wanted to learn more about being innovative. I wanted to learn more about the creativity side, and more of how I can help others work with people. I knew I wouldn't want to be a therapist. I thought if I went into therapy, I'd be crying at the end of the day every day, or I would be drinking or both. These were not my idea of a satisfying life.

Wright

In Speech Communication what specifically did you study during your master's research?

Linger

Working on my master's degree, I studied teacher, trainer and speaker communications. I knew I wanted to be a great trainer and speaker. I really concentrated on studying how teachers, trainers or speakers communicated in front of the room to create an environment that most motivated their learners and audience members. I wondered how they excited people to do more work, and what behaviors they showed in front of the classroom? How did they use that one tool that everyone has—communication—to get their message across?

I remember when I was growing up there were some teachers who everyone loved. Those teachers created a challenging environment where everyone, regardless of their diverse background, could learn and grow. My friends and I seemed to learn so much when we took the classes with those teachers. With most of the rest of the teachers, few students learned a lot and wanted to strive to do their very best. I wanted to know what was the difference. What did those teachers do? Why does everyone like to take their courses even though they offered more challenging courses? Everyone liked to take classes from the great teachers because we all learned so much. I was curious what great teachers did. I wondered what is the difference? What makes some trainers and speakers better than others? Great teachers create an environment that allows and encourages diverse individuals and groups to succeed.

After several years in the working world I realized that great leaders also created an environment where everyone, regardless of their diverse background, could learn and grow. I realized that great teachers are great leaders and great leaders are great teachers.

Wright

How did having the master's degree lead to your earning a doctorate in adult education, training and development? That's a long commitment, isn't it?

Linger

I am selfish. I will admit it. I wanted to be a great teacher, trainer and speaker. Even thought it took over seven and a half years, I felt it was one of the best investments in time and money I could make.

At first I didn't want to study at the doctoral level. At San Francisco State, my advisor and mentor, Dr. Rudy Busby, actually talked me into earning my doctorate degree. From the first week in the program he said, "So, when you go for your doctorate..." I remember saying, "Wait a minute. I just want to get a master's degree and go find a job where I can earn more money." He kept saying, "When you go for your doctorate." He persisted in telling me, "You have what it takes you have to go on."

At first I found many excuses and said things like, "There's no way. I'm not a good enough learner. I can't sit still and concentrate for that long. The master's degree is two and half years, and I don't want to commit to five more years of studying." But Rudy kept at it! After a while, I started thinking, "Well, okay, maybe this is a good idea. Maybe I can do this." Because he kept encouraging me, by my second year I simply assumed that I was going to apply for doctorate programs. I think having that mentor—a person who really believes in you when you don't believe in yourself—really makes a difference in your career.

Once I made the decision to earn a doctorate I thought, "If I am going to do this study something I really enjoy." That choice lead to the doctorate in adult education because I was fascinated with what motivates diverse people to perform at their highest level. Also, I wondered how different people learn. Then, I looked into how teachers communicate. I took it one step further by asking many other questions like, "How do adults gather the knowledge? How do they retain knowledge? What makes them want to develop themselves more? What makes them want to learn and what makes them not want to learn?" We are always learning. Are we learning fast enough to keep up with the market? Are we learning as a way of life?

Wright

So what specifically did you study in adult education while working on your doctorate?

Linger

I studied communication and motivation for adults. When we ask children to learn something, they say, "Cool! Let's go learn it." When we ask an adult to learn something they will often cross their arms in front of their chest and ask, "Why do I need to learn this?" This fundamental difference was a wonder for me because I was one who learned to love learning. After undergraduate school I didn't learn much. Soon I changed and found myself saying, "Learning is great! This is a lot of fun!" What took me from, "Well, I like to learn but never did anything about it," to sitting in a room right now with over 400 books on the shelves? I read all the time, always looking around for new information, always going into bookstores, and always going to the library because I really enjoy learning. The Greek philosopher Aristotle wrote, "Learning makes us feel more alive."

The world is diverse. For example, many people read the newspaper every day. That's a way of gathering knowledge. They are learning about the world around them. Some want a little bit more depth and take responsibility for their learning. Great leaders want to gather knowledge about the world around them. Different people have different ways of learning. It has been my experience that, all over the world, the most successful and happy people are always learning and growing.

I want to help bring back a lot of this high level diversity, leadership and motivation knowledge to the U.S. Now it is especially important since China is opening up. Training and speaking in the

U.S., the U.K., and Europe are an important part of my business plan. It is an exciting part of the business plan, and my clients have been welcoming the information. People there are really excited about understanding the differences in diversity so they can apply them to their own companies and markets.

Wright

How has your academic research transferred to add value to your business practice of training and speaking?

Linger

My academic research transferred to add value to my business practice of training and speaking in many different ways. First, I have applied what I learned about the two types of research to look at data and information more objectively. Next, I learned many new ways to motivate others to find new ways to help diverse employees and customers connect and communicate with one another. Also, I studied methods of communication that help individuals surpass their highest levels of performance and then applied this knowledge to business.

There are two predominate types of research, qualitative (the quality or description of a person's experience) and quantitative (large quantities of data from many people or sources.) The interesting thing is the emotional reactions that each group of highly "objective" researchers has toward the other type of research. For example, I have heard qualitative researchers claim that qualitative is the only way to research. Also, I have heard quantitative researchers say the same about their discipline.

I feel they are both important. If we only look at the qualitative experience we find diverse responses among each respondent but we can miss the trends we see from the majority. If we ignore qualitative research in business then we could miss the one or two diverse ideas that could truly inspire employees, customers or markets.

If we only look at quantitative research like surveys we find what most (i.e. 80% or 90%) of the people respond, but we don't know what the others feel and why they don't agree with the majority. If we ignore this research we could missunderstand the trends of the majority of responses. If we only look at quantitative research in business we could miss the opportunity to apply the great ideas that came from the quality of experience research.

In business I have found that those who can apply both types of information gathering are the best leaders at every thing from management to marketing. These leaders work well with diverse groups.

Also, during my academic research I studied many different ways leaders motivate others. Looking at the adult market, I found that learning how to teach, train and speak well were the gates—the gates to helping adults become great. By gaining the knowledge and skills so I could create a motivating environment, I found I could really connect with my audience, training seminar or class.

I found that applying the research in my work, I could teach many different topics, but the key was still to make that connection with the audience to help them strive for greatness. For example, today I was leading a project management seminar for adidas Greater China, in Hong Kong. Seminar participants were from Germany, England, Mainland China, Taiwan, Hong Kong, and U.S.A. With that rich mix of people and a topic like project management, there were many differences in opinion from the diverse backgrounds. The great thing was that their diverse backgrounds helped them, as a group; develop very clever solutions to the challenges I created for them.

This follows the theme that new ideas come from differences. New ideas come from different perspectives people have when they look at problems. Also, they come from mixing and crossing different experiences. The newest concepts and biggest steps forward come from the most unusual ideas. They come from a good mixture of people, backgrounds, cultures and ideas that are different.

Diverse backgrounds come through in differences in what we call "come from." Working with diverse groups we need to remember that each person is coming from a different point of view and is going toward, or fulfilling, a different set of needs. At times members of groups act just like kids, but I have to give them credit when they take responsibility. When we learn to make decisions with diverse groups of adults we create a much more rich working environment.

Working in Asia has been wonderful for me because most every organization has asked me to come back and train or speak for them. In the training and speaking business, one of the best endorsements I can receive is to be asked back by my clients.

Wright

Great.

Linger

As I mentioned before, when I did my academic research I looked at adults and how they learn. I studied different types of learners and audiences to understand how to help them find value in their own way. Every audience is different and every person sitting in the audience is different. I thought that if I can help each person in a diverse audience to meet his or her own needs, I can help everyone get more out of the training. When they walk out of that training room at the end of the day, they have more value and take it back to work.

The fundamental idea, from my research, is that we are communicating with human beings. We often forget about that idea now. When we are at work, my computer is talking to your computer instead of me talking to you. I'm trying to help companies change and understand ideas like, "Hey, I'm a human being. You're a human being. You're my customer and I really want to connect with you as a customer." If every customer is different and you are striving to be diverse in your thinking this makes an incredible difference to the bottom line.

One area of emphasis in my doctoral research was helping people surpass their past achievements by reaching what we call optimal experiences. Mihaly Csikszentmihalyi researched these highly productive states in different cultures around the world. Optimal experiences are when people is so totally involved in what they are doing that a bomb could go off in the next room and they wouldn't notice.

I looked at how teachers, trainers and speakers communicate to their audiences so that the learners were totally involved in the learning experience. The most important point is that these high levels of experience are very motivational. These levels make people feel really good after they've felt it so they want to come back to these experiences. Now, instead of just training a group we can get them respond by saying, "Hey, this is an incredible feeling. I want to apply what I have learned to get this feeling again!" Then after the training is over, they are far more likely to apply what they have learned.

If great leaders are great teachers then the best leaders can create this same experience for their employees, right?

Wright

Right.

Linger

They can inspire employees to get totally involved in a project so they can reach optimal experiences. Great sales people and great marketers have the ability to bring people to these high levels of motivation. Looking at diversity those who are great at creating highly productive environments are masters at diversity. The masters accept others as they are and help each individual strive to do her or his absolute best. Everyone has access to the statistics to do their jobs. The best communicate better than the rest to get their people and customers to strive to surpass their past performances.

Wright

I don't know how to define optimal experience, but there have been times when I have experienced what you are describing. The question is, how do you define optimal experiences or what are the characteristics of these experiences? How do leaders communicate with diverse people to help them to be motivated to reach these optimal experiences?

Linger

First, it is important to look at how leaders use communication to connect with different people. Then, we can look at the characteristics of optimal experiences.

There are two modes that leaders use and these are verbal and nonverbal communication. Let's start with the verbal communication leaders use to motivate others. First, they give personal examples and talk about personal experiences from outside of the work context. Second, they ask questions and encourage others to talk. Third, they get into discussions based on what others want to know even if it is from outside work. Fourth, they use humor. Fifth, they are warm and have others refer to them in ways that are most casual for their culture (i.e. they use first names if that is appropriate.) Sixth, they talk with employees or customers outside of the work context. As you can probably guess great leaders use all of these in moderation as each situation needs.

Next, let's look at nonverbal communication leaders use to motivate others. First, they move around and don't sit behind a desk. Second, they use gestures when talking. Third, they use vocal variety when they talk to others. Fourth, they use appropriate eye contact and facial expressions when talking. Fifth, they talk with passion and enthusiasm.

The key is that leaders communicate differently to diverse people. Leaders seek out and hire people who are different from themselves. In fact, they know that the best ideas come from crazy, oddball people. But, great leaders can motivate these different people to be the best at what they do.

With a basic understanding of how leaders communicate with diverse groups, let's look at the characteristics of this optimal level of experience. Leaders create an environment that others can be totally involved in the task at hand and experience the following characteristics. These leaders help their staff or customers to: 1) only concentrate on and complete the task at hand, 2) have clear goals and get immediate feedback, 3) become so deeply involved in a task that they feel the task is almost effortless yet they feel that they have a sense of control over their actions, 4) become so deeply involved in a task they loose limiting concerns for themselves and forget about outside worries and frustrations, and 5) become so deeply involved in a task that their sense of time is altered so tasks that take a few hours seem to take minutes and vice versa.

Again, the best leaders are masters at communicating with diverse groups to help individuals and audiences reach this optimal level of motivation. These leaders are masters at using communication to help others strive for greatness and enjoy the process.

Right now the most successful companies in China are the ones that really look at the culture and the people. The successful companies ask, "What do the people in China want?" and "What do they need?" The unsuccessful companies may ask these questions, but then they say, "Our method worked for us in the past. We'll do it our way." Then these companies wonder why the market is not responsive.

Wright

There seems to be a growing concern about companies going abroad and their success when they do that. Do you have any examples of companies that are successful at doing business with diverse cultures?

Linger

I have two examples of companies doing business globally that have been leaders at responding to diverse markets and employees. One company is retail chain and the other is a bank chain.

There's a local brand clothing company called Giordano here in Hong Kong. Giordano is selling to quite a few different cultures right now. Giordano is similar to Gap by having good clothing at a great price and they change their styles very quickly to follow market trends.

Their philosophy is a local brand for every culture that they go into instead of being a Hong Kong brand. So, when they go to Singapore, they're a Singapore brand. When they go into Malaysia, they're a Malaysian brand. When they go into Mainland China, they're a Mainland China, brand.

This effort to be the local brand wherever they are has been very effective for them. Their achievement is that they are successful at fighting the push toward uniformity within the company. This creates success in the different, diverse markets.

Wright

Great concept.

Linger

Another leading company is my client H.S.B.C., or what we call Hong Kong Bank around here. A while back, I led a diversity workshop for H.S.B.C., one of the fastest growing brands in the world. They're number 37 in brand recognition for all brands around the world. Two years ago, they weren't even on the list of top brands in the world. Their main slogan is that they are "the world's local bank." By making their brand "the world's local bank," they appeal to markets and people and yet they give people the confidence by being a world wide organization. Leading a diversity seminar with them me really feel good because they're constantly living the diversity part of their brand.

In their business plan they apply diversity to help different people and address different needs. By doing this, they're giving back to the community in the local areas that need their services. As part of their business plan they are contributing to education for people in economically depressed areas. When we talk about corporate social responsibility and giving back and not just taking, they're really setting a great example of being global and giving back globally. Part of their success is that they made diversity part of their business plan by putting it into their vision and mission statements and living the brand with the work they do.

Wright

Are leadership skills any different in Asia than they are in the United States?

Linger

Yes, leadership seems a little different here. Leadership is more subtle. First, those who have leadership positions are not questioned or challenged as much as in the U.S. Second, the cultures are more collective and the groups are more respected. People take more time to make sure everyone in the group agrees with decisions. This results in stronger commitments from everyone in the group.

Wright

I see.

Linger

It's more of a connected and committed team and in turn they have a stronger work ethic. Maybe it's just Hong Kong but they work very long hours over here.

Wright

Well, this has been a great conversation, Dr. Linger. I've really learned a lot. I could talk to you all day about the things that I do not know about the Asian culture. Perhaps one of these days we'll meet in the United States or in Hong Kong, and we'll sit down and have lunch and you can teach me as much as you will.

Linger

I have enjoyed this interview also.

Wright

I really appreciate this time you've taken with me. Thank you so much for being with us today on *Leadership Defined*.

Linger

Oh, well thank you very much, and I look forward to working with you again.

Wright

Great.

Linger

It's been a lot of fun and I hope that I can add value to our readers.

Wright

Great! Today we have been talking to Dr Warren Linger. He's recognized as a leader in diversity and culture trainer and speaker working to unite businesses and customers around the world. As we have found out today, he really believes about this around the world thing. He understands that everyone has different needs and he has devoted his life to learning, understanding, and developing ways to meet and exceed those needs. Thank you so much, Dr. Linger. I've really enjoyed it today.

Linger

Well, thank you very much, David.

Warren Linger has been recognized as an outstanding professional trainer and speaker who evokes passionate responses from those attending his seminars and workshops throughout the world. Warren's innovating, motivating, entertaining, interactive, and dynamic presentations are filled with high impact, useful information designed to give solid direction and help to those who want help achieving higher levels of success and leadership in their lives. Being a human possibility architect who created an international training and speaking firm, Warren understands that everyone has different needs. Warren has devoted his life to learning, understanding, and developing ways to help individuals and organizations achieve ultimate experiences in achieving their goals and dreams.

Dr. Warren Linger

World Class Value Training and Speaking

Linger Research International, Inc.

606 Kinwick Centre

32 Hollywood Road

Central, Hong Kong

Direct +853 2854-2720

www.linger-research.com

Chapter 5

VERONICA J. HOLCOMB

THE INTERVIEW

David E. Wright (Wright)

Today we are talking to Veronica Holcomb. Veronica is the president of VJ Holcomb Associates, an Executive Development and Training Consulting Practice. For the past three decades, Veronica has worked in Leadership Development almost exclusively as an Executive Coach. She has coached hundreds of clients from a variety of organizations and interviewed thousands of individuals at all levels on what it takes to be a successful leader. *Transforming Challenge To Opportunity*™, Veronica's trademark company slogan, captures perfectly her work as a Leadership Development coach and trainer. Veronica specializes in helping senior leaders and management teams discover and capitalize on their strengths to lead and perform at higher levels of impact and influence. She works with top performers and teams from Fortune 100 companies and specializes in combining personal insights with a proven model of structured analysis, reinforcement of strengths, and strategic action for increased effectiveness. Known for her integrity and warmth, her clients experience an impressive record of achievement, producing better communicators, better motivators, and stronger leaders. She's the author of *Ready, Set, Grow! 10 Success Strategies for Winning in the*

Workplace. She is an award winning Field Manager with Inscape Publishing Inc., a speaker with the American Management Association, and an adjunct feedback coach with the Center for Creative Leadership.

Before beginning her consulting business in 1985, Ms. Holcomb's professional experience included Director of Training and Organizational Development for a division of 4000 members at a major financial services firm in New York City. In spite of all her accomplishments, Veronica is most proud of her success as wife to Richard and mother to Stacey and Danielle. Veronica, welcome to *Leadership Defined!*

Veronica Holcomb (Holcomb)
Thank you very much, David.

Wright
You've been working in the field of Leadership Development for quite some time now. Can you give us a sense of how many leaders you've worked with?

Holcomb
I have worked with thousands of leaders. I've coached hundreds one-on-one, taught thousands in workshop format and interviewed a few thousand over the years.

Wright
So what makes for a great leader in your opinion, and can you offer some examples of what a great leader would be?

Holcomb
In my opinion, great leaders are people who have an extraordinary vision for the future - a vision that is ultimately for the good of people. They can mentally walk people into that future providing direction and hope. They are people of great integrity and principles and by their example, call everyone to a higher standard. They are role models and understand their responsibility to serve others. They're consistent *and* flexible. They connect with people at all levels.

Leaders are teachers. They attract and effectively use the talents of others granting authority *and* responsibility. They provide others room to grow. They recognize their responsibility in establishing an environment in which to grow other leaders.

They produce results through their influence on others. They demonstrate thankfulness for those who support them. Their leadership encourages and inspires others to take risks. And when they falter, the great leader is there to explore how and why it happened. They demonstrate value for human life more than numbers or possessions. They readily sacrifice for others.

Great leaders understand the value of stepping back to plan, celebrate and rest. They know when to confront and when to withdraw. They effectively handle people who don't want to get on board with them.

Great leaders make a positive difference and they leave a *legacy* of great leaders.

Great leaders are unfortunately, in short supply. No one person can be excellent in all that I've articulated. Nevertheless, there are a number of leaders that I admire. I'm quite impressed by David Neeleman the CEO of Jet Blue Airways, Joe Torrey, manager of the NY Yankees, Secretary of State Colin Powell, and Mary Kay Ash, former CEO of Mary Kay Cosmetics.

These men and women have achieved extraordinary results. Their track records speak for themselves. But more importantly, these people really exemplify integrity, concern, and care for people, and the ability to grow leaders. Great leaders are great teachers. Through their integrity, their ability to inspire others, they influence the world.

Wright

You must have seen many changes in Leadership Development along the way. Can you describe some of them for us?

Holcomb

Leadership Development is very different today than when I first started over 30 years ago. Who is being developed has changed. Thirty years ago, the number of women and minorities in my programs were very limited. I worked primarily with white men in their 40's. These men were wonderfully talented, competent and successful "drivers" who had come to a place in their careers where the next step required more statesman-like behavior. They lacked the more subtle skills required to be successful at higher levels. I worked with them to understand the impact their behavior was having on others. We then worked to fine tune critical areas and develop additional skills so they would have a greater behavioral repertoire from which to choose. This was my target group for over a decade.

Today, the workplace is much more diverse. I work with men *and* women from many different ethnicities and generations. I have always enjoyed my work, but it's a lot more interesting and exciting today.

Another difference in Leadership Development is the proliferation of instruments, programs and processes. Today, we take for granted Upward Feedback or 360° Feedback. Years ago, it didn't exist. People today recognize the value of giving feedback to others and are more open to doing so.

Wright

What do you believe are the greatest concerns for leaders today?

Holcomb

Survival. Leaders are under tremendous pressure to produce results. In today's competitive environment, leaders need to work with the best people available and be able to encourage their best performance.

Wright

If you had to put your finger on one critical component for effective leadership, what would that be?

Holcomb

Integrity is *the most critical* component.

Wright

Integrity?

Holcomb

Yes, absolutely. A leader can produce incredible results. But without integrity it's hard to sustain. Just ask Martha and the former leaders from Tyco, WorldCom, and Enron.

Wright

Have you come to this understanding because of all the recent revelations dominating the news today?

Holcomb

Not really. I am appalled at the moral shortcomings of these industry captains, and like most Americans would agree that ethics and integrity have a place in the workplace. But my unwavering belief in integrity comes from the observation that leaders can't develop leaders without it.

In recent years, I have become more and more disappointed and frankly frustrated with inability or unwillingness on the part of senior leaders to develop other leaders. They just don't seem to get it. Some may not see it as part of their role. Some do, but they are under such tremendous pressure to produce the numbers, Leadership Development takes a back seat. Oftentimes, what effort they do make is not well received.

Most large organizations have a set of values they print in their literature and on their walls. But when the leaders aren't walking the talk, people tend not to believe or trust them. When followers do not trust, believe or have confidence in their leader, it's very difficult for them to believe that the leader trusts, believes or has confidence in them. Leadership development under these circumstances is difficult.

Honesty and strong moral conduct is critical, but the major problem lies with every day kinds of things such as blowing off a scheduled meeting, following up on promises, demonstrating respect to a subordinate who's made a mistake, listening.

Wright

There are so many books, workshops and programs on leadership development, why are so many leaders in the dark about it?

Holcomb

The literature can be all over the place. If you pick up ten books on leadership or read ten chapters in this book you'll probably find ten definitions of leadership and ten approaches to Leadership Development. That's why it is so important to start with understanding who you are, what you stand for, and work from there.

Leaders must first be committed to their own growth and development. Making time to do that is difficult and understanding what to do can be challenging as well. There are certainly a number of resources available but it has to be important to the leader. Leaders who are concerned with leaving a legacy understand the necessity to develop others who can carry on when they are gone.

If an organization does not reward and support leaders for developing others, development is not likely to happen in any significant way. At Jet Blue Airways, Leadership Development starts at the top and works down throughout the entire organization. All leaders attend Leadership Development programs, which include classroom workshops and one-on-one coaching. David Neeleman, CEO, says, "Leadership Development is critical because it's critical to the success of the company and its ability to outperform the competition."

Another reason many leaders miss the mark on Leadership Development is because of the notion that leaders are born, not made. It's what I call the Silver Spoon Theory.

Wright

Tell me more.

Holcomb

The Silver Spoon Theory suggests that leaders are special people who have come into the world with innate leadership ability, potential or... a *Silver Spoon*. And, having been born with this special gift or talent, one can become a successful leader.

I saw an advertisement for the National Spelling Bee on television a few years ago. The announcer said, *"Today's great minds, tomorrow's leaders."* The sponsors were suggesting that these children with special intellectual gifts will make great leaders. I'm not convinced that there's a correlation between one's ability to spell and one's ability to lead.

Wright

They may just have great memories. We do seem to be committed to this theory, the Silver Spoon Theory.

Holcomb

Absolutely.

Wright

So what is the alternative?

Holcomb

The first thing is to understand the fallacy of the Silver Spoon Model. Let's work with the example of two David E. Wrights. Imagine they are exactly the same in terms of their intellect, education, upbringing, DNA...everything. One David *works* at developing himself as a leader and the other does not. Who will be successful? It seems obvious; the David who *worked* at it will be the success.

One's success in leadership or any endeavor is, for the most part, decided by determination—S*heer Determination*. You've got to want to be successful. There has to be a real drive, desire, and discipline to execute your strategy. Think about the successful leaders you know and you'll realize that this is what they have done.

Wright

I heard the inflection in your voice when you said determination. You preceded it with *sheer*.

Holcomb

Yes I did.

Wright

So, what is it that drives *sheer* determination?

Holcomb

That's a good question. There *is* a force that drives determination and its called confidence... you have to believe in yourself.

Confidence comes in part as a result from your experience with success. When you achieve success in any endeavor, e.g., leadership, athletics, relationships, your confidence is strengthened. When your confidence is strong, you're able to bring more effort and energy to the table.

You must believe that you can accomplish your goals in order to muster up whatever the required level of effort. Donald Trump was once asked what he looks for when selecting a leader to work for him. Without missing a beat he said, "Energy! Being smart has to be a given. What I look for is energy."

Sheer Determination is a type of energy, which begins with confidence and belief in oneself. Belief allows one to make a strong effort and achieve a level of success. Success then bolsters one's confidence.

Wright

Are you talking about self-image?

Holcomb

Only in part. You must be able to see yourself accomplishing your goal. But it's more than visualization; it's a belief and faith in yourself. This does not come naturally because we're not born with confidence.

Wright

Is it confidence in one's self or someone's confidence in you?

Holcomb

It's both. Since we're not born with confidence, it must come from somewhere. Confidence can be developed in a couple of ways.

Confidence comes in part from *Positive Self-Talk*. When we speak our positive belief in ourselves to ourselves it strengthens our confidence and allows us to step out a little further to tackle an area where we might be fearful. We can use *Positive Self Talk* to avoid coming down on ourselves when we've made a mistake.

Another way of developing confidence is by engaging in a developmental process. This type of process is similar to weight lifting. For example, if I want to strengthen my biceps, I might start performing bicep curls with five-pound weights in order to challenge the muscle. If I'm diligent and consistent, at some point that muscle will no longer be challenged so I'll graduate to a heavier weight, perhaps seven or eight pounds. In time, even that weight will no longer be challenging, so I'll graduate to 10 pounds and then 12. I will continue to graduate to heavier weights incrementally and modestly in order to challenge and build my biceps. All the while, I am also building my confidence.

Wright

You seem to be really sold on the idea of confidence. Could you tell our readers more about why confidence is so important?

Holcomb

I meet and work with far too many people who live their lives well beneath their potential. They do so for a variety of reasons but at the root of most of it is their lack of confidence. Frankly, I'm quite troubled by the lack of support people receive from their leaders. If leaders are genuinely interested in developing their people, there is hardly anything more important for a leader to do than to strengthen the confidence of their people.

Confidence also comes from the *Supportive Relationship* a leader can provide; consequently, when leaders believe in their people, their people can believe in themselves. When people don't believe in themselves, they don't muster up the energy required to do outstanding work. In far too many situations, people work in environments where they're criticized and unsupported by their boss. The result is lack of confidence, desire, discipline and drive. This lesser effort will most certainly produce leadership behavior that is "lesser" in nature. Mediocre leadership further reduces one's confidence.

I see this again and again. So when I have a chance, I *really* jump on my soapbox, and go on a rant. There is nothing more important than a leader's ability to build the confidence of their people. As I said, when leaders believe in their people and their potential to grow and develop, their people will believe the same and go on to do things they hardly knew they could.

Wright

You know it makes a lot of sense. Could you tell our readers how integrity fits in?

Holcomb

When people trust and believe their leader to be a person of integrity they will accept their leader's trust and belief in them.

When a leader *lacks* integrity, followers will have difficulty believing this leader truly cares about them and their development. There's always a cloud of doubt in the atmosphere; not enough to prevent followers from coming to work and even making things happen. But, the lack of integrity will prevent them from being fully energized, empowered and working at their full potential.

Wright

This power thing is an aphrodisiac. I think it must be really, really hard to use my integrity button all the time. What do you think?

Holcomb

Of course it's hard. That's why one *must* have people to whom they are accountable and put systems in place to fight against what just might be "human nature."

I'm not sure many leaders have thought much about how critical a role integrity plays in their success and the success of the organization. When I've asked leaders if they have an unchangeable moral code or standard that guides them through various situations, the answer is a disappointing "no." Their standards change depending on the situation.

Those who do have a strong moral compass usually develop it because of their parents and/or a religious background.

Wright

John Maxwell suggests that as you proliferate in an organization (in terms of leadership, power, and influence) your rights, perks, privileges should diminish—for the good of you and the organization.

Holcomb

I agree with him. You have choices. You can choose not to have a mansion, fancy cars, expensive jewelry, lavish parties and such. Please don't get me wrong, I like nice things as much as anyone, but when you start to feel "entitled" to these because of your rank and power, you're sliding down a slippery slope.

Taking the easy way out is what can lead to excess. It starts small, with little things. Lesa Lardieri, VP Pfizer, describes those small steps as "shaving" away your integrity. It's dangerous because you can't be sure how deep you're going and once you've cut away, you can't get it back.

I'm sure many of the fallen leaders we've been reading about recently would return all of their excessive perks in a heartbeat for a good night's sleep—in their own bed.

Wright

Yes. Tell me, how are you defining integrity.

Holcomb

Integrity is honest, moral and ethical behavior. It's an understanding of your core values and beliefs and living them. It's consistency, being complete and whole and, as John Maxwell would say, making certain that your words and your music match.

Wright

I can see that it's a challenge in areas other than corporate. Do you think that's true?

Holcomb

Sadly, it is very true. Integrity is lacking in business, professional sports, the church, education, government, relationships, and families. It's a huge issue, and I believe it limits our impact as a society.

I visualize it this way. Imagine a triangle, which we've divided into thirds with two horizontal lines. Let's title the base of the triangle, *Integrity*. The next or middle section we'll call *Inspiration; and* the top or apex we'll call *Influence*. When leadership is based on a solid foundation of integrity, followers will develop belief and trust in the leader. If the leader walks the talk and develops their people, followers will have confidence in themselves. With that, the leader can effectively inspire them to perform their best and achieve extraordinary results. That result brings us to the top of the triangle, which is Influence, the ability to effect change in our sphere of responsibility. When we turn that triangle upside down, which we often do in this culture, we first focus on and applaud performance or a person's ability to influence the environment. An upside down triangle cannot maintain that position. It will eventually topple.

Imagine what it would be like to work in an environment where integrity really mattered. Our world would be a very different place.

Wright

Do you think some of these leaders are getting off track because they don't believe in the whole life theory; that every part of your life should be in balance? Are they just going for the performance and that's it?

Holcomb

It does appear that leaders for whom integrity is important have a world-view based on their moral and ethical beliefs and those who get off track do not.

Unfortunately, in our society we often care more about the performance than the content of one's character. I once sat with a CEO discussing a junior executive of his who needed coaching. This fellow was extremely abusive and difficult to work for. The CEO confessed this bad behavior really didn't matter to him because the junior executive delivered what he wanted.

I have worked with many executives who learned through my coaching process they were behaving in ways that were career limiting. Many had never been told what they learned through coaching. It really makes my blood boil that someone could be allowed to work in a career 20-30 years and not be told what he or she needed to grow and develop. But again, it didn't matter because their performance was more important. This is a serious shortfall on the part of the leader.

There are many examples of highly successful and visible leaders whose character leaves a lot to be desired. But when the organization or society's needs are being met, we overlook at lot. To play off a quote from Winston Churchill, *"we get the leadership we deserve."*

Wright

Do you think by the time the people come to you for coaching and consultation, this is one indication that they're really serious and they want to tackle all these questions of confidence, honesty, integrity, and production? Or are they just there because the company sent them?

Holcomb

It's both. Most are there because the company has sent them, but once they arrive and they see the benefits and the advantages of working through this type of process, they're on board. They recognize it is to their benefit to fully understand how they are coming across to others and what is getting in their way.

The more seniority a leader has, the less in touch they are with others. People tell them what they want to hear and oftentimes, that information is far from the truth. In my coaching process, I interview colleagues, peers, subordinates and bosses. And the feedback I share with them is attributed. So if I spoke to John about you David, I would say, "David, I spoke with John and this is what he said." This type of feedback is constructive and concise. I assure my clients that we're going to get "The Truth." It is very difficult for people to share this kind of information with one another, but they will share it with a third party. I then deliver the information in a way that is clear, constructive and comfortable for my client. It's a wonderful opportunity to deal with these issues and situations in a safe environment.

Wright

Well, before I ask you the last question, let's talk a bit about your book, *Ready, Set, Grow! 10 Success Strategies for Winning in the Workplace.*

Holcomb

I'd love to!

Wright

Is *Ready, Set, Grow* available in bookstores or on amazon.com?

Holcomb

Yes. Look for it in the fall of 2004.

Wright

Great! Congratulations on that and much success to you. Now, tell us, what is the answer to this challenging issue? I'm talking about the issue of integrity, being a great leader, trying the best you can to take your company to great heights while keeping all the moral and spiritual and ethical questions in check.

Holcomb

Draw a line in the sand and do not cross it.

Wright

That simple, huh?

Holcomb

It's just that simple, and equally as difficult. It's a good idea for leaders to sit down and think about where to draw that line. When life presents challenging situations, and it will, they know where they stand. It's also important for a leader to consider what success means to them Not crossing that line may require them to give up or sacrifice an "opportunity."

I know many people who are extraordinarily successful in business but are rarely home with their families. The price they pay is considerable. I know others who would be considered average performers at work but are leaders in their homes and communities and have raised healthy, balanced children who will make a positive contribution to our society.

Great leaders who desire to leave a legacy will draw that line in the sand not cross it.

Wright

Well, what an interesting conversation. You've given me a lot to think about today. I really do appreciate the time you've spent with me, and I think I agree with you. This is a question that each of us has to deal with, but you've given me a new perspective. I'm going to start drawing more lines in the sand.

Holcomb

Thank you.

Wright

Today we have been talking to Veronica Holcomb, president of VJ Holcomb Associates, an executive development and training consulting practice. And as we have found out, she knows an awful lot about the issues that confront prospective leaders in the world today. I really do appreciate you sharing these ideas with us and I hope we can talk more about them in the future.

Holcomb

I would love to.

Wright

Thank you for being with us on *Leadership Defined.*

About The Author

Transforming Challenge To Opportunity. This phrase captures Veronica J. Holcomb's life's work as a Leadership Development Strategist and Coach for the past 30 years. Ms. Holcomb specializes in helping individuals discover and capitalize on their strengths to lead and perform at a higher level of impact and influence. Known for her integrity and warmth, Ms. Holcomb's clients affirm an impressive record of producing better communicators, better motivators and stronger leaders.

Veronica J. Holcomb

Phone: 718.981.1568

www.vjholcomb.com

Chapter 6

RICK HOUCEK

THE INTERVIEW

David E. Wright (Wright)

Rick Houcek's singular company purpose is: *To provide high-octane, world-class strategic planning systems for business and life,* helping Top Gun leaders, teams and individuals to succeed "on purpose, most of the time," rather than "by accident, some of the time." He does this four primary ways: (1) facilitating his *Power Planning*™ strategic planning retreats for small and mid-size companies, (2) leading his *Passion Planning*™ workshops for ambitious individuals on personal life planning and goal setting, (3) delivering high-energy motivational keynotes, and (4) one-on-one success coaching.

He has coached entrepreneurs, CEOs, presidents, and senior executives for over 10 years, and is former president of Ross Roy Advertising, an Atlanta ad agency and division of the $700 million Ross Roy Group. A University of Missouri graduate, he is a member of the National Speakers Association and has been recognized in *Who's Who Among U.S. Executives* and *Who's Who in Georgia.*

Rick is married and passionately devoted to his soul mate, Robbie, adores his awesome grown twins, Chip and Val, and has four fanatical life passions: his family, his personal health and fitness, helping others prosper through his business and friendships, and playing

competitive baseball on a traveling men's team. Rick, welcome to
Leadership Defined.

Rick Houcek (Houcek)

David, I'm honored to be here.

Wright

In today's unpredictable times—a struggling economy, high un-
employment, domestic and worldwide terrorism, media watch-
dogging, plus the zaniness of business closings, sales and mergers—
what's the biggest problem leaders face today?

Houcek

None of the above. It's the perception among followers that leaders
are corrupt. And every leader—including the majority who are honest—must face this music. Whether they like it or not, every leader is
scrutinized by their followers. Look at it through the eyes of the followers. The employees at Enron believed their leaders when they said
the company was profitable, the retirement funds were secure, ad
nauseam. Then—*wham!*—The discovery is made of lies and misdeeds.
Those employees were trusting and got betrayed. There have been a
similar string of events at WorldCom, Adelphia, Tyco, and a host of
others nabbing all the front-page headlines. And it's not just business—it's in organizations of all kinds. We see improprieties in
recruitment practices by college athletic coaches, abuses at military
academies, even the Catholic Church has been ravaged by scandal. So
now every employee in every company is asking himself: "Hmmm, my
CEO seems honest enough, has all the right moves, gives all the right
answers—but so did those guys from Enron, and look what they
turned out to be. Enron employees probably trusted their leaders like
I trust mine, and they got fooled and lost everything. I wonder if my
CEO is a crook and it just hasn't been discovered yet." *That's* what's
going through the minds of employees everywhere. It's discussed
among employees offline—over lunch, in restrooms, over a beer after
work, even at the dinner table between spouses—but never directly
with the CEO. And every leader better wake up to that. But the irony
in your question is: leadership corruption isn't characteristic only of
troubled times. Crimes at the top have been happening for centu-
ries—in times of peril and prosperity—and will continue. The vigilant
leader never forgets that his decisions and actions always will be
scrutinized for their honor or their deception.

Wright

If it were possible to declare one kind or style of leadership that rises above all others, what would it be?

Houcek

There is one: leadership by example. Probably not what you were expecting, but it's the only one that has *ever* mattered. Funny thing is, it's not really even a style, and it's not one that any leader chooses consciously—it just *happens* whether they like it or not. Whatever a leader says or does is considered the acceptable norm for organizational behavior. A leader's words and actions—whatever they are—become her example. And that is what the organization will follow and emulate. Mother Theresa was a quintessential "leader by example"—we should all set examples the way she did. Let me put it another way: everything a leader says, thinks or does gives her followers permission to do likewise. No matter what. Case in point, let's say the company values on the wall declare: "We will behave with integrity and the highest professional ethics at all times, in all dealings"...but the CEO announces in a meeting "We're in a cash crunch, so let's delay paying our suppliers. Dodge their calls as long as possible and don't tell them we're in trouble. And if you have to, pay only the loudest complainers." That sends a clear message to employees that deception is okay, which, of course, violates the values. But if you take the high road and live by the values—which is expected or you should take them off the wall—the decision should be to talk openly to suppliers up-front, telling them of the cash situation and working out a payment plan that meets both parties' needs. *That's* the integrity move. And the CEO who misses it loses all credibility and shouldn't be surprised when employees follow suit with their own unethical decision-making. I've said for years that "CEO" is a meaningless title and should be changed to CES—Chief Example Setter—it's a much more accurate description of reality.

Wright

If we believe the news media, ethics among leaders is rampantly low. But to be fair, aren't there times when deciding to violate a company principle may be the right thing to do?

Houcek

There might be. And the only acceptable reason is *when it serves a greater good*. Which means two things: first, you better have your values written down and highly publicized internally so everyone is singing off the same song sheet; and second, you better list them in priority order, so in a crunch, you only cut from the bottom, never the top. An example might be a U.S. president who commits government dollars to a particular cause when war breaks out and funds must be diverted to national defense. Are we going to put our soldiers in jeopardy with poor training and inferior weaponry because a pledge was made to fund lesser important programs? Of course not. At the time the pledge was made, it was sincere, but new events caused the priority sequencing to kick in.

While that makes sense for budgeting, it's different for *core behavioral values*. I believe if you truly think you might violate one value in favor of another—and values *are* promises—you should seriously consider whether the one you would violate is even a value to begin with. Why put it on the list if you know in advance your commitment is questionable? I prefer to treat values as absolute tenets, never as matters of convenience. I would add that breaking a promise, when necessary, must be done carefully and properly. Some people break promises and never tell those affected, or tell them arrogantly with no explanation—both are horrible leadership mistakes. Understand the other party has an expectation the commitment will be fulfilled—one you agreed to—so a delicate, courteous, genuinely apologetic explanation is in order.

Wright

How easy is it to spot a bad leader? Are there some telltale signs?

Houcek

Besides the obvious—telling lies or getting caught with fingers in the cookie jar—there are a couple of glaring red flags to me.

First is a leader who, when crisis hits, abandons company values and makes decisions in his own personal best interest. In my world, that's worse than just "bad," it's downright underhanded. A chimpanzee could make high-integrity decisions when times are good—that takes no will power or good sense. But the mark of an ethical leader is the one who will make the same high-road decision in a hailstorm of crisis. Show me someone with a history of making decisions like that, and I want him running for president of the United States.

The second red flag is when a leader trumpets to staff: "Our number one objective is to make a profit." I know trouble looms ahead on that one. When will CEOs get it that making profit, though very important, is a privilege you earn only as a result of doing what the company is really in business for—*creating and keeping customers*—to ensure longevity of the enterprise? When the sun comes up, no matter what products or services you sell, you better be making the decisions and taking the actions that create and keep customers. On some days, you may even have to *forfeit* profit to do it. But if profit is your number one objective, above all others, you just gave your employees permission to abuse customers if necessary, so long as they don't lose money. They'll even think their jobs depend on it. In the short term you win financially, but in the long term, you'll lose customers, which is akin to severing the artery to the heart, and you'll bleed to death. That's tragic mismanagement. I even hate to see "profit" written in a company mission statement or in the core values. It sends a horribly wrong message to employees. It's even worse when it's on the lobby wall over the receptionist's head—*that* sends a catastrophic message to customers. When I'm a customer and walk into a business that blares the profit goal in the lobby, my first thought is, "I may get screwed here."

The only exception to this is if your values say something like: "Our #1 Priority is achieving the loyalty of our customers as a result of our non-stop, diligent efforts to delight them with superior products and services—and only when we have accomplished that will we deserve a fair profit return for our efforts...etc. etc. etc." *That* would be okay, because it sends the proper message to both employees and customers. If wording to that effect appears in any company's values, I've never seen it.

Wright

When a new leader takes the helm—either by replacing the old leader or in the starting of a new business—what is his <u>first</u> obligation?

Houcek

There's not just one—I think there are several. There's a first obligation of *behavior*, a first obligation of *action*, and a first obligation of *attitude*.

The first obligation of behavior is to *establish an atmosphere of trust* throughout the organization. Proclaim in no uncertain terms that trustworthy behavior is the minimum expectation of individual success, and live by that example yourself. Was there a more trusted leader than Robert E. Lee of the Confederacy? His generals and soldiers had such faith in his honorable nature; they would follow him into battles, with odds stacked heavily against them that meant certain death for many. Establishing an atmosphere of trust, as Lee did, will require clear examples, since simply saying the words doesn't cut it, and because everyone defines trust differently. Cite specific examples of what both trustworthy and untrustworthy behavior are, relevant to your business, and challenge your people to take it deeper, with more concrete examples. Such as, announce that missing a deadline and saying nothing in advance is untrustworthy, but that informing others who are affected, with time to react and prepare, is a responsible act. Missing the deadline may still bear consequences, but owning up to it in advance is nonetheless an act of trust.

Second is the obligation of action, which is to *define reality*. It never ceases to amaze me how many different perceptions of reality exist in any organization—probably as many as there are people. Externally, there's the reality of the marketplace, the reality of the competitive environment, how your products and services are perceived, what is your unique and compelling customer advantage, et al. Internally, there's the reality of where your profitable growth will come from, how you measure company and individual success, what are the standards of excellence it takes to be on the team, and more. One caveat: while the CEO should make sure these definitions of reality get done and communicated company-wide, she shouldn't create them alone. For greater effectiveness, she should involve a team of dedicated company leaders and thinkers to get buy-in and commitment. There is simply no substitute for buy-in. Without it, you're swimming upstream. While at the helm of GE, Jack Welch was known to be particularly adept at gathering teams to define reality.

Third is the obligation of attitude, which is to *require a company-wide "learning culture," a constant willingness to improve by all employees*, starting with the CEO. Tell everyone exactly what you do on a week-by-week, month-by-month basis to learn, grow and improve— books you've read, workshops you've attended, tapes you've listened to—so they see you leading by example. Announce that everyone will have a personal development plan—created in tandem by themselves and their supervisor—specific to the needs of their job. Yes, this even applies to those who don't have aspirations to advance to higher levels—they too must be willing to improve. Back up your commitment by budgeting for education. Make this "learning culture" a part of the hiring process too. Probe deeply in interviews to sift out evidence that your candidate is someone who routinely learns, grows and improves—by choice, not by force. If no evidence exists, they don't fit. Also make this a part of the performance appraisal process for onboard employees. If they've not taken action on their development plans, maybe they don't fit. Don't kid yourself, an organization of stagnant people is a stagnant organization and will be buried alive by aggressive competitors. If you've ever shopped at Nordstrom's or spent the night at a Ritz Carton hotel, you know both have a penchant for unmatched customer service. Neither got that way by sticking their heads in the sand on improvement—they accomplished their legendary reputations by constant and never-ending learning, growing and improving. It's in their DNA and they will not settle for less.

Wright

Leading well seems incredibly challenging, since the failure rate is so high. What would you say is the most difficult task a leader faces on an every day basis?

Houcek

Bar none, it is realizing that, to be effective in her role, she must constantly inflict pain and suffering on her people. Why? Because central to a competent leader's success is her willingness to *drive change*. But human nature is to resist change, so employees tend to fight it and get angry about it. Therefore, driving change means creating pain for others. Many leaders won't do this; it's outside their comfort zone. To lead well, you better *get* comfortable with it. You better first get outside your own comfort zone, and then expect others to get outside theirs. Or you stagnate. If you can't, you'll pay a horrible price: if you're the owner, you'll lose your best people. And if you're a hired gun leader, you'll first lose your best people, then you'll lose your job because the owner will terminate you. Colin Powell said being responsible means pissing people off. It's unavoidable and comes with the territory. If you can't handle it, it doesn't make you a bad person, but it will make you an ineffective leader.

Wright

Thirty years ago, you couldn't find a book on leadership. Now, bookstores are backed up with books, cassettes, CDs. There are even videos, seminars, workshops, peer groups, you name it. What's all the hubbub? Leaders from long ago seemed to get along just fine without it. Why so much educational material now?

Houcek

Several reasons. But first, let's don't kid ourselves into thinking they got along just fine way back when. They didn't. They tripped and fell, repeatedly, just like leaders of today. But there was far less media scrutiny and publicity of their blunders. Leaders have done dumb things throughout history—most are just lucky enough to not get found out—there was no investigative reporting and there's only so much room on the front page.

But back to your question: The reason there's such a tonnage of available how-to information on leadership today is, I think, just the natural progression of time. Heck, there's more information available on *everything* today, and there will be boatloads more in the years to come. Leadership hasn't been singled out.

All that said, there is nothing simple about effective leadership—it isn't everyone's strong suit—so learning tools are critical. The old adage "Oh, he's just a born leader" is preposterous. It's nonsense to believe a newborn infant is blessed with some innate abilities to lead others, even if the child comes from a long line of leaders. Leadership is, and always will be, a *learned* skill. Some learn bad habits and become bad leaders. Others, who are really committed to excellence and aspire to become exceptional leaders, study, study, and study more, the behavior of winners. That's where the quantity of leadership learning material becomes helpful. I'm an avid student and learner of leadership effectiveness, and devour new material.

Wright

What's your favorite leadership book—that you'd tell someone to read if they could only read one?

Houcek

Sorry, there are two, and they're both exceptional. Bar none, the best of all time, in my estimation, is *How To Win Friends And Influence People* by Dale Carnegie. That one may be surprising because no one thinks of it as a leadership book—but it is one, in spades. I read it once a year during December and I've done so for the last 15-plus years. Second is *The West Point Way of Leadership* by Col. Larry Donnithorne. Until I read it, I was of the mistaken opinion that the purpose of West Point was to train soldiers. It isn't. It's to *grow lead-*

ers, and they've grown more than any other single institution in the world.

There are other good books, but those two are so high above the rest, I'll stop there. I would hope this book, *Leadership Defined*— the one this interview is being done for—would soon be among the most-acclaimed leadership books too.

Wright

It's almost frightening—the complexities of leadership, the vast quantities of learning materials, the risks, the constant criticism, and now the questions of low integrity. When taken in total, it seems so overwhelming. Why would anyone want to become a leader in today's world?

Houcek

Not everyone should because not everyone is cut out for it. It requires courage beyond what most can fathom. I'm hard pressed to think of a harder decision a leader has to make than to stay the course when the tide of public opinion is swinging the other way, and even some of your staunchest supporters are changing sides. Consider every U.S. president who has led during wartime. There's usually strong support at the beginning. But at some point, the people of our peace-loving nation get tired of the fighting, sometimes forget why we're involved, want to return to peace, and ultimately get angry with the current administration—whichever party is in office—and want out. Imagine being president when *that* tide shifts. It would be so easy to throw in the towel and pull out. Why fight it when the masses against the war are becoming louder and angrier? Maintaining the war effort in the face of that dispute, criticism, ridicule, and anger is horrifically difficult. What few people realize is that Abraham Lincoln—who many historians consider our best and most effective president—was highly unpopular, even with members of his own party, up until very late in the Civil War. The North was losing, newspaper reports constantly ridiculed him, he was the target of a daily barrage of criticism, his decisions were relentlessly second-guessed, and his re-election was considered a lost cause. But Lincoln was so convinced that his highest presidential obligation was to preserve the union, he staked his political reputation and re-election on his belief that the war should continue until the union was saved, not divided. Staying the course, when the masses want to go the opposite way, is not for the squeamish. You better have a cast-iron stomach because you're in for public humiliation the likes of which you've never seen—all directed at *you*. In politics, at least the criticism is out in the open. It's worse in a business, because it's mostly invisible. You don't know who is really on your team and who's faking it. There is no media machine cranking out quotes with names attached to them. It's all under the table, and you won't know who to trust.

Wright

As a leader yourself, if you could pick one and only one single tool with which to lead effectively, what would you choose?

Houcek

A CEO friend of mine answered that one day very eloquently. He said, "Give me just one honest person in my organization who will tell me the entire truth every time, and tell it to me fast, and I could lead effectively forever." That's hard to argue with. Like many leaders, he had been plagued with getting inaccurate and untimely information from his direct reports. Why this happens is simple to understand. Some people won't challenge the CEO, so they tell her what they think she wants to hear, even if it's untrue or a stretch of the truth. Result: the CEO gets jaded information and makes flawed decisions. Another reason: Some people are scared to death to bring bad news to a leader for fear of getting shot. That's mostly the leader's fault, by the way, for creating a shoot-the-messenger atmosphere. Sometimes, though, the leader didn't create it—the employee may just fear authority figures. The quality of leadership decisions and actions is highly dependent on the accuracy and timeliness of information. Surround yourself with a second tier of courageous and forthright individuals who will *tell it like it is*—then make sure you do nothing to shut down their candor.

Wright

Since a leader is responsible for seeing that operating results are achieved, it's no doubt important to be a good motivator. What are the best motivational skills a leader should possess, to help light people's fires?

Houcek

This may surprise you: *None!* Being a good motivator is a dead-end street, and I don't believe leadership should involve motivating others. When an employee needs to be motivated, a siren should go off. It's not a sign the leader is a lousy motivator, it's a sign the wrong employee was hired. Leaders should create quality hiring processes to make sure only *self*-motivated employees are invited in. Employee candidates who require others to motivate them shouldn't make it past the first interview, and should certainly never be hired. All that said, let's boil it down. Regarding motivation, a leader really has four key responsibilities. First, hire only self-motivated people, the kind who light their own fires. Second, create an inspirational workplace environment and culture where self-motivated people can flourish and win. Third, remove those *non*-self-motivated folks who slipped in under the radar, which will happen, by the way, because even the best interviewers get fooled periodically. And fourth, and this one is critical, don't *de*-motivate employees. That's where leaders often shoot themselves in the foot, and may not even realize it. People can get de-motivated by many things a leader does, like word choice, behaviors not matching company values, decisions impacting employees that are unexplained, miscommunication, no communication, repeated indecision, breaking commitments, allowing chronic non-performers or non-value compliers to stay, gestures and body language that show displeasure—and of course the big three—lying, cheating and stealing. And on top of all those, dozens of other little things. So the leader's role is more about creating inspirational environments for self-motivated people, not motivating non-motivated people.

Wright

You mention lying, cheating and stealing. Aren't those tough to prove? How many times do employees have the necessary evidence— or the courage to stand up and accuse—when they suspect dishonorable CEO behavior?

Houcek

Seldom, if ever. But that's not the point. It doesn't take real physical evidence—it only takes the *perception* of evidence for the leader to lose the support and confidence of the troops. That's why leaders must realize the importance of building quality relationships with *all* constituents—employees, the leadership team, customers, owners, everyone. Let's go to the core. The main ingredient for a successful relationship of *any* kind, between *any* two people, is trust. If you don't have trust, you don't even have a relationship—you're only acquaintances. When the chips are down, you'll go only to people you trust. Likewise, they'll come to you. So the biggest CEO crime is a violation of trust or integrity—or the perception of one. But let's drill deeper still. One of the most important documents in any organization is the list of core values. Trustworthiness should no doubt be one of them, but there should be others. Leaders have a right to create this list and mandate them, but I think that works best only in a new company. In an established company, I lean toward forming a team to create the behavioral values. Once complete, they should be enshrined and posted for all to see, in multiple locations. All employee activities should be built off the values—hiring, coaching, performance appraisals, rewards, punishment, and when necessary, termination. If you're not enforcing the values, take them down. Most important, as leader, you must live the values on a day-by-day, decision-by-decision, action-by-action basis.

Wright

What's your biggest pet peeve about leaders, one that really infuriates you?

Houcek

Dodging a direct question by answering a different one. That drives me nuts. While I denounce lying, at least a lie is a direct answer to the question. Dodging isn't even an answer, it's a deflection, and frankly it's insulting. It happens most in times of crisis, fear or uncertainty, when what people need most from the leader is straight talk, honest answers. Leaders, especially politicians, are heavily trained and particularly adept at handling media interviews by going in armed and dangerous—which means, having their own agenda points to get out, regardless of the question asked. In other words, they're trained to deflect tough questions away from the issue and onto the point-of-view they want communicated. While this may seem smart on their end, it looks and feels like a lie on the receiving end. Viewers watching on TV get angry with this. Do politicians really think we're that stupid? If I were an interviewer, I would hang on like a pit bull, asking the same question over and over again, until I got a straight answer.

Now don't get me wrong, media interview training is a great idea. Some interviewers ask questions that are clearly intended to stump the leader, make them look dumb, off-guard, and stumble for an answer. Others are worse—they presume guilt or blame without evidence, making the interviewee appear to be lying. Still other questions are downright stupid or insulting. Anyone in her right mind would want to be prepared to handle those. But I don't mean those—I'm talking about the fair, insightful question that deserves a straightforward, honest answer. Dodging those is integrity suicide. Answer the question you were asked, directly, then if you want to make additional points that suit your agenda, it's okay. One final point on this: "I don't know" is an acceptable answer when you really don't know. Don't fake it. Isn't it smarter to risk disappointing your followers in the short-term with your lack of knowledge than to risk losing their trust forever with a dodge or a lie?

Wright

It's often said that leaders should "set the tone for the organization." What exactly does that mean, why is it important, and how do you do it?

Houcek

It means the leader establishes the culture of organizational behavior. No one is in a better position to do so because no one's decisions and actions impact a wider body of people in the company. Why it's important is because the culture defines what is acceptable and unacceptable behavior, so it represents the very fabric of the organization. How do you do it? There are a host of ways a leader can influence the culture—many through her own behavior that I've already mentioned.

But let me offer two more. One is to have stump speeches at the ready. Pick two, three or four primary points—they could be goals, values, issues of importance, or success stories—and any time you are gathered with staff, those are the points you will constantly harp on. You'll get sick and tired of hearing yourself say the same old things long before your people will have heard them even once. Repetition is key. Remember, the topics you choose will define key culture points, because once folks realize what's important to you, that's what they'll focus on too. The very best at this were our Native American ancestors. They excelled at passing on tribal history, stories of forefathers, laws, tenets, beliefs and values—through passionate repetition of the spoken word, primarily through campfire stories from tribal elders to the young. They relied solely on this spoken method of teaching and wrote nothing down. And yet it worked wondrously. An Indian's historical roots and spiritual culture is ingrained deeply in his soul. Nothing is forgotten. We could certainly learn from their example.

Second is to put important axioms on paper for clarity—and post them everywhere. These too could be goals, values, issues of importance, success stories, or inspirational thoughts. While I wish it could be accomplished the Native American way—without writing anything down—the truth is, in our fast-paced, greatly-changed, distraction-laden society, people spend far less time learning one-on-one from mentors. Plus, they're inundated with thousands of messages every day, each competing for their attention—so remembering the ones you want them to remember is asking a lot. Effective leaders must realize this and know that when a new follower joins the team, it is incumbent upon her to shake the newbie out of his confusion and indifference and drill into him, repeatedly, the values, laws, and history of the clan. Having them on paper makes them visual and easier to drink in.

Wright

Okay, last question. What three final pieces of advice—that you haven't already covered—would you give to today's leaders?

Houcek

Only three? I'm just getting rolling.

Okay, first, *never ask anything of anyone you haven't done yourself or aren't willing to do yourself.* And let them see you do it. This is central to what made Vince Lombardi a respected leader. In my own experience, I once came back from a client meeting, walked by the conference room where three administrative assistants had the entire table filled with direct mail pieces, envelopes, and stamps, and had an assembly line of folding, stuffing, stamping, and sealing. I took off my jacket, rolled up my sleeves, asked where I could squeeze in, sat down at the table, and enjoyed the next 30 minutes of delightful conversation with them while we handled a very important client mailing project. One remarked how surprised she was the president had time for such a menial task. I said, "To me, it's the most important thing I could do at this moment. Our clients are gold to us, you're on a tight deadline, I've got a few available minutes before my next meeting, and you're fabulous people to spend time with. Where else should I be?"

Second, *give credit to others, don't steal it for yourself.* Many years ago, I worked for a CEO who, during a team meeting, listened attentively to the good ideas of his staff, then at the end he announced his chosen option and presented it to the assembled team as his own original idea—and it had just come from a VP at the table only minutes before. We sat there with jaws on the floor. It was the main topic at the bar that night and was all over the office by lunchtime the next day. He crucified himself. Overcoming the effects of that idiotic behavior would require months of high integrity action—and there would still be some people who would never forgive or forget. Ronald Reagan had a sign on his desk: "It's amazing how much you can get accomplished if you don't care who gets the credit."

Third, *love to lead*. The greatest leaders have a passion to be in charge. Not because power has corrupted them, but because they're driven to make a positive difference. General Patton had it, Margaret Thatcher had it, Colin Powell has it. If you don't love to lead, you owe it to yourself—and to your followers—to find another line of work. There's no shame is stepping aside to let an abler person run the show.

In fact, I'm going to cheat and add a fourth point, since I just touched on it: *know when it's time to leave*. That's a tough decision because we all believe we have a few more good moves left in us. In fact, to me, that's when it's the perfect time to ride off into the sunset. An old Hollywood entertainment rule-of-thumb says: *leave 'em wanting more*. Not a bad prescription for leaders. Not bad for interviews either. And on that note, taking a dose of my own medicine, I'll say "adios."

Wright

Ahhh, a man who practices what he preaches. Today, we've been talking to Rick Houcek. Rick, thank you for sharing your thoughts on leadership.

Houcek

It's been my pleasure, David. Thank you.

Rick Houcek's singular company purpose is: To provide high-octane, world-class strategic planning systems for business and life, helping Top Gun leaders, teams and individuals to succeed "on purpose, most of the time," rather than "by accident, some of the time." He does this four primary ways: [1] facilitating his Power Planning™ strategic planning retreats for small and mid-size companies, [2] leading his Passion Planning™ workshops for ambitious individuals on personal life planning and goal setting, [3] delivering high-energy motivational keynotes, and [4] one-on-one success coaching. He has coached entrepreneurs, CEOs, presidents, and senior executives for over 10 years, and is former president of Ross Roy Advertising, an Atlanta ad agency and division of the $700 million Ross Roy Group. A University of Missouri graduate, he is a member of the National Speakers Association and has been recognized in Who's Who Among U.S. Executives and Who's Who in Georgia. Rick is married and passionately devoted to his soul mate, adores his awesome grown twins, and has four fanatical life passions: his family, his personal health and fitness, helping others prosper through his business and friendships, and playing competitive baseball on a traveling men's team.

Rick Houcek, President

Soar With Eagles, Inc.

5398 Hallford Drive

Atlanta, Georgia 30338

Phone: 770-391-9122

Fax: 770-393-0076

Email: Rick@SoarWithEagles.com

www.SoarWithEagles.com

Chapter 7

BILL BLADES

THE INTERVIEW

David E. Wright (Wright)

Today we're talking to Bill Blades, a professional speaker, trainer, consultant, and author. Bill speaks from experience. While serving as vice-president of sales and marketing for a food manufacturing company, he increased sales 150 percent from $13 million to $33 million in only four years. His firm was named Small Business of the Year. He also served as Finance Chairman for Newt Gingrich, former Speaker of the House of the United States Congress. Bill is the author of the best selling *The Mother Of All Enterprise* as well as a featured author with attorney F. Lee Bailey in the book *Leadership Strategists*. He has served on the faculties of the Graduate School of Banking of the South and College of Estate Planning Attorneys, the National Association of Sales Professionals, and he also lectures at universities including American Graduate School of International Management, the number one rated international graduate school in the United States. Bill Blades welcome to *Leadership Defined*.

Bill Blades (Blades)

Thank you, David

Wright

What do you feel is the most important value in any organization?

Blades

Without a doubt, it is communication style. And communication is present in organizations with good and bad leadership. Either a leader paints a clear picture of the company's vision for all the employees to embrace, or he or she adopts a "my way or the highway" communication style.

A study conducted in 2001 looked at over twenty thousand exit interviews and found that the number one reason people left a job was poor supervisory behavior, or in other words, bad bosses. And, one of the biggest factors cited in these interviews was poor communication skills.

With every interaction, employees become either more engaged or less engaged with their work and the organization. If the interactions are more negative than positive, you will produce disengaged individuals who become more and more disconnected from their work. Then, they settle in to a routine of apathy, and usually end up costing the employer a chunk of money.

Every leader must realize that each one of their employees is part of the company's financial assets. For those assets to perform at maximum levels, the executives must focus on creating and nurturing a great environment within the organization. And, a huge part of that environment relies on communication.

Wright

What communication traits are found in bad leaders?

Blades

Everyone has heard the statement, "I'm the boss." You can often find bad leaders shouting this statement at people, which is not only unprofessional, but it's also obvious that the leader lacks respect and vision of organizational goals. And people naturally translate this into, "I don't value you."

Everyone knows that to teach dogs certain behaviors, treats and praise work better than whips. I'm not sure why more leaders don't approach people in the same manner. When you verbally abuse someone, they usually withdraw. Being loud, getting red in the face, and pounding the desk has gone out of style, that's if it was ever in style.

Poor leaders are also quick to assign blame and point fingers. They don't understand that they should share the glory, and accept the blame. All leaders need to understand that mistakes are part of life. Everyone makes them. But when a leader criticizes someone, the whole organization loses part of its potential. In actuality, bad leaders create zombies by destroying the potential of their employees.

The Glengarry Glen Ross style of management, which fosters competition rather than teamwork, is dead. The Equation Research Survey revealed that ninety-six percent of 377 executives interviewed believe that yelling can never be an effective management tool. The message is many leaders need makeovers. Not in the form of adding new methods, but identifying what methods need to be modified or taken away.

Wright

What communication traits do you find in the good leaders?

Blades

Strong leaders, no matter the economic environment, display respect, trust, integrity, and reliability. But perhaps honesty is the most important quality a leader must possess. By being honest with themselves and their employees, good leaders foster an inspirational work environment that supports good behavior and innovation.

Another effective approach that good leaders often take is servancy leadership. This means they lead by asking what their followers need in order to be successful. Essentially, this approach treats every employee almost like a client. Good leaders must figure out what each of their employees need, what makes them tick, and what they ultimately want to achieve. This approach leaves employees feeling empowered, respected, and important. And it makes them want to work harder toward the goals of the organization.

Good leaders also have vision. They maintain a steady focus on a long-term approach to a successful business that can weather the evolutionary nature of the economy. By combining that focus with great communication skills, the major battles are won.

Wright

How important is culture of an organization to their overall success, and how do leaders influence this culture?

Blades

Outside of having a great product, culture is everything. It determines the ultimate success or failure of every business. In simple terms, culture means everyone going in the same direction, with shared beliefs, behaviors, and assumptions, for every single co-worker and client.

Everything, including culture, starts at the top. The top executives and the top managers are responsible for what happens in an organization, and they are the ones to blame when things go wrong. Therefore, leadership determines the culture, and culture determines performance. So improving the behavior of the leadership should be the initial course of action for a struggling business.

A large part of the culture is dictated by communication. Not just in what the organization itself communicates, but how it communicates it. A leader can chew on people all he or she wants, but all that accomplishes is a short-term drop in morale and a long-term drop in revenues. A constructive culture on the other hand, will drive people to better performance. Unfortunately, many leaders take a passive approach to the culture of their organizations. And many times the business leaders don't know any better. In these cases, an outsider perspective may be extremely beneficial.

Wright

How does a leader's positive attitude affect their organization?

Blades

The positive leader takes time to express a genuine interest in people. And he does so because he feels it is the right thing to do. The positive leader listens to people, and understands their concerns. He knows that he isn't always right and makes an effort to find solutions, even when he is actually part of the problem.

And positive leaders aren't concerned with what they can get out of people. Rather, they focus on how to invest in their people and how to help them succeed. They focus on the positives, not just to be nice, but because it leads to enhanced performance. They consider keeping a positive attitude as setting employees up for greater success.

Leaders can check themselves for a positive mindset by tracking the number of times in a workday they pay a compliment to one of their employees. A good leader should strive for at least five compliments per day.

A positive attitude can make a great difference in a person's ability, and not just as far as leadership is concerned. For example, when one negative job candidate with more skills and ability goes up against a positive job candidate with a shorter resume, most leaders would choose the positive person without a second thought. That person's positive attitude will carry over into eagerness, creativity, and better communication skills and results.

Wright

What types of training are most important for good leadership development?

Blades

ASTD conducted a study and found that over eighty percent of managers in the United States became managers without any formal management training. Either the leader inherited the position through the family, was promoted because someone died or retired, or maybe the person was the most qualified candidate at the time the position opened, but he or she wasn't really ready for the responsibility. But these situations often can't be avoided, so sometimes people are thrown into leadership positions without the right training or coaching to properly prepare them for the job. And many times, leaders must come to this realization on their own and seek out training and mentors to help them succeed.

Most importantly, every new leader needs a mentor. Either before they move into the leadership position or just after they've taken on the new responsibility, someone needs to tell them the truth about what they need to do to be successful. The best mentors usually come from outside the organization, but they are always straightforward and honest.

Wright

Should good leaders focus more on long-term or short-term goals?

Blades

Good leaders should focus short-term on interim goals. These are the small steps necessary for reaching the big goal. And accomplishing the small, short-term goals give everyone in the organization a confidence boost. But ultimately, the long-term goals should be more important to a good leader, who focuses on the disciplines of their business with patience and perseverance. These leaders account for the details and the follow-through required for reaching the smaller goals, while always keeping one eye on the long-term.

Good leaders also know that no firm can be instantly successful, and that one or two quarters do not make the success or failure of an organization. Effective leaders know that long-term efforts yield higher returns than cutbacks.

One of these long-term efforts should always be education. Leaders must understand that a huge competitive differential is a well-educated workforce, which takes time and persistence to develop. They also realize that the only thing worse than educating an employee that eventually leaves the organization, is not educating someone and having them stay.

Babson College conducted a twelve-year study which found that the only thing successful entrepreneurs had in common was a willingness to launch, or to stay out in faith. One of history's greatest leaders, Frederick the Great, said it best, "Audacity, audacity, always audacity." Whether in robust or recession times, organizations always need visionary leaders who are committed to creating an exciting future for themselves and for others.

Wright

So, why are leaders open to certain degrees of risk?

Blades

They need to teach their people to take risks without the fear of punishment for mistakes. A good leader encourages their people to innovate solutions, and does not berate them for mistakes. Just because of their authoritative position over their employees, leaders naturally intimidate many people. And the leader may not mean to strike fear into their people, but they do. So therefore, leaders must acknowledge this power they possess, and strive to reposition themselves as approachable and understanding.

Wright

What's the main difference between a manager and a leader?

Blades

Leaders focus on people. Most managers control and focus on the bottom line, while genuine leaders focus on people and the future. Although the bottom line is important, the people in an organization have a direct effect on success. Therefore, keeping the people happy will increase the bottom line.

Also, managers thrive on catching people making mistakes, where leaders think, "What can I do to make this better?" For example, when a manager catches one of their employees doing something wrong, they might call them into their office and reprimand them. But a leader embraces the philosophy that failures are necessary for finding success. They allow their employees to try new methods, and may actually hold people accountable for doing so. Then if something doesn't go as planned, everyone can examine their actions and learn from the mistakes as a team.

Wright

Finally, what actions do leaders take to foster teamwork?

Blades

Just by embracing this philosophy that mistakes are a learning experience, leaders foster teamwork among employees. This philosophy also supports peer-mentoring relationships that allow employees to work together towards better solutions. Plus, when everyone knows mistakes are acceptable, they connect with each other through sharing experiences and having fun. No one can accomplish maximum results unless the process is fun. When people have fun, they throw more of themselves into their work—just because it's fun. Enthusiasm moves mountains.

Good leaders also invest considerable amounts of time in coalition building. This process requires listening, support, and encouragement so people aspire to greater things. Also, if any of their people try to hurt another person or team, leaders act fast to stop those negative behaviors. The leader wants a unified team—and voice.

Leadership for the Success

The universal ideal leader does not exist, but all good leaders possess certain traits. Listening to concerns with an understanding ear, a positive attitude, 100 percent honesty, and an approachable personality are the foundations of the quality leadership any organization needs to reach a higher level of success. And with an understanding of these characteristics, leaders can improve their methods and lead their organizations to rise above the competition. By applying these good leadership traits, any leader can be ideal.

About The Author

Bill Blades is an international speaker, consultant and author. He has served in many leadership positions, including the U.S. Army, materials management, plant management, political campaign management, chief of sales and marketing, and C.O.O. and C.E.O. positions.

Now he heads up William Blades, LLC, a sales and leadership consulting firm based in Scottsdale, Arizona. He is the only person in history to serve as chairman for both the National Speakers Association Sales Professional Emphasis Group and the Institute of Management Consultants' Marketing Special Emphasis Group.

Bill Blades, CMC, CPS

William Blades, LLC

Phone: 480.563.5355

Email: bill@williamblades.com

www.williamblades.com

Chapter 8

DR. WARREN BENNIS

THE INTERVIEW

David E. Wright (Wright)

Today we are talking with Dr. Warren Bennis. He is a university professor and a distinguished professor of business at the University of Southern California and chairman of USC's leadership institute. He has written 18 books, including *On Becoming A Leader, Why Leaders Can't Lead,* and *The Unreality Industry,* co-authored with Ivan Mentoff. Dr. Bennis was successor to Douglas McGregor as chairman of the organizational studies department at MIT. He also taught at Harvard and Boston Universities. Later he was provost and executive vice president of the State University of NY—Buffalo and president of the University of Cincinnati. He published over 900 articles and two of his books have earned the coveted McKenzie Award for the "Best Book on Management." He has served in an advisory capacity for the past four U.S. presidents, and consultant to many corporations and agencies and to the United Nations. Awarded 11 honorary degrees, Dr. Bennis has also received numerous awards including the distinguished service award of the American Board of Professional Psychologists and the Perry L. Ruther practice award of the American Psychological Association. Dr. Bennis, welcome to *Leadership Defined.*

Dr. Warren Bennis (Bennis)

I'm glad to be here again with you, David.

Wright

In a conversation with *Behavior Online*, you stated that most organizations devaluate potential or emerging leaders by seven criteria: business literacy, people skills, conceptual abilities, track record, taste, judgment, and character. Because these terms were somewhat vague, you left them to be defined by the reader. Can we give our readers an unadorned definition of these criteria, as you define them?

Bennis

There's no precise dictionary definition that would satisfy me or maybe anyone. I'll just review them very quickly because there's a lot more we want to discuss. Business literacy really means: do you know the territory, do you know the ecology of the business, do you know how it works, do you know where the plugs are, do you know who the main stakeholders are, and are you familiar with a thing called business culture. People skills: This is your capacity to connect and engage, because business leadership is about establishing, managing, creating and engaging in relationships. Conceptual abilities is more important these days because it has to do with the paradoxes and complexities; the cartography of stakeholders that make life at the top (more than ever) interesting and difficult, which is why we've had such a turnover in CEOs and leaders over the last few years. Track record: Now, if I want to know about a person, if I were a therapist, one of the first questions I would ask is, "Tell me about your job history." That tells me a lot. On the whole, as my dad used to say, "People who get A's are smart." People who have a successful track record tend to be effective. We don't always go on that, because sometimes these people don't grow. But, if I had only one measuring stick, it would be that one: Tell me your job history. Let's talk about whether it looks successful or whether the person views it as successful or not. It's hard to define, but it's about whether or not you have the capacity a good curator has, a good selector has, to know people. It's always a tough one; God knows we all make mistakes. Your taste means your capacity to judge other people in relation to the other six characteristics. I think taste and judgment are combined. I dealt with them separately because I thought taste was specifically the selection of people in an intuitive and objective way, but also in a subjective way. It has to do with the range of such things as being bold vs. being reckless. It has to do with the strategic implications and consequences of any decision and what you take into account in making any decision, especially the tough ones. The easy ones are different; everyone looks good in a bull market. It's when things get tough, vulnerable, difficult and in a crisis mode that judgment really counts the most. Taste and judgment are the hardest things to learn, let alone teach. Character: Here I have in mind a variety of things such as size of ego, the capacity to listen, emotional intelligence, integrity and authenticity. Basically, is this a person I can trust? That's what character is all about.

Wright

You said that businesses get rid of their top leaders because of lapses in judgment, lapses in character, not because of business literacy or conceptual skills. Why do you think this is true?

Bennis

It's true simply because it's true. Look at the record. I wasn't just stating a hypothesis there that looks to be proved. I was stating experiences with leaders, and I'll give you three quick examples. Let's look at a recent one. Howell Raines—the top job in journalism in the world—had great ideas, great business literacy, and all the things in the top five. He did not have taste, judgment, or character. This is a guy who had an ego the size of Texas. He played favorites, had the best ideas, was a terrific newspaperman and no one would argue with that. But, his way of treating people, of not harnessing the human harvest that was there, and being bullying and brutalizing and arrogant and unable to listen, that's what I mean by character. Eckhart Pfeiffer was fired after seven or eight very good years at Compaq—he had terrific ideas, but he did not listen to the people. He was only listening to his "A" list, who were saying, "Aye, aye, Sir." His "B" list was saying, "You better look at what Gateway and Dell are doing; they're eating our lunch on our best china." He didn't listen; he didn't want to listen. That's what I mean by character. Let me just stay with those two examples, I don't think it's ever about conceptual abilities, ever. There may be some examples I don't know about. But, with over fifty years of leadership research, I don't know of any leader who has lost his job or has been ousted because of a lack of brainpower.

Wright

You said that teaching leadership is impossible, but you also said leadership can be learned. How can that be?

Bennis

Let me qualify that. I teach the stuff, so no, it isn't impossible to teach you. As is the case with everything, teaching and learning are two different things. One has to do with input into people; the other has to do with whether or not they get it. You know very well, and your listeners and readers know very well, that there's a difference between listening to a lecture and it having any influence on you. You can listen to a brilliant lecture and nothing may happen. So, there's a disconnect to teaching and learning. Actually, how people learn about leadership varies a lot. Most people don't learn about leadership by a Ph.D., or by reading a book, or by listening to this tape, although that may be helpful; they learn it through work and experience. You can be helped by terrific teaching, like a recording, like a tape, like a book, like a weekend retreat. Basically, the way people learn about leadership is by keeping their eyes open, being a first class observer, having good role models and being able to see how they deal with life's adversities. You don't learn leadership by reading books; they are helpful, don't get me wrong. I write books; I want them to be read. The message you are trying to get out to your people, to listen to and to read is also important. I think it's terrific. That's my life's work. That's what I do for a living, and I love it. I'll tell you, it has to be augmented by the experiences you face in work and in life.

Wright

Trust me, I have learned after reading many of your books that they are teaching materials.

Bennis

Thank-you. I hope you also learn from them, David.

Wright

As I was reading those books, I wondered why I did the things you said to do, and they worked when I did it. It's simply because I learned by doing.

Bennis

Thank-you. I'm really glad to hear that.

Wright

Since leadership is where the big money, prestige and power are, why would seasoned business executives, who are monitored more closely than the average employee, let character issues bring them down? One would think it would be like a person who constantly uses profanity, just deciding not to curse in church.

Bennis

I wish it were that easy. It's a really good question. I wish I knew the answer, but I don't. I will give you a real quick example. Howell Raines, as I said before, executive editor of the New York Times— people would die to get that position—was an experienced newspaperman, and there was a 17,000-word article about him in New Yorker, June 6, 2002 (he had been on the job since Sept. 2001, so it was written not a year later). The article exposed him; it was a very frank and interesting article. It called him arrogant, a bully, playing favorites, all the things I said earlier, and also called him a hell of a good man and a terrific editor. He'd been around the track; he had business literacy up the wah-zoo. He was as good as they get. He read that article and everybody at the New York Times read it. Do you think it might have made him want to change a little bit? Did Julius Caesar not hear the warnings, "Beware the Ides of March?" Did he not hear, "Don't go to the forum?" There were so many signals and he wasn't listening. Why wasn't he listening? Didn't he go down to the newsroom and talk to those people? No. The most common and fatal error is that because of arrogance; they stopped listening. It could happen internally, as in the case of Howell Raines, or like Eckhart Pfeiffer, who wasn't listening to his "B" list tell him about Gateway and Dell. I don't have the answer to your question, but I will tell you, someone ought to be around to remind these people of the voices, stakeholders and audiences that they aren't listening to. That's a way of dealing with it; making sure you have a trusted staff that isn't just giving you the good news.

Wright

I've often heard that if I had been Nixon, I would have burned the tapes, apologized, and moved on.

Bennis

Absolutely.

Wright

I think it's the arrogance factor; you really hit the nail on the head when you said that, to put it in my simple terms. How does one experience leadership when they haven't yet become a leader?

Bennis

How do you become a parent for the first time? There's no book that you are going to read on becoming a parent any more than there is a book you are going to read on becoming a leader that will prepare you for that experience. You're going to fall on your face, get up, dust yourself off, and go on. The only thing you're going to learn from is your experiences and having someone around you that you can depend on for straight, reflective back talk. A lot of it is breaks, it is chance. Some of it isn't that, but if there's one thing I want to underscore, nobody is prepared the first time they are going to be in the leadership position. You're going to fall on your face, you're going to learn from it, and you're going to continue that for the rest of your life.

Wright

At one time, I had a company with about 175 people working for me; we had business in the millions. I just kept making so many mistakes that afterward, I did wish that I had read some of the things you had written about before I made those mistakes. It sure would have been helpful. In your studies, you found that failure, not success, had a greater impact on future leaders, that leaders learn the most by facing adversity. Do you think teachers at the college level make this clear?

Bennis

I can't speak for all teachers at the college level. Do you mean people teaching leadership and business management at the college level?

Wright

Yes.

Bennis

I don't know if they do. But, I would imagine things are much more difficult and complicated today because of the kinds of things that business leaders are facing such as: globalization, fierce Darwinian competitiveness, the complexity of the problems, the regulatory pressures, the changes in demography, the difficulty of retaining your best talent, the price of terrific human capital and then keeping them, the ability to help create a climate that encourages collaboration, and then there's the world danger since 9/11.

Wright

In my case, I just remember the equations and things in the courses I took, like controlling and directing and those kinds of things, and I don't remember anybody ever telling me about exit strategies or what's going to happen if my secretary gets pregnant and my greatest salesperson is the one responsible for it. Who do I fire? As the owner of a small company that's growing at a rapid pace, what can I do to facilitate the competencies of the people I have chosen to lead this into the future?

Bennis

Your company is how big, again?

Wright

I was talking before about a real estate conglomerate. Presently I have a speaker's bureau/servicing agency and publishing business, and employ about 25 people, and we also use about 50 vendors, which I look at as employees.

Bennis

Yes, they are, aren't they? That's a good way of thinking about it. There are several things you can do in any size company, but with a small company, you can get your arms around it, conceptually, anyway. The leader/owner has to model the very behaviors that he wants others to model. If you are espousing something that is antithetical to your behavior, then that's going to be a double bind. That's number one. The second thing is to make leadership development an organic part of the activities at the firm. In addition to encouraging people to read, bringing in people to talk to them and having retreats, every once in a while, look at leadership competencies and what people can do to sharpen and enhance into those capacities that are needed to create a culture where people can openly talk about these issues. All of those things can be used to create a climate where leadership development is a part of the everyday dialogue.

Wright

If you were helping me choose people to assume leadership roles as my company grows, what characteristics would you suggest I look for?

Bennis

I've implied some of them early on, as we discussed those seven characteristics. I've become a little leery of the whole selection process; there is some evidence that even interviews don't give you really valid insight. I think what I would tend to do is look at the track record. Talk about that with the person, where they think they have failed, where they think they have succeeded. Try to get a sense of their capacity to reflect on issues and see to what extent they have been able to learn from their previous experiences. See what you can make of how realistically they assess a situation. Most people rarely attribute any blame to themselves; they always think, "The dog ate my homework." It's always some other agent outside of themselves who is to blame. Those are the things that I think are going to be characteristics of emerging leaders among men and women. That's what I would look for, the capacity to reflect and learn.

Wright

When you made that comment about interviews, I don't feel as inept as I did before this conversation. I'm 64 years old and the longer I live; I just feel that when people come in and interview, I want to give them an Academy Award as they walk out. People can say almost anything convincingly in this culture. It's very, very difficult for me to get through, so that's one thing I really had not thought of. It seems so simple; just follow the track record.

Bennis

I have had the same experience as you. When I was president of the university and making lots of choices all the time, my best was hitting 700, which means I was off three out of ten times. I think my average here was 60/40; it's rough. It's even harder these days because of legal restrictions, how much you can say about their references, how much they can reveal. We have to pay attention to selection level, no kidding. We can overcome mistakes in the selection level by the culture and how it will screen out behaviors that are not acceptable. That's our best default; the culture itself will so educate people that even mistakes we make will be resurrected by the culture being our best friend and ally.

Wright

As a leader, generating trust is essential. You have written extensively on this subject. Can you give our readers some factors that tend to generate trust?

Bennis

People want a leader that exudes that they know what he/she is doing. They want a doctor who is competent; they want a boss who really knows their way around. Secondly, you want someone who is really on your side—a caring leader. Thirdly, you want a leader who has directness, integrity, congruity, they return calls and are trustworthy. They will be there when needed and they do care about you and they do care about your growth. Those are the main things. It's not just individuals involved. A boss must create a climate within the group that provides psychological safety, a holding pattern where people feel comfortable in speaking openly. I think that's another key factor in generating and establishing trust.

Wright

It is said that young people these days have less hope than their parents. What can leaders do to instill hope in their employees?

Bennis

All the leaders I have known have a high degree of optimism and a low degree of pessimism. They are, as Confucius said, purveyors of hope. Look at Reagan, in a way look at Clinton or Martin Luther King Jr.; these are people who have held out an idea of what we could become and made us proud of ourselves, created noble aspirations, sometimes audacious, but noble. Leaders have to express in an authentic way that there is a future for our nation and that you have a part in developing that future with me.

Wright

Dr. Bennis, thank you for being with us today, and for taking so much time to answer these questions.

Bennis

Thank you for having me.

Warren Bennis has written or edited twenty-seven books, including the best-selling *Leaders* and *On Becoming A Leader*, both of which have been translated into twenty-one languages. He has served on four U.S. presidential advisory boards and has consulted for many Fortune 500 companies, including General Electric, Ford and Starbucks. *The Wall Street Journal* named him one of the top ten speakers on management in 1993 and 1996, and *Forbes* magazine referred to him as "the dean of leadership gurus."

Warren Bennis

m.christian@marshall.usc.edu

Chapter 9

ALISON R. BROWN

THE INTERVIEW

David E. Wright (Wright)

Today we are talking to Alison R. Brown. She is president and principal consultant of ALMEC International. The company provides management and employee training and development strategies that enable organizations to improve internal communication and establish cooperative relationships. Certification and on-sight training programs are available in topics such as workforce diversity, leadership, supervisory skills, and managing conflict. Clients include Columbus Public Schools, U.S. Bank, American Red Cross, and the Ohio Department of Health. Alison is an instructor in executive education at Capital University. She is a part time instructor at Central Ohio Technical College where she teaches management development. In 2003, Alison was nominated for Ohio Business Person of the Year, a prestigious award that has been given since 1956 and Small Business Person of the Year, an award given by the Greater Columbus Chamber of Commerce. She is featured in *Mission Possible*, Vol. 3 with Stephen Covey and Deepak Chopra. Alison is contributing author to *Real World Leadership Strategies That Work*. Executives from IBM, HP, Verizon, Prudential, and the Principle Financial Group partnered with her for her contributions. She is a graduate of the Minority Business Executive Program at the Tuck School of Business at Dartmouth. Alison, we're pleased to have you with us today for *Leadership Defined*. Welcome!

Alison R. Brown (Brown)

Thank you so much for extending the invitation. I'm really pleased to be here.

Wright

Alison, before we dive into issues specifically related to leadership, would you give our readers a little background? You haven't always been an entrepreneur, professional speaker, and author, have you?

Brown

No, actually I have not. I started out in a corporate job that I stayed in for 18 years. I resigned from the position in 1995 to launch a business because I was really at a point where I was ready for my career to go in another direction.

Wright

Can you remember back for us to one of your first experiences as a leader and tell our readers how that went, what mistakes you made, if any, and what you learned from the experience that might help our readers today?

Brown

Yes, absolutely. The experience that comes to mind was when I was supervising employees that had never had a female or African American supervisor. When I realized how closely everyone was watching me, I knew it was imperative that I lead by example. I took the time to learn about their professional needs and worked hard to meet those needs. For some, they wanted additional responsibilities above and beyond what was already required of them. Others wanted development opportunities in order to be considered for promotions. I had to make certain I didn't become friends with the people I was supervising. That would have been easy to do, especially given the fact that I was only a couple of years older than most of them. Developing friend's means you may develop favorites and then there's going to be a problem with the rest of the employees. Confidentiality and trust are important to me. I wanted my staff to be able to talk to me openly about challenges that were affecting their performance. Sometimes the challenges were work-related. Other times they were times the challenges were work-related. Other times they were personal. Looking back, I really should have worked harder at developing stronger relationships with my peers, which were the other supervisors in the division. I became engrossed in the job and the need to prove I was the best person for the job.

Wright

A lot of times down through the years I have...when you said that about confidentiality, down through the years I've got this terrible habit. I forget when people tell me not to say things. And if I do say it, it becomes a matter of trust issue.

Brown

Yes.

Wright

They say, "Well, I can't trust you." And I'm thinking, "Yes, you can. I just forgot."

Brown

Oh, I understand.

Wright

It's hard.

Brown

It is hard. The interesting thing was it got to the point where employees would call me at home. They wanted to talk about something confidential. They weren't always willing to walk into my office because everyone would know that a conversation had taken place. I gave them the option of calling me at home on the weekends or in the evenings, and that worked really well. I always told them, "Now, you've shared this with me and you've asked me not to say anything to anyone. If somehow this information comes back to you, it's coming back because you've repeated it, not because I've repeated it." I needed to make sure that they were clear about that.

Wright

You fall into a unique category of leaders, Alison. You're African-American and you are, of course, a woman. I know diversity is a com-

plex topic that often polarizes people, businesses, and communities.
So what is your perspective on diversity?

Brown

Well, I agree with what you're saying about the polarization because that's definitely true. What I've seen in my career and with the
corporations we've worked with is the difficulty someone from the majority group has in relating to a perspective on diversity from
someone representing the diverse group. We have to think about the
fact that we have built in biases. All of us do. Generally speaking,
we can't always understand the perspective of the other person because we are operating from a different frame of reference. We start
to think, "Okay, the individual can't possibly be objective because
anything they say is naturally going to be in favor of the group they
are a part of." It takes a lot of critical thinking and analysis to really
sort through and understand what's factual and what isn't. With the
changing demographics, not only of the workforce but also the customer base, diversity is a topic you really can't get away from. You
can't avoid the topic no matter how much some of us would like to.
The energy that is used to resist diversity could be used to understand and manage it. You want the end result to be a productive
workforce, satisfied employees and profitability. You want employees
that are able to reach the goals that you're setting forth. The fascinating thing is if you look at some of the commercials and magazine
ads today, it's obvious that corporations are starting to understand
what they need to do to reach certain demographic groups, and
they're also realizing that the groups have tremendous buying power.
As employees the groups have a lot of talent, skills, abilities, and
creativity. As a leader, it takes a different set of skills to communicate
with and manage a diverse workforce. One of the courses we offer is
entitled *Building an Inclusive Organization*. It shows companies how
to develop the cooperative and collaborative relationships they need
to reach the objectives they are trying to reach. The course also gives
managers an opportunity to practice some of the skills immediately.
It's very cutting edge. We have taught multicultural education in the
public school system. Teachers work really, really hard but they are
having some challenges in trying to reach and relate to a diverse
student population. It's fascinating too because one of the things that
was mentioned repeatedly when we were teaching the multicultural
education course was that students need to know the teachers care.
If they know that, everything in the classroom environment changes.

The teachers are up against things like cultural and language barriers, the lack of relationships with parents and with communities.

Wright

Let me follow up with this same theme. Do you mind if I quote you from one of your books?

Brown

No, go right ahead.

Wright

In your book *Real World Leadership Strategies That Work,* you talked about perceptions when it comes to women leaders in the workplace.

Brown

Yes.

Wright

And the quote is this: "For example, once women are promoted, there perhaps may be a power inequity brought about by the sheer numbers of men competing against them. It would be a mistake to under estimate the influence of such perceptions. Women are sometimes categorized or labeled if they are aggressive, assertive, outspoken, opinionated, detail oriented, sensitive, not assertive enough, too quiet, etc. Once a label is attached to a person, it takes energy and effort to see that person in a way that contradicts the label." You know I've heard it said that labels men are assigned, like tough and hardnosed and unyielding are seen as positive traits. But those same traits in women leaders are often seen as negatives. Is that what you're implying? And if it is, what can women leaders do to change this perception?

Brown

What I was referring to were women who are promoted or hired into positions that have been traditionally held by men. What may happen in either instance is if the majority of her peers are men, there may be challenges in trying to fit into the group. There's also a section in that book entitled, *In the Eyes of the Beholder.* The perceptions we have of others are very powerful. Those perceptions become the reality for each of us. I think we should compare how we are presenting ourselves against the requirements of the particular job senting ourselves against the requirements of the particular job we're in and the image we want to present. We need to take into consideration the career path we happen to be on. Tools like 360 Degree feedback help determine where adjustments need to be made. In high school I always viewed myself as being very shy. Years after graduation, I realized my former classmates viewed me as having quiet strength. They were looking at me from a totally different perspective. It's important for us to measure and assess where we are and to determine what direction we trying to go with our career. Some of the labels that have been attached to us can be very detrimental to our ability to move forward.

Wright

Back to your book on leadership, which by the way I think everyone should go out and buy right away.

Brown

Thank you.

Wright

And in case our readers want to do that, how could they get in touch with you?

Brown

There're several ways. They can visit our, website which is probably the quickest way. The address is www.almec.com. You can order online by clicking on either the products or services or the books page. An autographed copy of the book will be shipped right away. We can be reached at 614-755-4960 or by e-mail, which is alison-brown@mindspring.com.

Wright

Great. Now back to your book. You have a section on a difference between leaders and managers. First, do you think most people in business believe there is a difference? And the second question would be: what is the difference between a leader and a manager?

Brown

Well, I think the view of leading versus managing is starting to change. When you think about it, whether a person is teaching K-12, teaching at the college level or managing a diverse workforce, you still need leadership qualities. Companies that contact us realize there's a difference. They know that the success of the organization is dependent on their ability to develop and guide the workforce in a direction that contains costs, increases productivity, and helps the organization remain competitive. One of the key differences between leaders and managers is how they view and interact with the people that they are guiding. Leaders tend to be more effective with people and they think on a more global perspective. Managers are more efficient with systems, and they may tend to think more inside the box and focus primarily on what's happening on a day-to-day basis.

Wright

Near the end of your chapter in the *Real World Leadership Strategies That Work*, you described three areas of leadership that everyone should focus on dealing with change, integrity, and mentoring. Would you elaborate for our readers on these three areas as they apply to leadership?

Brown

Yes, as it relates to change, leaders are change agents. They have a vision for the direction that the organization needs to go. For the vision to become a reality, change always has to occur. Connected to the vision are strategy, the goals, and objectives. Leaders need to know when to change the plan, based on internal and external factors. The factors may affect the organization over the long or the short term. The work environment needs to be prepared for change. I equate this to a person that is going to have surgery. There is prep work done prior to the actual surgery.

Wright

Right.

Brown

There's a process the organization must go through prior to the change. This involves making sure the key people are part of the decision making process, information is requested from and communicated to employees, communities and customers, the proper assessments have been done, and a pilot of the project has been scheduled. You need to test it before you roll it out to the entire organization. Leaders also need to know when to abandon the change and move in a different direction.

Wright

So...

Brown

To lead with integrity means to be honest and accountable. I talked about this in my last book, *Real World Leadership Strategies That Work*. As a leader you're always going to encounter conflicting interests, agendas, and goals. You need a reliable process, for analyzing complex, high-risk decisions. This is something we help organizations with. All of us have preferences and a method for reasoning. Leaders sometimes need assistance with gaining an ethical edge in terms of moral and social responsibilities and competitive positioning. It takes a strong confident leader to be willing to become a mentor, or to support the implementation of a formal mentoring program within the organization. More organizations are starting to understand the benefits of mentoring. It's important you have people in the pipeline that are ready to step into leadership roles as people retire, leave the company for an extended period of time, transfer to other positions, or resign from the company to accept a position somewhere else. I wrote an article on mentoring that was published by The Consultant's Forum, a professional emphasis group of SHRM. The article was written from the standpoint of mentoring as a reciprocal relationship. The mentor has a lot of knowledge to share with a protégé that can aid in their growth and development, but in turn the protégé can give the mentor the benefit of their knowledge and expertise and skills. These three areas may be in the form of technical expertise, generational understanding and cultural insight. Leaders need to understand the benefits of mentoring and know that the benefits can greatly outweigh the risks.

Wright

I recently did a book on faith, *Conversations on Faith*, with some of the greatest theologians of our time, and I can't help but thinking this dealing with change, integrity, and mentoring is almost like that Christian mentor, not mentoring program, but just plain program that they have. You know the church changes all the time. Even people change when they accept certain tenants. And then honesty, accountability would be your integrity. And then mentoring is they're passing it on.

Brown

Yes, absolutely.

Wright

You know it sounds like this would be a great thing for all leaders to think about, especially the passing on.

Brown

I agree. You want to make sure that when it's time to pass things on, the people you're passing things on to are ready. It just like succession planning in the corporate world. You want to make sure that as you're handing the baton off, whomever you're handing it to is ready to take it and then to hit the ground running.

Wright

We are in the middle of a presidential election year, as you well know. Many say that the President of the United States, whoever he or she could be is in many ways the leader of the free world, which is an awesome responsibility for anyone to bear. Given the gigantic task before them, what fundamental leadership qualities do you think are essential for a person who desires to be the president?

Brown

In some ways I think of the president in the way I think of the leader of a corporation. .... The leader of a corporation has to be concerned with the company image, balancing the budget, strategic planning, and balancing the goals of the organization with the needs of the communities, customers, suppliers, and employees. Effective communication skills, I believe, are very high on the list because there's so much power in the spoken word. People tend to have long memories. The President needs to have a strong team because it's challenging but necessary to balance the needs of the general public, communities, organizations, corporations, the public sector, and foreign policy. Most places where you work you have a job description. Should there be one developed for the President? Who should enforce and evaluate the President's performance? Should the evaluators be a group that would be equivalent to a board of directors? What accountability measures should be in place if performance isn't matching the job description? Should the evaluators be made up of individuals from each of the represented groups? How should they be selected? Being skilled in negotiating, exercising tact and diplomacy, ethics and the ability to mediate would be important skills for the leader of the free world. There would be tremendous challenge in trying to honor the promises you made to get elected with the pressure of peers (once elected) trying to persuade you to go in a direction that is in conflict with the promises.   Just like a corporation, as a country we need some measures of accountability in place to make sure we're on track with the direction we want to go as a country. The majority of the public has never held a public office. There's probably an education we all need in order to understand what is taking place and why.

Wright

I was just thinking as you were speaking about the framers of the Constitution I think they called them congruents. The problem with the evaluators is they've become so partisan that they can't evaluate anymore.

Brown

I understand how that could happen. That's why the group needs to be made up of a variety of people from the general public, corporations, organizations, and communities. If you have a mix of people and a way of screening them, the evaluation could be done in a more unbiased way.

Wright

Right.

Brown

Yes.

Wright

In closing, what advice would you give young men and women who desire to grow as leaders in practical terms and based on your experience as a leader, what can people really do to improve their leadership skills?

Brown

Leaders can keep the lines of communication open. Be receptive to giving and receiving feedback. Set up mentoring programs that are reciprocal relationships. Take calculated risks. Learn about the cultural groups that make up your workforce and your customer base.

Make sure your actions and words are aligned. Reward the team with something they value. Have an open door policy. Remove barriers so people can contribute to their full potential. Don't be intimidated if someone on your team knows more than you do.

Wright

Well, what an interesting conversation. I have learned a lot here today, Alison.

Brown

Thank you so much!

Wright

We've been talking to Alison Brown, president and principal consultant with Almec International. Alison, it's really been a pleasure. Thank you so much for your words of wisdom and encouragement.

Brown

I appreciate being given the opportunity to share my expertise.

Some Final Thoughts

There are no easy answers to the leadership dilemma we now face in this country. As companies adjust to doing more with less, strong leadership becomes even more important than it has been in the past. The competencies leaders needed previously are not the same as the competencies needed today. Current leaders are not always equipped and in some cases have not been groomed to handle the challenges they are faced with. The global economy and the changing demographics create a very different playing field. Companies are concerned about recruiting and retaining leaders who can help the organization remain competitive, have vision and have the ability to come up with a strategy to implement the vision. It means taking the blinders off, getting our heads out of the sand, and realizing things will never go back to being the way they were.

Leadership strategies should focus on educators, executives and entrepreneurs. Educators must have the skills to teach in a multicultural world and make sure students are getting the tools they need to be able to function as employees or as entrepreneurs. As small businesses grow, employment opportunities are created. Executives must understand the journey and be willing to go through the process in order for their organization to be the best it can be. Organizations are driven by profits and the bottom-line but in reality it all comes down to people. They are truly the greatest, most valuable assets. As the saying goes, the sum of the parts is worth more than the whole. Leaders that disregard the fact that we live in a multicultural world are doing themselves and their organizations a disservice. Leaders that see the strength in this will be able to guide their organizations in a way that sustains them well beyond this century.

About The Author

Alison R. Brown is a professional speaker and principal of ALMEC International. The company provides training, development, coaching, 360-Degree feedback, surveys, mentoring programs and assessments. The consulting firm has worked with organizations of 500 to 55,000 employees in the areas of workforce diversity, multicultural education, management skills, facilitation, focus groups and on-site certification. Alison has guest lectured at the Ohio State University, Otterbein College and Jefferson Community College.

Alison R. Brown

ALMEC International

PO Box 420

Pickerington, Ohio 43147-0420

Phone: 614.755.4960

Email: alisonbrown@mindspring.com

Email: alison@almec.com

www.almec.com

Chapter 10

JACK BARRY

David E. Wright (Wright)

Today we are talking to Jack Barry. Jack is a Business and Leadership Consultant with extensive frontline leadership experience. His experiences span the U.S. Navy, Fortune 500 Companies such as IBM, Xerox and Harris through mid-size companies and even entrepreneurial start-up companies. He has held a number of key positions in both public and private companies, including CEO of a software company and CEO of an information services company. Recognition of Jack's leadership abilities has resulted in him serving on the Board of Directors of nine companies. He also serves on Grove City College's Entrepreneurship Advisory Council. In 1995, he was selected by a committee of the Secretary of Defense to participate in the Defense Department's Joint Civilian Orientation Conference. His philosophies regarding leadership, customers, employees and shareholders have been developed based on first hand experiences and successes. Jack, welcome to *Leadership Defined.*

Jack Barry (Barry)

Thank you, David. It is a pleasure to be here.

Wright

Jack, your career in the computer, software, networking and services industry spans 38 years. Would you tell us a little about your experiences?

Barry

It would be my pleasure. I have been blessed with a rewarding career in a dynamic industry. As with all careers it has had its share of successes, challenges, frustrations and risks, but it has always been exciting. I actually consider my career beginning with the four years I spent as an officer in the US Navy aboard a destroyer. That experience was invaluable in preparing me for the business world. In the computer related industries I spent the first 19 years of my career working for Fortune 250 or larger Companies. In December of 1984, I left the position of Vice President in a Fortune 250 Company to become the CEO of a struggling young company. I had thoroughly enjoyed the large company environment but this move was the beginning of the most challenging and gratifying years of my career. I consequently spent the next 16 years leading mid-size and growth companies. The common denominator of these companies, regardless of size, was that they all marketed domestically and internationally, primarily to large customers and had to interface with senior customer management. Since January 2001, I have stayed active in the industry through consulting and Board of Director commitments. In addition to my management duties, I have had the privilege to serve as a member on the board of directors for nine companies, four as an inside director and five as an outside director. Collectively these experiences have provided me with valuable insight into a variety of leadership and management styles. This has been a tremendous asset in formulating my own leadership philosophy.

Wright

So you were CEO of two companies that were recognized leaders in their respective markets. Would you provide a little insight into these companies?

Barry

They were actually quite different. One was a struggling young software company that in four years we built into a leader in the data transfer market. The other was a mature service company that in 5 years we successfully reinvented with a new strategy. In both cases it was necessary to establish a new company culture based on a new business strategy and new methods of meeting business objectives.

Wright

What leadership challenges did you face in establishing a new culture and strategy in these two companies?

Barry

When establishing the direction of a company, the CEO has a threefold leadership challenge; the employees, the customers and the shareholders. Each will be interested in the new vision, objectives, implementation and projected results from a different perspective. The CEO must be able to convey a consistent strategy in the terms of each group's interest in order to gain their support. A good leader must therefore understand the perspectives of his/her various constituents and address their concerns and interests.

Wright

Did you give equal importance to all three groups?

Barry

Yes, all three are equally important but the employees are the key to the successful implementation and maintenance of any strategy. Consequently, I initially spent more time in that leadership area than I did the other two. As the strategy implementation progressed my time was more equally spent between all three. Because of the importance of employee performance on any strategy, my comments in this interview will be primarily focused on the leadership of employees. To a large extent the employee leadership challenges were similar to the personnel challenges I had encountered as a naval officer, VP Marketing, business unit manager and sales manager. The same leadership principles are also relevant to coaching, leading a committee at church or any other leadership situation. In a short period of time a leader has to set the direction, obtain buy-in and earn the respect of their constituents. The leader then has to set the day-to-day example.

Wright

So let's see if I understand you correctly, unless the employees are set in place and the people are following you, the other two are just absolutely unnecessary.

Barry

That is not really what I meant. The customer is always a business's greatest asset and investors are necessary to fund the implementation of a new strategy. The employees, however, must successfully implement the plan to have satisfied customers and provide a return for the shareholder.

Wright

So based on your experiences, what would you say is the foundation for your leadership philosophy?

Barry

As a result of my cumulative leadership experiences, I have created my own definition of leadership. It is, **"Leadership is the ability to create an environment and provide direction that stimulates others, to employ their creativity and stretch their talents to overachieve defined objectives."** Leadership is therefore the critical factor in both creating a winning culture and implementing a successful plan. Leadership respect must be earned. It cannot be delegated or assigned. It does not come with a promotion, any specific position or authority. Respect is earned through the overall actions of the leader. I practiced this philosophy as a CEO and continue to express it as a consultant.

Wright

You mentioned stimulating employees to overachieve and earn leadership respect. How does a leader begin these initiatives?

Barry

The leader has to begin by setting the stage to create the desired business environment. As previously mentioned, the employee is the key, so it is important to understand the employee. It is prudent to start with the fact that employees spend a major portion of their life at work with their employer. People by nature want to be proud of the company where they work and their contribution to its success. Success is contagious and if people believe in the strategy they will strive to make a meaningful contribution. It is the leader's job, therefore, to develop a vision that has a sustainable competitive differentiation and effectively communicate it to the employees. The leader must then solicit the creativity and knowledge of the entire company to refine the plan. People support what they help create. The plan should be a stretch, but with the appropriate performance, attainable. The success of the plan is dependent on the CEO establishing the appropriate expectations with the customers, shareholders and employees. The plan should also define the processes necessary for success. Employees want direction and an orderly way of performing their duties. Customers like to do business with vendors with whom it is easy to work. The easier it is for a company to operate and interface with its customers, the greater its chances of success. Once the plan is finalized the leader and the employees must live the intent of the plan.

It is the leader's responsibility to keep this planning process as simple as possible and to ensure the process doesn't disrupt the day-to-day business operation. The plan needs to be completed in the shortest possible timeframe. From the very beginning, the leader has to be an effective communicator. Communications is the key to obtaining initial employee buy-in and participation. The ultimate success, however, will depend on whether or not the company leader gains and maintains the respect of his/her constituents.

Wright

Are you saying that gaining the respect and confidence of the leader's constituents is necessary for a leader to have the optimum opportunity to realize his or her objectives?

Barry

Yes, that is exactly what I am saying and it is true at all levels of leadership. People form their opinion about a leader based on his/her overall actions that include what the leader says, their demeanor, their integrity, their consistency, their decisiveness and the confidence they project. Employees want to feel their leader knows where they are going, has a plan to get there, and is going to be equitable with all of his/her constituents. Consistency and equality of treatment are critical to building a team. It is essential that the employees are confident that the leader is going to advance the company both ethically and legally. Every employee must fully understand that there are consequences for any employee who does not act accordingly. In order for a leader to gain employee trust and respect they must be visible to the employees and consistent in their actions. Leading from the ivory tower and managing through emails or memos doesn't get it done.

Wright

So how can a leader quickly let the employees know what ideals he/she represents?

Barry

David, I think in order to answer your question, it is important to explain what I believe and how I orientated my leadership. I believe in a customer centered, revenue generating culture. This means that the company must understand its customers, maintain satisfied customers and have an industry leading company and product differentiation. To convey this message there are two tools that have worked consistently for me; the mission statement and the operating principles. I realize that in many companies these are required exercises that end up in a manual somewhere and are not really used. In my case, I continually strove to lead by the intent of the mission statement and operating principles. I emphasized them in most company, customer and shareholder presentations. They were also reiterated in all company training sessions. The following is the basis of the mission statement for the companies that I led. It is a simple statement but it emphasizes the basic reasons we were employed; **"To provide industry leading solutions to customer perceived problems in the form of products and services at a fair price to the customer and a reasonable return to the shareholder."** I was able to discuss at considerable length the detailed philosophy behind each of the nuances contained in this statement.

Equally important were the operating principles that I practiced and enforced. These operating principles were based on **respect, performance** and **employee recognition.** The principle based on respect defined the respectful way the company was going to treat customers, individuals, shareholders, partners and competitors. It defined the company code of conduct and the spirit of goodwill. The performance principle addressed quality, operating efficiency, competitive differentiation as well as revenue and profit philosophies. The employee recognition principle defined how employees had to perform to be successful and be recognized. With these principles I could explain in detail how the company was going to operate.

Wright

I get to talk to a significant number of CEOs and leaders around the country and many, not all, complain about their employees' work habits. They describe having difficulty getting them to arrive at work on time and then keeping them working instead of gathering around the water cooler, lamenting "oh woe are we." What leadership characteristics and practices aided you to stimulate people to over achieve? I am really interested in this overachieving that you are talking about.

Barry

Overachieving for an individual is a difficult measurement to define because most expectations are established based on industry averages. It has been my experience, however, that most people underestimate their capabilities and set their expectations at a comfortable level. The challenge is to create an environment that stimulates them to upgrade their own expectations, which leads to overachieving based on previous benchmarks. The leader is in essence helping them create a "can do" and "will do" attitude. It has also been my experience that employees who understand the mission and operating principles of the company, as well as their own individual role, their potential opportunities and rewards, tend to be happier, committed and more likely to strive to overachieve. When the employee believes in something bigger than their daily routine, and wants to be part of it, they make an extra effort to be successful. Water cooler breaks are not bad by themselves. It is the tone of the water cooler conversation that is important. I operate under the belief that it is the responsibility of the leaders to set the tone for the company and/or their respective area of authority. The following comments will describe my leadership beliefs and the style that I am constantly striving to live by. It is also what I expect of all leaders in the company.

In order to create a can-do attitude in their area of influence, the leader must possess and consistently project a **sincere, positive, confident** and **purposeful** attitude themselves. This attitude reduces the possibility of accidentally sending the wrong message to those people who try to read something into the leader's every mood and action. The result is the leader spends a minimum amount of time on the nonproductive activity of addressing false rumors that are harmful to morale and productivity. A true leader **demonstrates leadership** in all situations regardless of whether it is with subordinates, peers or superiors. This does not mean that they are domineering, control addicts or have all the answers, but that they operate in accordance with the leadership definition I previously defined. A leader is always cognizant that the ultimate responsibility for the direction, decisions and results of their area of responsibility is exclusively theirs. Although employees want to contribute to the strategy and the implementation processes, they want a **decisive** leader that provides **direction**. Employee involvement is an excellent practice and produces a better finished product. What it does not mean is decision by committee. It is essential that it be obvious that the leader is **committed** and sharing both the risks and rewards with the employees. Customers and shareholders also want the company to have decisive leaders. A leader cannot always get the desired level of buy-in from employees, customers and/or shareholders in the desired timeframe. In such cases, the leader must make a decision, stand firm and manage through any consequences.

There is no leadership characteristic more important than **integrity**. It is important that the leader be visibly striving to achieve objectives that are in the best interest of the customer, employee and shareholder. Leadership is not about being popular, although a good leader is friendly and approachable; it is about doing, on a timely basis, what is best for the company's mission. Such actions are also the most beneficial to the employees as a whole. For example, good leaders put the best qualified people in the right jobs irregardless of friendships or former associations. They establish performance criteria for these positions, inspect the progress, reward good performance and take appropriate and timely action for poor performance. A leader will never get 100% agreement on their selections, but as long as the majority of the employees see the merit and sincerity of the approach this action can be instrumental in gaining the employees' respect. Leaders are **consistent** in how they treat others. This is a characteristic that I cannot emphasize too strongly. An employee may not like a specific answer given by the leader but it is essential that they believe that any employee asking that same question would have gotten the same answer. Leaders **communicate** frequently to those who are directly involved with the success of their operation. It is important that a leader be **truthful** in his/her communications. Employees want to know how the company is performing, what is working, what is not, and what needs to change. They want to know what is necessary to meet the company's objectives, including critical deadlines. A leader recognizes that communication is a two way process. Employee input and feedback must be encouraged. Employees want truthful and objective feedback on their performance. A leader doesn't wait until the annual appraisal to inform the employee about their performance. When an annual appraisal results in a disruptive employee situation, it is most frequently because the leader did not do the appropriate job of coaching and counseling through out the year.

A leader is a coach, and as such, provides the employee with performance feedback throughout the year. When done correctly the annual appraisal is a short experience with no surprises. A leader doesn't shy away from, postpone or defer difficult one-on-one conversations with individual employees. These conversations need to be held on a timely basis with the leader being frank about his/her position while at the same time being respectful to the employee. It is important to note that this practice should also be followed in other business situations like interacting with customers or shareholders. Leaders **champion** both the company mission and their subordinates. While they strive to achieve both at all times, there are times when the leader must place more emphasis on one than the other. Leaders **prepare** their employees to succeed. This means they provide timely training and inspect the subsequent implementation. The inspection practice is critical. Far too many leaders set objectives but don't regularly inspect the progress. Inspection is a key element in maintaining an overachieving environment.

Wright

Are you saying that overachieving comes from inspection?

Barry

No, but it is definitely a key element of the formula. I have observed that if employees have clear direction, understand their role as it relates to the overall strategy and know their work is going to be regularly inspected for timeliness and quality, they tend to be more focused and stretch to overachieve. It is equally important for a leader to **recognize and reward** his/her people. Recognition is objective and based on performance. Key measurements of a leader's ability to create and maintain the right environment are the success of the people they hire, the success of the people they promote, the morale of their subordinates and their ability to retain motivated people. In addition, leaders who successfully build businesses are not afraid to hire individuals that will challenge their own abilities.

Wright

Do you believe these same leadership principles apply to all companies regardless of size?

Barry

Absolutely, but the larger the company and/or the faster the growth of the company, the smaller the percentage of employees on whom a leader can have a direct daily impact. With size and growth, senior management spends more time on shareholder relations, financing growth, legal considerations, mergers and acquisitions, etc. The leadership principles I have described must be perpetuated by hiring or promoting key leaders that will operate in that mode. If the CEO practices these principles in his/her daily sphere of influence and insists that the other leaders in the company operate similarly, the leadership culture described will remain through growth and increased size.

Wright

Let me ask you what you might think is a strange question to ask a leader CEO, how important do you believe dress is to the effectiveness of the leader?

Barry

It depends on the situation and environment. Leaders have certainly emerged from the relaxed dressed codes of the last ten years. It is true that clothes don't make the person, but they do send a message. It is my opinion that regardless of the attire it is essential that the leader be perceived as professional and knowledgeable. It has been my experience that a leader can maximize his/her leadership effectiveness by wearing business attire when interfacing with senior management of large companies. I enjoy casual attire as much as anyone, but still prefer wearing business attire when dealing, with customers, shareholders or the outside world in general. I also prefer business attire to be worn by leaders' at large employee meetings. I subscribe to the philosophy that the leader should dress according to whatever they believe will assist them to be most effective in a given situation.

Wright

Do you feel leaders are born or made?

Barry

I believe that certain individuals are born with more natural leadership abilities than others. For example, some people have an intuitive decision making capability. It has been my experience that while some people have more natural leadership ability most people can learn to become an effective leader. So, my answer is both.

Wright

Jack, you have offered so many powerful leadership points, would you put them in some form of summary?

Barry

David, in this interview I have attempted to share my leadership philosophy. We could obviously spend countless hours discussing any of the points mentioned. Let me start by emphasizing that leaders are measured by results. Did they achieve the committed results in the committed timeframe? In order to achieve these results with any consistency leaders use all of the resources available to them and this includes the employees, customers and shareholders. The strength of a company lies in the performance of its employees so I have spent the majority of the interview discussing the leadership of a winning employee environment. To summarize, it is my leadership philosophy that a successful leader's top priority is building and growing a valuable company that consistently meets the expectations of it customers, shareholders and employees. There will of course be missed targets, but if the leader is sincere and on top of the situation the impact of these missed targets can be managed. Good leaders do not put the desire for personal gain above this priority. They believe that the way to achieve personal wealth and recognition is by leading in a manner that will provide the company with the best opportunity for long term success. In this context, leadership events such as an Initial Public Offering or subsequent financing is a milestone in the history of the company and not an end goal. Such events create new obligations to the new and existing shareholders and put emphasis on the current and long term challenges. Leaders constantly strive to improve the company's differentiation and competitiveness. They recognize that complacency is the deadly enemy of successful companies. A long term successful company can only be achieved by attracting and retaining talented and dedicated employees. Leaders constantly work at maintaining an environment that attracts and retains such employees. Leaders lead by example. This means leaders do the hard things; they do them right and on a timely basis. I would like to conclude by reiterating the overall theme; leaders put the interests of their mission and constituents first.

Wright

Well Jack, I really do appreciate this time you spent with us. I want to thank you not only for your time, but for your insights, which I think our readers are going to find invaluable.

Barry

Your welcome, David. I appreciate the opportunity to discuss a subject which I feel is of great importance. The future of our country and its economic well being depends on the creation of new companies and the growth of existing companies. Both require good leadership.

Some Final Thoughts

Leadership is essential at all levels of a company's infrastructure. All leaders are measured on results. Leadership is, therefore, all about achieving the desired results through people. In today's environment of rapid change, diverse backgrounds, opposing political views, ever increasing worldwide competition and the availability of an unparalleled quantity of information, leading a group of people to a achieve a common objective can be a daunting task. The necessity for good leadership may be more critical today than ever before.

Effective leaders take the time to understand their various constituents and communicate the vision, objectives, plan and results to each group in terms of their respective interests. Business leaders have three constituents; the customer, the shareholder and the employee.

In order for business leadership to be successful they must build on the following fundamentals; 1) the customer is a company's biggest asset, 2) the strength of a company is directly related to its ability to successfully integrate its employees, its processes and its unique differentiation and 3) the shareholders deserve a reasonable return.

If a company is going to enjoy long term success, its leaders must earn the respect of all of their constituents. This respect can only be earned through the integrity, the performance and the daily actions of the leaders. Good leaders communicate frequently with their employees. They let them know where the company is going as well as the expected performance and mode of operation. Leaders involve the employees in growing people and processes to ensure the desired results of the company. People support what they helped create. This does not mean decision by committee. Successful leaders recognize that the ultimate responsibility for effective and timely decisions is exclusively theirs. They do, however, utilize the expertise of their employees and all other resources in deriving the best possible decision. Leaders inspect the progress of key benchmarks on regular basis.

Good leaders make sure that everyone in the company understands their role in the company's processes and knows that their contribution is important to the company's success. In summary, I would like to close with my personal definition of leadership, *"Leadership is the ability to create an environment and provide direction that stimulates others, to employ their creativity and stretch their talents to overachieve defined objectives."*

Jack Barry is a Business and Leadership Consultant with 35 years of frontline management experience. His experiences span Fortune 500 Companies such as IBM, Xerox and Harris through mid-size companies and even entrepreneurial start-up companies. Mr. Barry held a number of key positions in both public and private companies including CEO of a software company and CEO of an information services company. Both companies were recognized leaders in their respective markets. Recognition of his leadership abilities has resulted in him serving as an outside director on the Board of Directors of five companies. He also serves on Grove City College's (Grove City, PA) Entrepreneurship Advisory Council. In 1995, Mr. Barry was selected by committee of the Secretary of Defense to participate in the Defense Department's Joint Civilian Orientation Conference.

Mr. Barry is a powerful speaker and has addressed audiences in multiple countries. His consulting reflects his commitment to a high standard of business ethics and is centered on three fundamental beliefs; 1) the customer is a company's most valuable asset 2) The strength of a company is its employees, its processes and its differentiation 3) that shareholders deserve a reasonable return. Mr. Barry's philosophies regarding leadership, customers, employees and shareholders have been developed based on first hand experiences and successes. His consulting engagements focus on the leadership, culture and processes critical to generating revenue.

Mr. Barry also has an association with Richard Tyler International, an internationally known consulting and training company, to jointly participate in a number of training courses and consulting assignments that focus on revenue generation.

Jack Barry

PO Box 630249

Houston, Texas 77263-0249

Phone: 713.974.7214

Email: JackBarry@JackBarry.Biz

www.JackBarry.biz

Chapter 11

THE INTERVIEW

David E. Wright (Wright)

Today we are talking to Mark Fulton, who is a leadership coach, business columnist, and professional speaker with more than 30 years of experience in education, broadcasting, management, and marketing. As a leadership coach, Mark helps business owners, executives, and professionals to be more effective by developing powerful relationships with their key people. Mark's coaching practice, Compass Leadership Coaching, teaches his clients to optimize workplace relationships by paying employees the "hidden paychecks" that will keep them loyal, motivated, and productive. Mark's column, *Business Sense*, appears regularly in *Inside Business*. His *Seven Sources of Successful Leadership* seminar has been delivered to various companies, associations, and government groups. Mark Fulton, welcome to *Leadership Defined*!

Mark Fulton (Fulton)

Thank you, David. It's a pleasure to be here.

149

Wright

Mark, as a former teacher, high school principal, broadcaster, training director, and marketing director, you've had opportunities to see the role of leader from many perspectives. How do you define leadership?

Fulton

Dwight Eisenhower said something that I think really captures the essence of leadership. He said, "A platoon leader doesn't get his platoon to go by getting up and shouting 'I am smarter! I am bigger! I am stronger! I am the leader!' He gets his men to go along with him because they want to do it for him and they believe in him." Considering this statement came from a man who was the supreme commander of the Allied Forces in World War II, president of Columbia University, and President of the United States, I think Eisenhower's description of leadership is worth examining. I believe he was way ahead of his time in his thinking about leadership. Simply stated, Eisenhower said that good leadership is not a matter of issuing orders and enforcing obedience. Instead, an effective leader inspires others to cooperate and to use their own talents to the fullest. I believe a good leader does that by building powerful relationships with the people that he or she leads. Leadership is all about relationships.

Wright

It sounds as though you're saying that a high-powered, authoritarian, in-your-face leadership style doesn't work.

Fulton

Well, David, it works to a point. If your aim is merely to get your followers to obey, you can accomplish that with a dictatorial leadership style. But detachment and intimidation don't inspire cooperation, creativity, and commitment among employees. As a means to building a team that is loyal, enthusiastic, and diligent, the authoritarian leadership style is highly ineffective.

There's a historical reason for this new focus on sensitive leadership. In the last few decades of the 20th century, corporate America experienced an extraordinary change in its relationship with employees. It used to be that a person could reasonably expect to give his or her best effort and unqualified loyalty to an employer and expect in return the promise of long-term employment. Well, increased competition, diminished internal resources, and the turmoil created by mergers, reorganizations, and downsizing erased the bonds between employer and employee and replaced them with a new mindset on both sides: We will do whatever seems best for us.

That's why the old authoritarian leadership style doesn't work anymore. Managers at every level of an organization have found that employees demand to be treated as individual personalities who possess unique needs and expectations. Companies have also discovered that ignoring those needs and expectations will motivate their best and brightest people to go looking for an organization that will satisfy them. The expense of losing highly trained, competent employees is a terrible drain on a company of any size.

Wright

A lot of popular business books on leadership have focused on concepts such as emotional intelligence, values-based leadership, mentoring and coaching. How have these leadership techniques paid off in the workplace?

Fulton

When I was a wet-behind-the-ears television street reporter at the ripe old age of 28, I worked for a veteran news director named Dick Minton. Dick chewed tobacco, swore a blue streak, and expected his reporters to get the whole story and get it right. Even though I was a bit intimidated by his persona, I felt that he really cared about me as a person, that he wanted me to succeed for my own sake, as well as for his news department. I don't believe he ever read the book *How to Win Friends and Influence People*, but he certainly knew how to instill confidence, how to motivate his people, how to get his people to excel, and how to encourage us when we felt that we had failed. He also made sure that we kept things in perspective. He had us laughing at ourselves all the time and at life in general.

I wanted Dick to be pleased with my work, not because he was my boss and might fire me if I messed up, but because I liked and respected him. And I wanted to make him look good to the station's management. That's how I believe relationship-based leadership really pays off. It turns employees into stakeholders, who take ownership of their piece of the corporate pie, and they do their best to deliver quality work. Their motivation shifts from "What's in it for me?" to "How can I help us succeed?"

Wright

So the secret to unlocking employee productivity is a matter of treating people well and letting them know that you care about them as individuals?

Fulton

Well, it's a start, but a leader who really wants to unlock an employee's discretionary effort has to find out what hidden paycheck currencies that employee wants to be paid.

Wright

Discretionary effort? Hidden paycheck? What do you mean?

Fulton

Discretionary effort is the effort employees can give to their work if they choose to do so. Employees know what they need to do to keep their job or get a raise, but that's not all the effort they can give. Surveys have shown that most employees can be from 25% to 50% more productive if they are properly motivated to expend the extra effort that is theirs to give or withhold.

The hidden paycheck is paid in currencies that have nothing to do with money and benefits. A national survey was conducted a few years ago that asked supervisors how they would rank 10 job satisfaction factors in order of importance to employees. The 10 factors were: equitable pay; good working conditions; job security; feeling "in" on things; a fair discipline system; full appreciation for contributions; knowing that management cares; opportunity for growth; empathy for personal problems; and challenging work.

The supervisors who were surveyed ranked the top five of those 10 as: equitable pay; job security; good working conditions; a fair discipline system; and opportunity for growth. Now here's the interesting part. A national sample of employees was asked to rank those same job satisfaction factors. Their top five in order were: feeling "in" on things; full appreciation for contributions; knowing management cares; challenging work; and a fair discipline system. Interestingly, equitable pay, which was the supervisors' top choice of what they thought employees wanted, didn't even make it into the employees' top five. Based on these results and other similar surveys, it's evident that the hidden paycheck currencies that employees value the most are a mystery to most managers. Identifying and delivering the hidden paycheck that employees really want is critical to keeping them satisfied, motivated and loyal.

Wright

It's easy to go out and find some books on how to be a sensitive leader, but people often learn better by observing and imitating someone they admire. Were there people in your life who modeled this style of leadership?

Fulton

My mother and father were my first leadership role models. They taught me values that formed the foundation of my character. They introduced me to the Christian faith, where I found the ultimate leadership role model: Jesus Christ. In my early adult years, my understanding of Jesus' life and teachings expanded. I began to see him not only as God's son and my savior, but also as an outstanding example of truly enlightened leadership. Author Laurie Beth Jones wrote a great book entitled *Jesus, CEO*. In it she illuminates the leadership characteristics that Jesus demonstrated during his earthly ministry. As I read that book, I was amazed by her insights about Jesus' self-mastery, his dynamic personality, and his relationship skills. As I read other books on effective leadership, I saw the same traits being mentioned again and again. Integrity, humility, sensitivity, positivity, and creativity are just a few of the leadership qualities that I've integrated into my leadership coaching practice and my seminars. These qualities serve as guiding principles for anyone who wants to be an effective leader.

Wright

Guiding principles? Is that the concept behind the name of your coaching practice, Compass Leadership Coaching?

Fulton

Yes. I think a compass is a perfect symbol for how we navigate life's experiences and for how we make decisions about our own behavior. An actual compass is a handy device for determining where you are and where you want to go. If you're lost in the woods or you're drifting out to sea, a compass can save your life by pointing you in the right direction. I like to say that we all have an inner compass—I call it a life compass— an innate navigational tool that's governed by our own unique combination of intellect, common sense, intuition, knowledge, experience, and spirit. All of these components work together to help us evaluate and respond to the circumstances of life.

Your life compass helps you judge what others tell you. It steers your emotions in constructive directions. It guides you in making the hundreds of decisions that you face every day, and it's a primary tool for achieving personal excellence as a leader. Just like a real compass responds to the earth's magnetic field, your life compass responds to your character, which is a combination of guiding principles that I mentioned earlier: integrity, ingenuity, positivity, and so on. Think of these character traits as forces that influence your life compass and make it point you in the right direction.

Of course, as with any mechanism, your life compass requires you to have a certain amount of knowledge and skill in order to use it effectively. That's where I come in as a leadership coach. I help my clients understand, develop, and use their life compass to reach the goals they've set for themselves and their business or career.

Wright

So how do I use my life compass, as you call it, to be a better leader? Are there specific skills I need to develop?

Fulton

Yes. As I mentioned, I believe leadership is all about relationships. So any skills that help you relate more effectively with people will help your life compass work better. One such skill is what I call leadership intelligence. Leadership intelligence is actually a combination of three kinds of intelligence: emotional intelligence, behavioral intelligence, and relational intelligence.

As you mentioned earlier, emotional intelligence should be a pretty familiar concept to people in the business world, thanks to authors such as Daniel Goleman, Robert Cooper and James Autry. Their books explain that emotional intelligence is actually more important than the intellectual aptitude measured by an IQ test in determining leadership success. In other words, how smart you are isn't as important as how sensitive and perceptive you are to the emotions of others. Your head knowledge may help you make intelligent decisions, but it's your heart knowledge that will enable you to engage the people who will be involved in implementing those decisions that you made.

Building a climate and a culture of caring in an organization relies on the two sides of emotional intelligence: understanding and managing yourself and identifying and responding to the emotional needs of others. Self-mastery comes from developing your self-awareness, self-control, and self-confidence. Effective people skills rely on empathy and social expertise. Emotional intelligence is what drives your perception about yourself and others. If I know why I'm feeling a certain way about something, I'm better equipped to understand how others feel under similar circumstances. So being in touch with myself gives me perspective on others. It helps me step into the other person's shoes and see things from their perspective.

Behavioral intelligence, the second component of leadership intelligence, is at least as old as Socrates, who instructed his students to seek to understand themselves before trying to understand others. Later, Aristotle identified separate personality styles that he believed determined human behavior. Today, there are several behavioral style assessment instruments based on Aristotle's philosophy. One of them is the DISC behavioral style survey, which sorts people into variations of four basic personality types. Understanding that we are all programmed to have certain behavioral preferences when we face a situation is the beginning of behavioral intelligence. One person may be by nature a dominant driver—someone who likes to take charge. Another may be inspiring and influential, preferring to engage people and win them over. Another may be steady and supportive, preferring to serve on a team rather than lead it. And still another may be careful and correct, preferring to work alone and take responsibility to attend to details. Once you understand how these different behavior styles affect your perception and interaction with other people, you can use that intelligence to lead people more effectively.

The third kind of leadership intelligence is relational intelligence, which relies on the other two: behavioral and emotional intelligence. I mentioned this earlier while talking about discretionary effort and the hidden paycheck. Now more than ever employees are comparing what they get out of a job with what they put into it and deciding whether the transaction is an equitable exchange—whether there's balance. In return for hard work and loyalty, employees expect a decent paycheck, reasonable benefits, and those hidden paycheck currencies. Relational intelligence leads you to look for signs of which currencies your employees value the most. Different employees value differ hidden paycheck currencies. Some value trust more. Some want acknowledgement more. In fact, there are objective surveys that actually measure those expectations on the part of employees.

Building powerful relationships with your key people by employing emotional, behavioral, and relational intelligence isn't just a nice idea, David. It's an absolute necessity for boosting your company's productivity and profitability.

Wright

Can you give our readers an example of someone you believe demonstrates leadership intelligence?

Fulton

Yes. A perfect example of leadership intelligence for me is maestro JoAnn Falletta, the music director of the Virginia Symphony Orchestra and the Buffalo Philharmonic Orchestra. I wrote a column comparing her leadership style with her musicians to that of a corporate chief executive.

When I asked JoAnn to describe a conductor's most important responsibility, she replied, "Inspiring people to pursue excellence. A conductor is a catalyst to get the team to give its best performance." Throughout our conversation, JoAnn talked about the importance of respecting her musicians, earning their trust, encouraging them to understand the importance their part plays in the overall performance of the orchestra, their importance to the team. JoAnn strives to inspire leadership in key members of the orchestra. She said, "I rely on principle players to be part of creating the vision for the concert. I let them shape the character of a performance and make decisions about the work environment for the organization. Their voices are heard and they know it." Now that's behavioral and relational intelligence at work, David.

JoAnn pointed out that her approach to leading an orchestra isn't universally practiced. In fact, it's very rare in Europe, where some conductors take a much more authoritarian approach to conducting an orchestra. She believes that an orchestra led by a conductor who is focused on power produces a different kind of music. Musicians under an authoritarian tend to be more careful and cautious, and they don't put all of themselves into the performance. JoAnn Falletta actually goes out of her way to challenge her musicians. As any good leader will do, she encourages them to stretch their abilities and expand their understanding. She said, "I challenge them with repertoire, with music that requires different skills. I want them to take risks. I encourage them to think as if they were playing without a conductor, as in a chamber music ensemble. I want them to listen to the other players and hear from their colleagues."

Of course, that's not to say that JoAnn Falletta provides no guidance. She said, "I establish the frame. Musicians move in and out of the frame. I give them the freedom to be different. Some people like more structure. Others like more freedom. When someone takes a risk and succeeds, others are inspired to do likewise." JoAnn Falletta creates an atmosphere for her musicians in which good things can happen, and that's real leadership intelligence. There are lots of examples of historical and fictional figures that serve as great leadership models.

Wright

How about an example of a fictional character that defines leadership as you see it?

Fulton

One of my favorite movies is "Casablanca," and one of my favorite characters is Rick Blaine, played by Humphrey Bogart. Rick is a hard drinking, cynical American who runs a nightclub in Casablanca in 1941, when Morocco was the crossroads for spies, traders, Nazis, and the French Resistance.

Like most people, I used to focus on the tragic love story of Rick and Ilsa Lund, played by Ingrid Bergman. What escaped me until recently is how Rick relates to his employees in the film. Even though he's a tough and brutally frank guy, who doesn't hesitate to thumb his nose at the Nazis, Rick noticeably softens when he interacts with Sam, Carl, Sasha, and Emile, some of his key employees. In each case, Rick demonstrates genuine affection, trust, and devotion. In fact, it's obvious that all the workers at Rick's Café American regard him with respect, loyalty, and fondness.

Early in the film, a young couple trying to escape from Nazi occupied Bulgaria attempts to obtain exit visas from Casablanca, but they have no money for the bribe that they need to get the documents. The lecherous local police captain offers to provide the visas in exchange for sexual favors from the wife. When Rick learns of this, he arranges for the husband to win enough money at the casino's roulette table to guarantee their departure. As word of his chivalrous deed spreads through the café, employees express their admiration for Rick's generosity.

Good leaders recognize and accept the fact that doing the right thing sometimes can have a high cost to their company. However, integrity is a leadership quality that inspires respect, trust, and loyalty among employees, emotions that can more than compensate for a short term financial setback. When you are faced with an ethical decision, remember who's watching. Remember that your employees look to you as a role model. If they observe that high moral standards are your modus operandi, then they're more likely to replicate them on the job.

When Rick's Café American is wrongly shut down by the Nazis, Rick keeps all of his employees on full pay. He clearly understands the impact this unanticipated business downturn can have on his people, and he does everything in his power to minimize its effect. For many employers sensitivity to employees' needs is a notion that has its limits. Okaying time off for a family emergency or accommodating babysitter challenges are often the extent of corporate largesse. But what would happen if a leader went beyond the crisis mentality and really sought to assist employees with some personal necessities? What if employer helped pay for a child's special education needs or helped a spouse get a job? I believe being creative with special gestures of kindness and generosity will be repaid many times over.

When Rick decides to help Ilsa and her husband escape from Casablanca, he realizes that he must sell his café and disappear in order to avoid capture by the Nazis. So he visits his competitor, Signor Ferrari, owner of the Blue Parrot, and he offers to sell his café with certain conditions. Sam and other key employees must retain their jobs. Even as he departs, Rick demonstrates a real interest in the well-being of his people.

Commitment to employees may seem like a naïve notion in this era of notorious executive pillagers. Certainly the corporate chieftains at Enron, WorldCom, and other disgraced companies showed little concern for workers whose retirement plans were devastated while the big shots received hefty severance packages. I think Rick would have taken those scoundrels for a long drive in the desert.

Taking care of good employees is never a bad idea. Winning employees' loyalty and inducing them to perform with excellence and enthusiasm requires a commitment on the leader's part to provide not only their compensation and benefits, but also hidden paycheck currencies such as acknowledgement, challenge, security, and trust. Who knows? If more employers followed Rick Blaine's example, they might inspire their employees to hoist their coffee cups and say, "Here's looking at you, boss."

Wright

Okay, those are two good examples of great leadership. But sometimes it's helpful to look at a thing's opposite in order to understand it better. How would you describe the characteristics of poor leadership?

Fulton

My earliest thoughts about bad bosses occurred when I watched "A Christmas Carol" on TV as a child. I remember cringing as poor Bob Cratchit took abuse from Ebenezer Scrooge at the beginning of the film, and then I smiled when Scrooge realized his former employer, Old Fezziwig, was quite a different kind of leader. I was especially pleased when Scrooge made amends with Cratchit at the end of the story. Nevertheless, as we all know, Scrooge has become an archetype of the insensitive, belligerent boss.

You've probably heard this joke from Henny Youngman: "You can't help liking the boss. If you don't, he fires you." Well, some bosses *are* a joke. Like Scrooge, they don't have a clue about building mutually rewarding relationships with their employees. They live in a world where productivity is simply an outcome of consistently applied pressure. I started thinking about my own employment history, and I came up with some characters that I believe a lot of employees have encountered at one time or another.

Sadistic Sam - Sam clearly takes great satisfaction from inflicting discomfort on others. He relishes flirting with female workers while flaunting his authority over the underlings who serve him. He enjoys barking orders, interrupting breaks, and criticizing clerks in front of customers. Meanwhile, his favorite employees can do no wrong, and they milk his blind spot for all it's worth. Sam is particularly tough on lifers; the poor employees who hope to keep their jobs until retirement.

Carping Carla - Carla raises criticism of employees to an art form. She berates staff members for being slow and inefficient. With an air of exasperation, she relentlessly reviews team objectives that haven't been met, while discouraging feedback. Expressing a word of encouragement is as foreign to her as giving alms to the poor was for Scrooge. Carla assumes that pointing the finger at others will keep her superiors from scrutinizing her performance too closely.

Paranoid Pete - Pete thinks his primary role as a manager is to squelch dissention in the ranks. Staff members who suggest alternatives to tried and true policies are treated as traitors and rabble-rousers. They are often punished with less-than-objective evaluations and undesirable work assignments. In a dispute, Pete typically takes the side of anyone who has a history of agreeing with him or who might be recruited as a spy to provide Pete with information he can use to keep perceived troublemakers in line.

Sycophant Sue - Sue is a master at sucking up. Anyone who can advance her reputation in the eyes of the CEO is a legitimate target for major brown-nosing. Her staff knows that any innovative venture is vulnerable to scuttling if someone higher up expresses the smallest doubt about it. Sue is actually a warm-hearted woman who's caught in a quagmire of corporate quicksand. She believes that the only way to keep from going under is to grab the coattails of anyone who seems to be successfully climbing the corporate ladder.

Egotistical Eddie - Eddie has never met a mirror he didn't like. Eddie operates his department as though it exists to remind the world of how wonderful he is. His staff understands that the greatest crime is to make Eddie look bad. Gratuitous complements are welcome. Fawning over his pet project is expected. Eddie thinks that taking a personal interest in his employees and treating them with kindness is beneath him and utterly unnecessary.

David, if America is to accept its role as the leading economic force on the planet, it must also uphold the standard of ethical, compassionate, and courageous business leadership. From Fortune 500 companies to the local fish market, leaders must set a worthy example for their employees. The Bob Cratchits of the world are watching.

Wright

Any final thoughts about defining leadership?

Fulton

There's a quote I particularly like from British Prime Minister Benjamin Disraeli. He once said, "The greatest good you can do for another is not just to share your riches, but to reveal to him his own." That's as good a definition as any for effective leadership.

Wright

What a great conversation, Mark. I really appreciate all the time you've taken with us here today. It's been interesting and I've learned a lot.

Fulton

Thank you, David. It's been a great pleasure for me, and I'm thrilled to be a part of the *Defining Leadership* book project.

Wright

Today we've been talking to Mark Fulton, who is a leadership coach, business columnist, and professional speaker with more than 30 years of experience in education, broadcasting, management, and marketing. And as you have found listening to this or reading this, he's a pretty smart guy and knows what he is talking about. You might want to listen. Thank you, Mark.

Some Final Thoughts

Leadership is a possession, not a position. It is not an inevitable consequence of being charge. In fact, there are plenty of people in positions of authority—business executives, elected officials, military officers, etc.—who lack leadership. Actually, leadership is a skill that anyone can develop and employ, regardless of his or her position.

Life is full of leadership opportunities. Circumstances frequently arise in our jobs, social circles, church activities, community groups and other settings that are occasions for us to step forward and influence outcomes. If you are a parent, you hold one of the most vital leadership jobs in the world. Even if you don't occupy a management position at work, you can still serve as a leader by being a role model for other employees to emulate.

Think of leadership as a river that runs through the landscape of your life. When it is properly employed, leadership shapes circumstances, wears down obstacles, enriches what it touches, provides power for producing results and moves people in positive directions. Your river of leadership is fed by many tributaries, personal attributes such as integrity, humility, sensitivity and positivity. How effectively you tap into your river of leadership depends on how well you have developed those qualities.

Of course, the world of business is a key arena where sound leadership is desperately needed. The corporate scandals involving Enron, Worldcom, Tyco, Global Crossing and others are merely the most obvious manifestations of corporate leadership failure. More commonly, leadership lapses are a product of inattention. Too often, business executives are so focused on beefing up the bottom line that they fail to deliver what their key employees want in order to be productive, satisfied and loyal stakeholders in their company.

Leadership coaching can help executives and business owners become confident and effective leaders.

About The Author

Mark Fulton helps companies transform their managers into leaders. Through his coaching, columns, seminars and speeches, Mark helps business people optimize the single most important factor in boosting workplace productivity and profitability: relationships. Mark's coaching practice, Compass Leadership Coaching, develops dynamic leaders who know how to energize and engage employees through powerful relationships. Mark's coaching clients and seminar attendees learn vital thinking, communication and behavior skills that will take them to the top of their field.

Mark Fulton

Compass Leadership Coaching

215 Brooke Avenue, Suite 904

Norfolk, Virginia 23510

Phone: 757.533.9650

Email: mark@CompassLeadershipCoaching.com

www.CompassLeadershipCoaching.com

Chapter 12

GEORGE RITCHESKE

THE INTERVIEW

David E. Wright (Wright)

We are talking to George Ritcheske. George has over 25 years' experience in leadership development processes with international professional service firms as well as energy, telecommunications, high-tech, and hospitality organizations. He works with leaders in enhancing their effectiveness and the effectiveness of their teams. Utilizing 360-degree feedback processes, assessments, and organization-wide communication processes, George facilitates exceptional retreats for strategic planning and implementation as well as leadership team development and structured off-sites for business problem resolution. As a professional speaker and workshop leader, George address such topics as: "True Leadership"; "The Challenge of Change"; "True Team- building"; "The Manager as Teacher, Leader, and Coach"; and "The Power of Differences." George is the co-author of the book *True Leaders: How Exceptional CEOs and Presidents Make a Difference by Building People and Profits*, published by Dearborn Trade Press in December 2001. The book presents ten leadership principles drawn from interviews with 27 CEOs and presidents. He earned his BA in Economics at Dartmouth College and his MBA at the University of Michigan. He is a member of the International Coach Federation, the Organization Development Network, and the National Speakers Association. He has been actively involved in community organizations including the Boy Scouts of America and Rotary International. George, welcome to *Leadership Defined*.

George Ritcheske (Ritcheske)

Thank you, David.

Wright

Why is it that there is such an outcry about the need for leadership?

Ritcheske

David, I think it's because we as a society have seen leaders who have broken their trust with the folks around them. We've seen it in businesses with the corporate scandals: the Enron, WorldCom, and Tyco fiascos, where we had leaders in place who seem to have focused on their own wealth and got caught up in the greed. They really didn't have a concern at all for the innocent people who would be affected by their actions. We've seen things in our churches, our schools, and our government where we have leaders in trusted roles who broke that trust. People are looking around and saying, "Where are the leaders who are protecting people? Where are the leaders who help develop people? And where are the leaders who really are looking out for the greater good rather than just trying to increase the money going into their own pockets?"

Wright

It is a little scary to take $50 million dollars as a CEO while your company is losing profits and you're laying people off. Why in the world would someone do something like that? I consider that to be stupid—talk about cutting off your nose to spite your face!

Ritcheske

We found, David, that very frequently, leaders of large organizations get caught up with being in charge. People don't tell them "no"; they believe they can do anything they want, essentially that they're above the rules. We saw that with Martha Stewart: she doesn't think she did anything wrong, and yet she was convicted for having obstructed an investigation. She couldn't tell the truth about what she had done; while she said, "I didn't do anything wrong," she also couldn't take responsibility for it. That happens frequently with leaders: they lose touch with reality and they think that is OK because they are important to the organization. Their rationale is, "if it benefits me, it will benefit the organization, because I'm so important to the organization."

Wright

So what do you think contributes to the confusion about leadership?

Ritcheske

The confusion is due to the use of the term "leadership." The term is used to describe a position instead of describing the person's behavior. True leadership is not about power, but rather about what a person does to influence people to move in a more positive direction. So we talk about leaders, and people immediately began to think, "OK, well, that's the Boss, the CEO, the president, the superintendent, the Governor." That's the confusion, because we can have a "leader" who is leading people in a direction that is really harming the greater good. Osama Bin Laden could be seen as "leader." He certainly is influencing people and he has people who are committed to his cause. Yet, the purpose of that cause is to inflict damage and harm on others, and that doesn't promote a greater good. What we need to do, then, to really understand leadership is to focus on what direction that individual is influencing people to move in: Is that direction promoting something that is better for society?

Wright

So, before we go any further, how do you define "leadership?"

Ritcheske

Leadership, true leadership, is influence: I influence people by what I do and what I say. But what I do conveys what I believe is important. As we looked at true leaders, we found them to be very interested in learning from others, which suggests both open-mindedness and recognition that knowledge increases their personal influencing capabilities. True leaders see acquisition of knowledge as information they can use to help the organization be more effective. The other aspect we discovered was that true leaders don't see knowledge as a source of power for themselves as leaders—they gain knowledge and then share it more broadly to increase other people's development, and through that sharing, leaders make a bigger impact within the organization. So there is very much this sense of leverage: I have access to information, and I want to continue to learn because I know that I don't know it all. As I learn from others, I also want to share my learning with other folks in the organization so that we can collectively apply our new insights to making our business better so we can fulfill our customers' needs in a more effective fashion.

Wright

Are there two or three characteristics that are the most important for a leader to possess?

Ritcheske

We believe there are, David. These characteristics are inherent in everyone, and we can build and develop them. The first one is what we call a strong humility: strong in that leaders know they have gifts and talents, and they want to use those gifts and talents to help the organization be more effective. The humility says, "I don't know it all, and I can't know it all. Therefore, I am interested in hearing and learning from other people." So that strong humility says, "I am not the best person in the organization, and I'm not the most important person in the organization. I am an individual in the organization, and I'm in a role where I can influence people to make better things happen." True leaders have both a strong sense of self and are humble. The second characteristic is an interest in people. Frequently, leaders get caught up in having to "tell" people. True leaders listen to people: they gather information, and then they are able to communicate in a fashion that connects with people's hearts and helps them see the benefit of moving in a particular direction. So people aren't there to be commanded, but rather to be engaged. The third one is that leaders need to have the courage of their convictions.

The business world is a cycle that goes up and down. Too frequently, leaders begin to make decisions on what they think will affect the stock price instead of recognizing that a leader stays committed to the organization's purpose and to doing the things that strengthen the organization's foundation and its capability to meet that purpose today and in the future. It's the courage to say, "Yes, we still need to be investing in our people even though the cycle is down." Then they will be ready when the cycle comes back up, and will be able to surf the wave rather than get crushed by it.

Wright

So what do leaders struggle with the most?

Ritcheske

Our experiences tell us that leaders struggle the most with communication.

Wright

Communication?

Ritcheske

Yes. They struggle most with communication because business leaders have basically been brought up in an environment where the myth is that if a leader says something once or twice, everybody else will follow it. And that's not true. Leaders need to announce, "We are moving in this direction; we're going to be developing a new product or service," and they have to ask questions of people at different levels in the organization. They need to ask questions like: "What does that mean to you? What's the impact on your area? What things do we need to consider in order to be successful with this initiative?" Each person in an organization is going to share his or her view and that view will be based on the individual's experiences and position within the organization. So each person that the leader talks to has a different perspective. The leader processes that information and then sits down with another group to engage in a roundtable discussion about the initiative.

In facilitating that conversation, the leader is raising the awareness of everybody around the table about the things that need to be considered. Then the leader recognizes, "Now we need to have people accountable for those aspects of the change initiative." Communication is listening, synthesizing, sharing, reinforcing, and assigning responsibility to follow through. That communications process can frustrate leaders. We've worked with a number of leadership teams who will say, "We understand the change initiative and it's a great thing to do, so why are we getting push back?" And our question to them is, "How long did you process the prospect of moving in that direction?" Ultimately it's a 3-month, 6-month, or 9-month process where the leadership team had interaction, debate, dialog, and argument about a commitment to move in that direction. After that, they have an expectation that "now that we've done that work, our people should just fall in line." And yet, time and time again, when an initiative is announced or a change occurs people want to know the "why" behind it. True leaders organize processes to help people discover the "why," understand the implications of that change, and earn commitment to make the change work.

Wright

So how does leadership differ in a not-for-profit organization?

Ritcheske

That question gets asked frequently. We are involved in community-based organizations like schools and churches, and we have found that the principles apply in the same way. But in a not-for-profit organization, there is a real emphasis on understanding influence. When you're working with people who could choose to go elsewhere, you can't command them. So there is a real recognition that leaders need to influence, and yet not-for-profit organizations frequently lack leaders who have the courage of their convictions to influence people to buy into the organization's philosophy. We have been involved in several not-for-profit organizations that have a heightened sense of respect for each person's opinion. Respect is necessary, but we end up with a democracy of 30 "leaders," which doesn't work. People have a say, but we need to commit to a course of action. Once we commit, just as in business, we have to create a plan where certain people have responsibility for certain actions and outcomes. So, people in not-for-profit organizations recognize the importance of influence and accept that when we agree, we have to operate like a business and create clear responsibility teams to carry out the plans. Accountability for results is still needed.

Wright

Let me ask you two questions in one here: What obligations to develop other leaders do you think a leader has and how did you really develop leadership skills?

Ritcheske

Leaders do have an obligation to develop other leaders. I believe that we in the United States have suffered from thinking of leaders as heroic leaders: Lee Iacocca "rescued" Chrysler. He was the "hero," he made it happen, and Chrysler would have died if it hadn't been for him. Well, Chrysler was never transformed as an organization; while he helped it survive, it never prospered and eventually got purchased by the Germans. So it isn't about heroic leadership, true leadership is about making the organization healthy, and one of the key ways to do that is to develop leaders at all levels. Jack Welch walked his talk at GE by saying, "We need leaders in all of our businesses," and he continued to invest in that. One of the best examples of his investment is that when Jeff Immelt was named as the new CEO to replace Welch, the other two internal candidates were immediately recruited by other major organizations. One went to 3M, and the other went to Home Depot. So they were so well regarded that, while they weren't chosen to lead GE, they were immediately chosen by the business community to lead two other important organizations.

Wright

I should say.

Ritcheske

That's what leaders need to do: they need to develop other leaders at all levels. Otherwise, there's *the* leader who made it happen, like Sam Walton, and there's an insufficient number of leaders coming up—so you end up with a large organization getting all sorts of bad press now because they're not doing certain things very well. How do leaders develop? Leaders develop through experiences, building on a framework that other leaders have shared with them. If I am committee chairman, I may see my role as a way to get the committee to carry out my agenda—that's a very self-centered objective, and yet most people end up trying to do that in those kinds of roles. Compare that to a leadership development experience, which says, "Your role in this committee is to help build better communication between these four departments." So I'm going to be conscious of how to promote true two-way communication between those departments. Now I'm not focused on me; I'm focused on the process and an objective that will benefit the organization even after I'm gone. If I move on to a different role with different responsibilities, those enhanced communications processes will be ingrained in the organization.

Within organizations, promotions are frequently based on a person's technical expertise—yet a leader's success in the new position really depends upon how well the leader can accomplish things through people, their "process" knowledge. They must have an understanding of how to communicate with people, connect with their hearts, and help them connect with others. Leaders must know how to motivate the team to strengthen the organization and move it forward.

Wright

Most people, in this culture at least, view leadership as a single person at the top or not more than two or three in a major, large environment. But you're talking about leaders at all levels. Why is it important to have leaders at all levels of an organization?

Ritcheske

I lived inside of organizations for 18 years, so I know the importance of leaders at all levels. People are constantly influencing others by what they say and what they do. Simple example: you're sitting around a table and people are gossiping about this guy who is really sort of a bad apple. You can sit there and participate in it, or you can stand up and say, "I choose not to participate in this conversation because it is gossip and it isn't benefiting anybody. If we're really concerned about that individual's impact on the business, then we need to go and talk to his boss because his boss is the only person who can do something about that." What I've just done is to say that gossiping is not acceptable and doesn't benefit anybody. I've offered a way to deal the concerns in a constructive fashion, and that's true leadership. That isn't about a position that I hold, it's about a conviction that I possess.

Leaders are needed at all levels of an organization because what the people do on an organization's front line defines that organization for its customers. When something goes wrong with your car repair, and you come back in and the person who's right there on the front line says "We'll take that off your bill and fix it free of charge," that's leadership. They've said, "We made the mistake, we're going to make it right, and you, the customer, are not going to be negatively impacted by it." Now I have a very positive sense of that organization because they care about me as a customer. That's true leadership in the moment. I was at a well known retail organization and had just purchased something from the shelf by the cash register. It rang up $1.00 higher than the posted price, and I said, "I thought it was only $4.00. "The cashier looked across the aisle and could see it was only $4.00, but said, "I will have to get my supervisor to handle this." The supervisor came over and said, "OK, go ahead and adjust it by the dollar." And I looked at the supervisor and said, "What should the cashier have done?" The supervisor said, "Well, she should tell somebody to change the price on the shelf so we get the right price." I said, "No, she should have immediately taken the dollar off for me." That's not true leadership. In that moment, the supervisor said, "We'll adjust it for you, but now we're going to go ahead and change it so we get the money we want." That leaves an impact on customers. We know business is about making profit, but do they make profit at the expense of fairness?

Wright

As we look at the bigger picture, how do you think leadership, or good leadership, or even better leadership would benefit our entire society?

Ritcheske

People develop through their experiences. When we have leaders at all levels helping people to become better contributors, we are helping them develop their competence, their confidence, and their character. People of good character will say "no" to things they think are wrong and, in a sense, it's that check and balance that needs to exist—in the pursuit of profits, people can get into some unethical or at least very gray areas. We need people who have the strength to stand up and say "no." Whistle-blowers are necessary, but within an organization it's even more important not to do anything that a whistler-blower has to report. The more we build true leadership within an organization, the more we encourage people to do what's right. As we really strengthen people in doing what's right, it helps our society because we're developing additional people, a critical mass, who recognize it isn't about the money—it's about doing things fairly and for the right reasons—and when we do them well the money will follow.

Wright

Let's get a little bit specific, about politics. What recommendations would you give to our political leaders after we take all that you've said about leadership into consideration?

Ritcheske

Political leaders, who are focused on staying in power, giving responses based on what the poll numbers tell them, are not true leaders. We need political leaders who will answer questions as they are asked, share the rationale for their point of view, and take the responsibility for things that work *and* things that didn't work. There are a lot of things that don't work, and society improves when leaders acknowledge them. I think we have built a political class more interested in staying in power than in truly making a difference in our society. Which is why, just as an example, David, I think Arnold Schwarzenegger has a greater possibility of making meaningful change as Governor of California than virtually anybody else who could have taken that role. He doesn't have to be in that Governor role: he already is a success and has made plenty of money in his lifetime, but he's truly in a role now where he wants to work for the greater good of society. He's not beholden to anybody, and he can follow through on his convictions.

Wright

It's a shame that, politically speaking at least, it's just kind of inherent in the beast—if they don't start running for re-election immediately after taking office, they're probably only going to be "one-termers." It's very difficult to get anything done in four years and it's just really sad, but you are right. I just wish there was another system so that the incumbent party wouldn't have to start working immediately to keep their jobs. Either that or have the personnel change every four years, no matter what. That might help, except it sure would look bad to the leaders all over the world.

Ritcheske

When I was in my MBA program, I wrote a paper about the disproportionate impact of special interest groups on our legislative system. I believe that special interest groups have a role in terms of influence, but it is much, much too powerful. We as a society need to be able to marshal ourselves to say, "This is what we need to have happen," and look for people who will help support making that happen.

Wright

Well it's powerful enough—seems that almost every person that loses his job on the Hill goes into the business of lobbying.

Ritcheske

Isn't that interesting?

Wright

And I tell you you're right. Well, what an interesting conversation. Hopefully another time you and I can talk politics. It's very interesting.

Ritcheske

I think that with leadership we need to encourage people to talk about not just *what* they believe but also *why* they believe it. When we really understand the underlying rationale, we are shaping other people's perspectives and we can build a greater consensus. I think true leaders are constantly working on building a broad-base consensus so that, as we execute our plans, we are putting our full effort into it. Time and time again, when organizations have the full commitment of everybody's time, talents, and gifts, marvelous things happen. Great accomplishments occur because people have had the "why" questions answered to their satisfaction and they are then able to fully put their talents behind whatever initiative to which they committed. It's worth it: the upfront investment in communications absolutely pays dividends because we now have people who are saying, "How can we make this work better?" rather than, "Why are we doing this at all?"

Wright

This has been interesting. I really appreciate the time you have taken with me this morning, George. Your ideas about leadership are extremely good and something that I would like to think about. Today we have been talking to George Ritcheske. He has over 25 years' experience in leadership development. As a professional speaker and workshop leader, he addresses topics such as: "True Leadership"; "The Challenge of Change"; "The Manager as Teacher, Leader, and Coach"; and "The Power of Difference." I think we have found out here today that he knows what he is talking about. Thank you so much, George, for being with us today on *Leadership Defined*.

Ritcheske

David, it's been my pleasure.

George Ritcheske is a consultant, executive coach and speaker with more than twenty-five years' experience in developing leaders and building high-performance leadership teams in financial services, insurance, real estate, manufacturing and service industries. He is adept at aligning workplace efforts with strategic plans to meet current objectives while implementing change for continued success. He captivates his audiences with stories drawn from his experiences in business, as a Scoutmaster and as a dad of twins.

George Ritcheske

Williams Square Center

5215 North O'Connor Blvd, Ste. 200

Irving, TX 75039

Phone: 972.304.6137

Email: george@trueleadercoach.com

www.trueleadercoach.com

www.true-leaders.com

Chapter 13

ROBERT MCMAHAN

THE INTERVIEW

David E. Wright (Wright)

Robert speaks, trains, and writes on time and life mastery, maximizing potential, and understanding and effectively using our psychological type to the fullest. Currently, Robert enjoys immensely his role as Leadership Development Specialist with T-Mobile in Thornton, Colorado.

Fans of University of Denver athletics know Robert as the public address voice of the Pioneers from 1995 - 2004. Robert has also taught working professional students for the last ten years as an adjunct faculty member of the Applied Communications Masters Degree Program at the University of Denver. Robert is best known, however, for sharing his expertise with thousands of people in hundreds of strategic seminars targeted to businesses of all sizes, from small nonprofits to Fortune 500 giants.

Hundreds of productive adults credit Robert with dramatic turnaround in their perspectives and performance. Robert, welcome to *Leadership Defined.*

Robert McMahan (McMahan)

Thank you, David.

Wright

Since most of your previous work focuses on productivity and making the most of our time and gifts, how did you become interested in leadership?

McMahan

The topics of time mastery and leadership are actually very closely aligned. From a young age I was involved in extracurricular activities, clubs, sports, and school. Early on, I found myself drawn to leadership in many ventures, so I had an interest in what made leaders successful. I wanted to know how they accomplished so much.

I quickly observed in my own studies and research that successful people find time for the important things. We've all heard the saying, "If you want something done right, find the busiest person you know." While I do not agree with the assessment that "busy" is a leadership quality, I do endorse personal productivity as a vital path to leadership effectiveness. How else do you explain successful CEOs, volunteer leaders, and philanthropists who find time to speak multiple languages, play musical instruments, contribute time and resources to their favorite charities, and still spend quality time with their families, all while leading organizations?

Wright

You just wrote of family time and leadership not being exclusive of each other. In your work you often credit your family with much of your success in your opportunities for leadership and in life. How has your close network of family inspired you to become the leader you are today?

McMahan

I believe we are who we are as a result of what we do with where we come from; how productive we are determines whether or not we capitalize and maximize our potential. I had productive, loving parents, and I feel blessed to have come from such an amazing family.

Although my mother and father were married straight out of college, they didn't have me until almost five years later and my sister, Jenny, nearly fours years after that. That five-year getting-to-know-you period was not the norm then, and I am convinced that this maturing time readied my mother and father to be the parents they became.

Nearly everything my mother and father did served as a role model for me. I can remember them telling me of an early job they each had working in the identical field and position as well as with the same employer, but my father earned 50% more money than my mother. They were employed as social workers by a Baptist orphanage. Although helpful to many in the 1960s, the church exhibited two qualities not rooted in equality, sexism and racism. These certainly ran counter to leadership, stewardship, and love. The church-based orphanage paid my mother a fraction of what they paid my father for identical work. Furthermore, when my father attempted to bring a black boy into this large north Texas children's home—this was a segregated orphanage, as was everything in 1964—the administration hit the roof. But my dad persisted, and that's what opened the doors to integration for other children there. My parents exemplified leadership, and they did so by facing up to a very large and powerful entity.

Growing up in Texas in the early '70s, the big issues were over race and gender. Before bussing, my mother taught second grade in a segregated black elementary school because she felt called to make a difference by offering her quality skills to an under-served area where it was hard to recruit teachers. One time my sister and I visited the classroom; I remember all of the kids looking at us in amazement because, outside of my mother, my sister and I were the only white folks they'd ever seen in person. My mother was expanding our world and theirs. That's leadership.

My dad, a former minister and social worker, later owned a consulting company where of the four top officers, he was the only Anglo, and two of the other four were very well qualified women. Not many business owners worked that way in 1970s Texas. Not that many, unfortunately, work that way today. Once again, leadership defined.

One other life lesson I recall vividly was when my mother took us to the old Big Town Mall in Dallas long after the civil rights struggles left the streets. She showed us the two sets of water fountains and restrooms; one set labeled "blacks" and the other "whites." Even though the official policy of segregation was gone, these vestiges still remained. We talked about how this made us feel and about how wrong segregation and racism was. Not leaving the learning and education to the schools and instead talking about this serious topic face-to-face exemplifies leadership.

My younger sister, Jenny, as a 10 year-old woke up at 5 AM to catch a bus so she could travel across town to an outstanding elementary school that was integrated, taught Spanish, and focused on learning as part of a community experience. None of her neighborhood friends could understand why Jenny made that commitment and seemed to never be home to play. Also, not all parents related to my mother and father's decision to allow Jenny to travel across town to school at her request. I was in middle school and was still sleeping while my sister was learning. She was younger, but she taught me many lessons like the importance of following through on commitments and having a burning desire to learn as much as possible, sometimes involving a self-imposed hardship. That's leadership.

Today, I owe much of who I am as a leader to my partner in life of nearly 12 years, my wife Denise. I learned from Denise about being the best leader you know how to be at work but then coming home to be the best caring partner you know how to be in your personal life. She taught me that being a phenomenal leader at work but lacking at home makes one lacking overall.

When we first married, we both had opportunities for promotions and relocations to two different states within six weeks of the other. Before a discussion could break out on which one to take, she spoke up in favor of my move and said "Let's go to Denver; I can make my career there." We did, and has she ever made a career here. From success at the director and vice president level in several nonprofit organizations to operating a successful marketing company today, Denise has succeeded immensely without complaint or mention of any concession. That's leadership.

The love, patience, and kindness Denise gives our infant son, Will, inspires me to be better at home, too. Denise models the principle of leadership beginning at home with those most important to us.

Wright

Well, it's easy to see how many close to you have influenced you for several years in your view of leadership. I'm curious about your philosophy of leadership today?

McMahan

I believe there are only two types of potential leaders: those who have the tools already, and those who see a deficiency in their resources but seek to build up their tool chest on their own. I see leaders as people who use the tools they've been given. They didn't really earn all of them; some they were born with, while others were cultivated with care.

Many a leadership writer puts stock in the great person theory. In other words, if you are tall, have a great voice, or are visually compelling, some might say leadership is more accessible to those people. I believe, however, it is what you do with your gifts, the work you put in to develop your talent that makes the mark of leadership. And it's a leader's role to positively and proactively affect other lives—to answer the questions, the solutions, and the problems that are posed to us.

I believe leadership to be where strategy meets empathy. One cannot only know how to lead from a book perspective; one also must understand what others experience in order to lead effectively. Leadership must be intentional, positive, and proactive.

People talk about missions, visions, and values. A mission is like a compass. Goals are today's maps to get where we need to go. Leadership is the volition to use the map and the compass to guide our communities forward toward the realm of most good.

Finally, what people do with what they have speaks volumes more when one comes from so little. The rags to riches stories are so compelling, especially when so many have so much yet do little with their natural gifts and birthright. I think that's why we celebrate those success stories. It reminds me of one of my father's favorite quotes from his grandfather, "Potential is something you ain't done yet." Leaders simply fulfill their potential and maximize their productivity.

Wright

Some of your perspectives are quite different from your fellow authors in this book. Do you believe it is possible to disagree vehemently with an avowed expert in leadership and also be an expert on leadership?

McMahan

I labored over whether or not to participate in a book project where I knew my key beliefs, core values, and vital concerns would not necessarily be shared by or even valued by some of my co-contributors. Ultimately, I decided that I would not be living up to the way of a leader if I walked away from an opportunity to dissent thoughtfully or to present a different perspective than, say Dr. Keyes or General Haig. Sometimes an open mind opens a diverse viewpoint. Based on the politics of the day, about 50% of the reading population might believe similarly.

Putting a diverse group of professionals together involves a certain amount of risk, especially in these polarizing times when "news" networks specialize in the sensational and editorial more than in the true hunt for accuracy, factual data, and clarity. Most books today are more polemic than thoughtful discussion. I believe, regardless of what sides of the aisle people sit or what viewpoint people come to see as truth, most people respect others who are principled.

Ultimately, it doesn't matter if one is left or right, conservative or liberal, democrat or republican. People of principle exist in all beliefs, and leaders of principle should only speak their mind to better our world.

I couldn't vote for Goldwater, and I didn't vote for Reagan, but I respect their leadership intent. Likewise, I believe Paul Wellstone and Barbara Jordon were admired even by their adversaries for their passion and for their principles, regardless of party popularity. A famous elected U.S. state official once said, "America needs alternating tides of liberalism and conservatism." I think what he meant was if as a country our leadership only voted with the liberal tide, we'd always be moving forward, never putting down roots; this would lead to a lack of anchoring in basic, core principles like concrete never allowed to set. However, if the leaders always voted from the conservative perspective, we'd never move beyond the tried and true and would stand the distinct possibility of being left behind by other nations due to our outdated ways and wouldn't adopt the progressive position that was so important in our nation's founding and future growth.

New research in business board behavior points to the number one cause of corruption, malfeasance, and irresponsibility on boards of directors as occurring when board members agree *too* often. Without dissent, who holds your viewpoints and perspectives in check? Leaders must weigh in on both sides of an issue, and parties on both sides of an issue must be willing to hear objectively all that is said. Oakley and Krug (1991) in their work on *Enlightened Leadership* also speak of a need for leaders to move issues forward and not engage in petty bickering or in complaining about past wrongs. Today more than ever we need dissent, and we need cooperation.

Wright

It seems balance plays a big part in leadership of a country or a company. In your career as a speaker, trainer, educator, and announcer, you've certainly come across people whom you call leaders, but many outside of a narrow, narrow circle wouldn't actually know. Let's meet some of these leaders.

McMahan

I have been blessed with many opportunities to work with great leaders. Picking any ten would leave dozens out, so I only highlight five in this chapter who have made a profound impact on my life.

Dr. George Wright taught history at the University of Texas in the 1980s. He took a large room full of sophomores in the fall of 1984 and in one semester taught us the real history of America from the Civil War that only recently is beginning to show up in textbooks. As one of a very few African American professors at UT, he was taking a risk by teaching history "from the bottom up." But he would have it no other way. His rigorous scholarship, tireless enthusiasm, and impassioned teaching style led to ovations at the end of classes and led me to attend graduate school as well as seeded the already bursting passion for speaking and teaching I was developing.

Governor Ann Richards entered office as governor in 1990. Even though I was leaving Texas to attend graduate school at Arizona State University that same year, I was fortunate to campaign on her behalf and meet her twice. Governor Richards always fought for the little people while maintaining watch on the bottom line, a hard feat for sure. She achieved the highest offices held by women in all of Texas history, and when she got there, she didn't back down. Her tenacity was amazing, and it spoke volumes about her drive. Even today in her 70s and out of politics, she works harder than ever to bring justice to those unjustly treated and empower those who are ready to make a change for the better in their lives. She truly is a fantastic mentor of leaders.

While an assistant coach at the University of Tennessee, Pam Tanner recruited several great players who won a national championship under legendary coach Pat Summit. Many would have been happy to stay and scoop up the wins and the credit as an assistant to one of the best coaches of all time. That was not enough, so she came to the University of Denver to lead a Division II program into Division I, a very tough task for anyone. In each of the first few seasons, she turned heads with her recipe for success. Coach Tanner hired the best assistant coaches possible because she knew she couldn't be everywhere at all times. She also recruited good players with the proper mix of athleticism and character. This is akin to Jim Collins', author of *Build to Last* and *Good to Great*, perspective of putting the right people on the bus. A student of the game and of coaching, Tanner never stopped learning, as she knew others were up late studying how to beat her team. If you ever watch a game with coach Tanner on the sidelines, you know that she coaches until the final whistle, even in a blowout, because she knows teaching time is valuable and must make the most of what she has. Finally, she was never satisfied with less than the best from herself and from others. To no one's surprise, Pam Tanner has been wonderfully successful leading her way and winning games.

In April 2004, George Gwozdecky became the only human on the planet to win an NCAA men's ice hockey championship as a player, an assistant coach, and as a head coach. But the truly amazing feat was leading a team that was in eighth place in their own conference only five weeks before the end of the season. The University of Denver men's hockey team of 2003 – 2004, led by Gwozdecky overcame huge odds, pulled together, and eventually became the hottest team on the ice in the last two months of the season. Even when others doubted, the confidence his team and coaching staff had in Coach Gwozdecky proved to be one of the most important elements in "winning it all." Not surprisingly, at the final awards night to end the season, all of the praise, accolades, and attention fell everywhere but on George. He is a true believer in the principle Keirsey and Bates (1978) made famous in their seminal work on leadership. They said that a true leader's job is "appreciation...all other responsibilities and actions can be cast aside as secondary, for, if a leader appreciates the people he cultivates, the rest will fall into place." And it did.

An 86 year-old man in Chico, California made a big impression on me. I met him at a seminar I was giving on time management. I was amazed that a man 50 years older than me at the time could need a course on time management. He was a doctor most of his life; then, at age 67, he went back to school for a master's in public health degree because he wanted to open a public clinic for impoverished people who could not afford healthcare. Finally, when I met him, he had purchased his old family orchard and was employing dozens of staff on 1,000 acres. He told me that he was at my seminar to learn. He said, "When I stop learning, I start dying, and I'm not ready for that."

Wright

It truly sounds like these leaders continue to have a profound impact on their world and yours. You've had the opportunity to work with leaders from many backgrounds. What would you say are some of the primary characteristics that define these people as leaders?

McMahan

These leaders, I believe, share many common characteristics. Among them are four I have identified: 1) **Single-minded purpose**—during their many moments of truth, each asks the question, "What is the *one* most important thing I should be doing now that will make the biggest difference on the outcome of the task at hand?" Whenever a person focuses on the power of one, she or he has mastered the moment, maximized time, and cornered productivity. 2) **Unquenchable thirst to be the best in their profession**—being second best is unacceptable. This pairs well with the single-minded purpose, for a single purpose focused on the wrong actions yields disaster in big doses. These leaders have identified their number one priority, and they follow it 100%. 3) **Self-confidence**—each leader has enough confidence to carry authority well, but not so much to alienate those they seek to serve. 4) **Lifelong learning**—a leader never knows enough. Each of the leaders I profiled knew that the single biggest secret to success is to know that learning more and studying hard come with the job description of a leader.

Leaders start and end every moment of truth by asking, "What is the one thing I should be doing, focusing on, believing in, or learning about in order to produce the results I seek?"

Wright

Those are important characteristics and would seem to define anyone we could imagine calling a leader. You speak highly of your current employer, T-Mobile, and of the ethical leadership in place there. This agrees with your talk about leadership as more than a set of principles, rules, or actions. In other circles, in fact, you have called for leaders to exhibit economic leadership, as well. What are you talking about?

McMahan

First, I am very fortunate to work for a company run fairly and exuberantly by principled leaders. It really is true that you can get more from life with T-Mobile. Many of my friends working elsewhere are not nearly as fortunate as I am.

Next, please hear me say that many chief executive officers are underpaid for their vital and rare form of leadership. However, the media of late have focused on the less ethical corporate chiefs, so that is also where my focus lies. These are the C-level employees I address in this section.

A CEO cannot perform without his or her subordinates. So if a CEO's base pay, separate from merit pay, increases, then the folks below him or her should also have their base pay raised by a fair and proportionate percentage; after all, who will make the gains that will reward the CEO? The line workers will. Now, I'm not talking about incentive pay that many CEOs rightfully earn for exhibiting solid leadership to take the company to another level. Once again, I refer mostly to the CEOs who lead a company into a deep hole and leave with millions of dollars lining their pockets only to abandon the company's other employees to a state of limbo for true leadership.

You hear so many people talking about paying teachers on their performance. Well, if the entry-level worker has a great year in many companies what happens? She gets a quarter more per hour, while some CEOs add up all the quarters of all the entry level workers and multiply them by a factor of thousands of dollars. That's not leadership. That's unethical, regardless of the employee's title.

Leadership is linking CEO pay to the pay of the lowest on the org chart. The saying goes, that "A rising tide lifts all boats." What other job in America gets multi-million dollar bonuses for non-performance but unethical C-level employees of poorly managed companies. Reform in this area is where positive peer pressure would be a welcome sight by many in boardrooms across America.

Wright

It seems like a fair expectation. Robert, you encourage leaders to use their position of power for corporate activism, and you espouse some pretty big activist positions outside of your work life. So what makes you qualified to weigh in on these heavy issues?

McMahan

Activism is a scary word to some people. Activism simply means involvement in something or taking action to bring about change instead of just sitting back and waiting for someone else to do the tough work. Most people agree on the importance of seeing an issue from all angles before making a decision. I think leaders, speakers, and authors have the responsibility to give people something to ponder and maybe spur them to action. As I wrote earlier, if everyone who sat in front of me agreed with everything I said, why have me speak, teach, or train?

Let's look at a few controversies from decades gone by that today are afterthoughts for most people because of activism in our past. Take the notion of creating America as an independent, free country; proponents of this new democratic republic were viewed as very controversial. What about other societal debates such as women's right to vote, own land, or hold positions in church? Consider subsequent stances on abolishing slavery and fights for equality through integration in schools, businesses and faith-based organizations.

In the heyday of each of these positions, most Christian churches, most businesses, most organizations, and most people in the majority opposed these ideas. What made them acceptable by today's standard was activism that was often seen as foolish zealotry in yesteryear. New rock formations only come from pressure. Change is the same. Food cooks better when put over heat. Let's add a little fire to the debate. Today's activism leads to tomorrow's positive change.

The issues of today are different, so we're told, but the same comments used in the past about blacks and women are now spewed at immigrants, gays, and others. I wonder what my world would be like today if activists did not fight for my liberties before I was born, before my ancestors immigrated.

If we don't push or question or cajole, who will? How will we climb to that next peak we need to scale as a country? We cannot, I believe, until we at least have most people in agreement with the concept of equality for all. On a level playing field, fair competition makes a much more enjoyable game.

Wright

You have written, "Leaders can only be hypocritical once," which I find to be very interesting. What does that mean to you?

McMahan

I'm embarrassed when I do something stupid or foolish, and my biggest hope is that I'll never do that same foolish or stupid thing a second time. We all have a responsibility to give back to the community in order to make sure society is well taken care of and everyone has a place. So many of the issues we have would not be issues, I believe, if we only did in private what we promised in public. Theoretically, for those who believe this way, if we all tithe 10%, no issues detract from meeting the societal need. Theoretically, if we provided as many volunteer hours in the classrooms as we spend criticizing classroom teachers, we would have fewer problems with our education system.

A central issue, I believe, is when folks do not live up to what they say is the solution; rhetoric cannot lift us high enough. In the 80s we used to hear about the magic of trickle down economics. This would have worked if the top bracket income earner had spent the money instead of saving it. One of the most important lessons today's workers need to learn is to save more, yet our government is telling citizens to be consumers and spend like there's no tomorrow, borrow 125% of your house value, etc. in order to buoy the economy. The reverse of hypocrisy is advocacy. Leaders advocate for the best position for the many, not the few. Leadership comes from investing in the community not in merely talking a good game.

Wright

You have been known to tell large groups of seminar attendees that no one has ever won a Noble Peace Prize by watching TV. Please explain to our readers what you really mean.

McMahan

Let's face it. TV is an absolute waste of time, unless we can use it as the technological tool that it can be to shorten the time it takes to learn or temporarily relieve of us of some of the day's pressures without becoming the focal point. Frankly, sometimes there's nothing better than sitting down with my partner after a long hard week of working and saying, "Hon, let's rent a movie." For everything there is a proper time and place. In 2001 *USA Today* reported results of a study showing that 51% percent of high school seniors watched three-and-a-half hours or more of TV a day; those are tomorrow's workers, tomorrow's employees. They are tomorrow's future leaders, and I don't know if watching "must see TV" is the proper way to prepare for our future.

In 2003, President George W. Bush stated that he did not watch the news. Many people gave him grief about that when he said it. I did not vote for Governor Bush, nor President Bush, but I think what he was saying was, "Look, I don't waste my time watching all of that drivel. I get the facts distilled from my advisors and that's what really matters." And so I think he had a really good message for us there of going to the real research, the factual data, not the unreal world of TV. Bush probably said it a little more succinctly and maybe a little more politically correct than I did, but that is exactly what I mean when I say no Nobel Prize winner ever got the award for watching TV.

Wright

When I was growing up, my mother complained about me talking on the phone too much. Then, I got a little bit older and she talked about me watching television too much. So now, my daughter, who is fifteen, can say she doesn't watch television and she doesn't talk on the telephone; but she IMs her people on the computer. So, she's using both the phone and the TV at one time.

McMahan

Your daughter is certainly not alone in her use of technology that neither of us could dream of at her age. I can't imagine where I'd be without my PCS phone and text messaging. Today, I believe we are seeing new technology as tool and recreation, and that's a powerful resource for people. It can really help us Bridge the GAP from where we are to where we want to go and I think that's a great addition to our tool belts.

Wright

Speaking of *Bridge the GAP*, that's one of the titles of a talk of yours, isn't it?

McMahan

Yes, The G stands for goal. The A stands for our actual performance where we are today. And the P stands for our potential success. If we take that goal, where we want to be, and subtract the actual performance we are currently enjoying, or not enjoying, the only thing that's left is the potential. And it's a simple formula that I use in this complex world. In a nutshell, we have G minus A equals P.

If working the GAP correctly, I will say to myself, "Hey, Robert, where are you and where do you want to be? Now what's the difference?" And the final thing I ask is, "What's the one thing I could be doing right now that would help me Bridge the GAP?" If I immediately start working on implementing those concepts to Bridge the GAP daily, I'll be the success today that I was meant to be.

Wright

It's true that time seems more and more fleeting. One of your specializations is time and life management. As our time is winding down for this particular chapter, perhaps we should end with your idea of what characteristics one should look for in a great leader regarding their use of time and resources.

McMahan

I don't know if many leaders can comment on who is the last survivor on the island, intern in the boardroom, or idol on the stage, but like I explained earlier, I have never heard of a Noble Prize winner leaving their research in a mad dash to make the final episode of the latest reality show. Leaders live reality every day, and the way they maximize their life and time is they focus on the power of one. I like to focus in my seminars on time management on the one thing that will make the most difference at that time to the isolation of everything else. And some people might say, "You can't do that. You can't just work on one thing at a time."

We all know the studies report that multi-tasking is really a fallacy. We are really working on one thing at a time; it's how quickly we transition from that one thing to the next more important thing that determines how efficient we are. No action items are ranked second on my list. My action items list is a composite of high priority tasks so I can start with one and proceed to the next important item; in essence my goal is to *mono-task* very fast.

My partner, Denise, says that she's got too many great books to turn on the TV; and I sure hope a few people feel that way about this great book. It's been a real pleasure and honor to contribute to *Leadership Defined*.

Wright

It's been my pleasure. You have been reading the words of Robert McMahan. He is a Leadership Development Specialist at T-Mobile.

I have been booking speakers much like Robert for about fifteen years now, and I'm always interested in getting quotes from what their clients say about them, so I can tell the meeting planners what kind of speaker they are. Of course, I have a lot of quotes from Robert's workshops and seminars, but there's one that I really do like. With Robert's permission, I would like to end this chapter with the quote. It says everything I'd ever want to say about a great speaker. A participant from Michigan said, "Robert was the best trainer I've ever listened to...I felt strapped to a rocket. Wow." That's pretty high praise.

McMahan

Thank you, David.

Wright

Thank you so much, Robert, for being with us in *Leadership Defined*.

Strategy and empathy are not mutually exclusive leadership traits. Stereotypically, strategy is seen as the hard, analytical skill that cannot coexist with empathy, the soft, emotional trait.

Professionals who prefer strategy often shy from empathy, while those preferring empathy tend to avoid use of strategy. A true leader will display characteristics from both in an attempt to balance their preference and meet the needs of their work environment.

Which style do you prefer?

Those who prefer the structured, analytical environment generally lean toward number crunching, hard facts, details, short-burst messages when speaking, and to-the-point responses. These folks are recognizable by the detailed reports they produce and affinity for technology.

On the other hand, those who prefer a more empathetic style often tell stories, share feelings freely, prefer loose organizational structures, like lengthy messages, and exhibit a highly expressive tone of voice. You'll know this group as people who give high-level treatment to details, prefer expressive, less-structured meetings and conversations, and desire in-person communication over email.

You might identify with one or both of these types of leaders at any given time. Chances are you prefer one trait to the other. So how do you learn to portray both effectively? Or do you need to be proficient at both?

Some leaders hire a complementary "right hand" to round out the blind spots. Others wishing to add to their own skill set will consider constituent needs and opt to practice skill integration by combining both.

Pay close attention to leaders you respect, and you'll notice that most of them prefer a blended style that represents their true disposition and the unique needs of the moment. Great leaders know much about many tools and practice both strategy and empathy for maximum impact.

About The Author

Robert trains business leaders and college students how to maximize potential through better time/life mastery. He has authored one dozen articles and book chapters on business topics. A Leadership Development Specialist for T-Mobile, Robert spends his days coaching, training, and consulting supervisors and managers in Thornton, Colorado. M.Ed., Arizona State University, higher education and adult studies. Robert is a member of National Speakers Association, alumnus of Up With People, and a 1998 graduate of Leadership Denver.

Robert McMahan

700 Colorado Blvd. #330

Denver, Colorado 80206

Phone: 303.363.1747

Fax: 303.364.1145

Email: Robert@RobertMcMahan.com

www.RobertMcMahan.com

Chapter 14

VINCE CREW

THE INTERVIEW

David E. Wright (Wright)

Today we are talking to Vince Crew who is an advisor, speaker, author, and founder of REACH Development Services. He consults with owners and executives on strategic growth and critical issues of leading people and organizations. With almost 30 years of experience in sales, marketing, and staff and executive management, his work is a blend of content and encouragement. Vince sees the success of any leader as the demonstrated ability to develop an enterprise by reaching up to higher goals, into his or her God given abilities and reaching out to others as an example of confidence and encouragement. And now, here are more of Vince's insights into the challenge of leadership. Vince, welcome to *Leadership Defined*!

Vince Crew (Crew)

Thank you, David.

Wright

What do you see as a leader's top priority?

Crew

I think it's taking care of the people who take care of the people. Not take care of the customer. Most leaders are so far removed from the customer, they're the last person they should obsess over.

Wright

Right.

Crew

But the people who take care of the customer, now that's different. You do that by giving your people the resources, the training, the education to get their jobs done, and then you provide direction and clear expectations. And you have to be an example of the values that are befitting the enterprise. That should be a leader's primary focus. All of that then helps to move toward the more tangible results of stakeholder or shareholder value depending on the nature of the enterprise.

Wright

So at what level do you consider someone to be a leader?

Crew

You know I think we're making leadership too complicated, too much information too fast, too many theories, research and the like. A leader is anyone that acknowledges their self-responsibility to perform, achieve, and encourage others to do the same. It's void of titles. I've seen people in some of the lowest paying unskilled jobs who exhibit stellar leadership traits. And then of course, we've all seen executives of companies and non-profits and even presidents of countries fail miserably as examples of leadership. So leadership is about doing. It's about moving forward and taking others with you and that happens at all levels.

Wright

Can leadership be taught? Are you or most people just born with it or have an inclination towards it?

Crew

Oh, that's the age-old question, isn't it? I don't think leadership can be taught. David, I think it can be learned. Now that's subtle, but I think it's a very big difference. There are tips and techniques and theories and guides, but the true achievement is brought about by experience. And that's going to include successes and failures, results, dead ends. That's how you develop your own leadership style and focus.

Wright

So what impacts leadership style and focus?

Crew

First of all style is what it is. You don't change it. It's what you are. It's who you are. It has been developed and reinforced by what has worked for you on your leadership journey, if you will. Now focus, I think that depends on several factors: where the organization is in terms of its life cycle; then what's happening externally to the organization; what's happening internally, and I guess another would be what the organization is ultimately trying to become. And then of course, you have to look at the leaders' life and where they are and their personal internal and external pressures, and together with that and what they're trying to become. So it's a simple process, if you will, but certainly not an easy one.

Wright

You mentioned "become" rather than vision or mission. Could you explain that?

Crew

I like the word "become." You see, I think becoming is more passionate and understandable. Everyone can see how they've grown over the years and how their lives have impacted others around them, and how others have indeed made a difference in their lives. A leader takes their enterprise and looks at what it can become. How can it impact others for the better? How will it improve the community, the industry, and the market place? How will things be improved by the success of the organization?

Wright

You've worked with business owners and executives, political leaders, non-profit executives, and various industries. What similarities and differences are there?

Crew

I think ultimately, David, leadership is about influence, persuasion, and example. Business leaders are responsible to boards and stockholders. Non-profit leaders are responsible to boards and stakeholders in their work, politicians to their political parties and voters. So ironically, even leaders must answer to someone beyond themselves; however, the simpler dimension in all of this is that they have to have a degree of responsibility to themselves, to their families, to their communities. They must be focused on bringing honor and meaning and progress to their personal and professional lives with their contributions. When you get down to those kinds of values, I think it's easy to see how I make transitions between industries and sectors working with leaders of all walks and means. The other thing I would add, and this became of interest to me in my graduate work years ago, are the leader's and their enterprise's stages of development. A young manager in a 75-year-old manufacturing concern has different interests and issues than a senior executive in a young startup company, or an outside professional manager brought into a third generation family business. So you see, once you overlay the realities of life cycle issues and aligning values and strengths, then that really becomes critical. The culture and politics of an enterprise is key. So this is why succession planning and other transition issues can be so difficult and very distinct regardless of the sector or size of the operations.

Wright

In your speaking or during your presentations, I know you talk about the three layers of leadership. How do you see this defining a leader's daily task?

Crew

Ah yes, the three layers of leadership. People—people are the foundational layer. Hiring better people, recognizing and rewarding conduct and performance that moves toward achieving the overall goals; developing skills at every level so the good skills get even better and stronger; retaining the best people, that's the first layer. Then communicating the promise is the strategic layer. Describing, in no uncertain terms, individual expectations. Talking and demonstrating the values by which your enterprise is to operate and be known is critical. Articulating that vision of what the market place will look like when your organization succeeds. Telling your people the direction in which the organization is headed is absolutely critical at this layer. In one of my books, *Keeping the Very Best*, I talk about these and other significant people management demands that simply need to be met by the leader at this level. Then, David, the third level, the third layer is performance. This is the execution side. This starts with individual dependability and accountability for each and everyone's contribution. Profit, however it's defined and measured, can change from industry to industry, but certainly, has some formula. There's something that defines it, and that is critical at this layer. Cash flow is the life blood of any living, breathing group of people engaged in a mission, and so money keeps people working and supplies purchased, facilities operating, and services rendered, and on and on. So that's just critical. And then the actual delivery is the final feature of this performance layer, accomplishing the goals, achieving the objectives, making the necessary adjustments along the way. So when you take these layers—people, promise, and performance—it forms a connection to the community of staff, neighborhood, town, industry, and profession. And the leader's role is to foster relationships.

Wright

You know most people define leadership in terms of how it moves an enterprise forward. In your view, what does the leader get other than the usual compensation and perks?

Crew

Excellent question! I think there has to be more than just money involved for any leader to continue. The stress, the pressure, it's all too expensive for only money. I have another book, which is a collection of essays and articles on a number of strategic areas, and in *The REACH Leadership Thought Guide Series*, I write about what I call the five gifts of leadership. The first gift is perspective, that ability to see from more than one side of an issue or opportunity, sometimes as an outsider, sometimes as an insider, but always as a person of conviction. A leader with perspective appreciates the struggles of the organization's past, but is still able to craft the direction for a promising future. Next is insight. This is solely the benefit of learning by experience, usually in years and in various situations. By doing so, ability for critical decision making, is gained. There's a sense that leads to depth and clarity usually when everyone around them is going nuts. Then there's direction. This is a powerful ability that provides a focused view of the organization's possibilities. Becoming more than it is and helping people realize their potential is the benefit of direction. And then I think another gift is certainly values, that unwavering North Star moral compass. It comes from upbringing and experience. It's affirmed by integrity and ethical conduct. And I think the last gift, the fifth gift, has to be trust. This is that certitude that attracts loyalty and support. It's that element that has led soldiers into battles regardless of the risks. It leads workers to rally behind strategic transitions no matter what the fears. It has garnered votes from people regardless of the odds of winning. Taken together, I think, you'd probably refer to those five gifts as wisdom or maybe even character. David, I think these are the defining traits of purpose, a purpose that brings meaning to the mundane day-to-day leadership tasks. I think they're gifts that are both received and given. They're the essence of personal conviction by leaders, by people who are privileged to lead other people in organizations.

Wright

What about the leader's challenge of strategic planning? We talked about long and short term. How do you suggest leaders tackle this issue given our rapidly changing environment?

Crew

I'm involved with so much of that lately. A brief explanation of my approach is that we look at a number of variables, pressures, and factors that play a part in the potential success of a strategy. This is combined with what's happening to the operations internally and externally. Transitions, I call them "points of pain," need to be examined. What about competition? What about government regulations? What about media scrutiny, customer trends, trends in the market or the industry? Regardless of what kind of obstacles are revealed, the responsive strategy these days is seldom a straight line. I'm finding with my clients that often there must be flexibility, extreme flexibility, in a plan, or even scenario planning whereby if something happens, then an adjustment needs to be made. And so that straight-line strategy just isn't realistic. Now I say flexibility, but that doesn't mean strategy-of-the-month club. Adaptability can be a good thing, but I think constant changing and shifting is very much a fatal thing, especially when you're trying to garner the support, enthusiasm, and energy of people. I mean we each have only so much to give, so a leader must determine what activity will yield the greatest return on that sacrifice and that hard work. I often tell my clients too, "just remember that the flawed plan that can inspire will outperform a perfect plan with no passion." So that's strategy.

Wright

Right. Do you think your leadership skills are transferable from situation to situation, organization to organization?

Crew

I guess my answer to that is probably yes and no.

Wright

Well, you can't have it both ways now.

Crew

Well, I'll tell you. I talked earlier about life cycle and culture and size and regulation and industry. There are simply so many variables that make up an enterprise, and the talents of leadership can be appropriate or inappropriate. Many years ago I worked for a computer PC manufacturer, and at some point in time, that manufacturer's Board of Directors felt a need to develop a more structured business model and overall formal strategy. There was a change in executive leadership, and a very well known, very successful leader was brought in from a very successful consumer beverage company, and he took over. His thinking was to look at price promotions, mass product availability, attractive merchandising—all the mainstays of a consumer products business. Unfortunately, he wasn't sensitive to the significance of channel distribution, support, and the incredible reliance on people that successful technology implementation requires. So the result was a loss of distributor network alliance, lost relationships, lost momentum, and to this day even the returning founder of the company has been challenged to make the company the leader it had the potential of becoming. So right guy, wrong industry, and wrong culture. Yes, some skills are transferable, especially people skills, but industries, life cycles, and other things weigh in. Some leaders are better at turnaround situations; others at maintaining established growth; others at dynamic expansion. There can be subtle and not so subtle differences from industry to industry, region-to-region, consumer perceptions, the need versus want you know as it relates to a product or service. So alignment of leader talents is so critical.

Wright

I know a man, Paul Meyer, down in Waco, Texas; he was the founder and CEO of Success Motivation Institute, he's been a friend of mine for many years. He told me one day, "David, if you envision yourself a great leader and you turn around and no one is following you, then you're just out for a walk." You know many people have favorite quotations or sayings that inspire and define leadership, so what's yours?

Crew

Well, I've got several, I guess. The first one that comes to mind is one of my grandmother's old sayings. "Grown folks ain't changin'."

Wright

That was a smart woman, you know.

Crew

She was indeed. I was blessed to have come from what we would refer to today as an extended family. Grandma lived with us, and it was just marvelous. I tell folks Grandmas are great inventions, and I wish God would make more of them. They just seem to have more time than moms and dads.

Wright

They tell me that the reason grandparents and children get along so well together is they share a common enemy.

Crew

That could very well be another astute observation of leadership—defining a common enemy. "Grown folks ain't changin'" was what grandma used to say after someone had disappointed her by making the same mistake or falling into the same pattern that they said they wouldn't. At some point in time, people are who they are. This is why I think hiring and matching talent with the task is so important. Just because a person is willing or able doesn't mean they're the best for the job, *unless they want to be.* Better put, don't think a little more time or training or whatever is going to make a person fit when they just don't have what it takes. Another one of my sayings, which I tell my consulting clients all the time is, "as long as you realize no matter what you decide, you're wrong, you'll survive being the boss." This is all about making decisions. Anyone in a role of leadership knows no matter what, someone will not agree. It's not a leader's job to build 100% consensus. I think their job rather is to build 100% movement. Those who don't want to move will be moved out of the way. It may sound harsh, but the most admired leaders know how to move people regardless of popularity contests. When I work with clients or speak to groups on retention issues, one of my favorite sayings is, "keep the best, circulate the rest." It's absolutely my experience, my philosophy, my observation, and counsel that every organization has losers. They come in by deceptions or faulty hiring practices, but they get in! Good leaders know how to get rid of them sooner rather than later. Great leaders know how not to let them in, in the first place. But great leaders also know that they can't know it all or do it all, so they must indeed surround themselves with good people, with the best people. Another saying just came to mind in my one-on-one meetings with a business owner or an executive officer, I'll often say, "Whatever works, works. Whatever doesn't, doesn't." It sounds very simplistic, but I can't tell you how many people, good people, strong people, honorable people are looking for one magic bullet or one magician to solve a problem, and there usually just is no one thing for every situation. As a strategy advisor, I can bring ideas, but ultimately it's individual implementation that deems whether it's practical or not. All ideas need to be modified to fit the individual circumstances, and sometimes no matter what, it just doesn't fit and you must try something else. Sure, it's frustrating, but that's also something, I think, that defines leadership. For the true leader, that frustration is quickly forgotten when the exhilaration of eventually finding something that does work. Those are a few of the quotations that come to mind.

Wright

As we come to the end of this interview, do you have a personal maxim that you can share with our readers, the things that you share with your clients?

Crew

David, when it comes to leadership, I think that would be my *REACH Leadership Directive©*. It comes from my years of working for leaders, working with them, and being one in my own endeavors. It is my guiding compass. I share it with my audiences when the topic and the setting are appropriate. I created the *REACH Leadership Directive©* early in 2004 after coming away from several days of an intense executive planning session with one of my client organizations, and here's what it says: "I know leadership is an attitude, not a title. It's a responsibility, not an assignment. Leadership is about learning, making decisions, and getting results. Today will bring moments when I can reach up to a higher standard, reach in to my God given abilities, and reach out to others as an example of confidence, faith, and direction. No matter what, I must continue to reach." Now, David, that's Vince Crew. That's my company, REACH Development Services.

Wright

It was worth the entire conversation to get that nugget.

Crew

Well, that's my approach to speaking, consulting, my one on one executive work, my writing. I guess in keeping with the title of this project, those words are my leadership defined.

Wright

Vince, I really appreciate this time that you've taken with me this morning. I've really enjoyed it and hate that it has come to an end. I've learned so much.

Crew

My pleasure!

Wright

Today we've been talking to Vince Crew. He is an advisor, speaker, and author. And he's the founder of REACH Development Services, and we have found out today why, with almost 30 years of experience in sales and marketing, I think he stopped and listened and looked along the way because he sure has enlightened me today. Vince, thank you so much for being with us on *Leadership Defined*.

Some Final Thoughts

The Age Old Question: Are Leaders Born OR Made?

After years of experience, research, and observation, I can give a resounding "YES!" Of course every leader is born... but more than that, they are *born to become...* and becoming a leader can only be fulfilled IF 3 things occur:

Nature - There is no denying the tendency of a child to be drawn toward activities, conduct, mannerisms, talents, etc. You hear comments like "he's a natural"—"she just seems to take to it"—"he makes it look so easy." These all point to something that can be *defining* to their lives.

Nurture - No matter the talent exhibited or the interest shown by a child, it's always a parent, neighbor, coach or teacher who is cited as the influence in that child's life. Adults who nurture provide the incentive to persevere.

Niche - Probably one of the least recognized dimensions of leadership is that specific field of interest the growing leader finds him/herself to be most comfortable. Some are better in smaller companies, others in charitable organizations, others in technical arenas, still others in direct people-oriented rolls, etc.? Ever notice a leader's ineffectiveness when taken out of *their element*?

So the concept of *making* leaders may be more about child rearing than anything else. Family environment, neighborhood, schools, churches, friends, etc. are conducive to developing good or bad leadership traits. These experiences can also yield good leaders of bad things. Some of the most powerful historical figures have not always been of good character, beliefs or conduct. They were leaders nonetheless.

So hug and encourage the children in your life; honor your parents; contact a former coach or teacher; make sure your spouse knows you appreciate their support. And thank you for contacting www.REACHdevelopment.com if we can assist in supporting your leadership efforts.

About The Author

Vince holds a M.S. in Marketing and Communication from Franklin University, a B.A. from Ashland University, and is a graduate of The National Planned Giving Institute at the College of William & Mary. Prior to establishing REACH Development Services in 1997, Vince Crew was COO/Development Officer for a senior healthcare foundation. His diverse background also includes the food, computer, and telecommunications sectors. Vince has authored several books, contributes to a number of professional association newsletters, and is a valued resource to the media.

Vince Crew

www.REACHdevelopment.com

Chapter 15

ALAN KEYES

THE INTERVIEW

David E. Wright (Wright)

Alan Keyes' powerful conservative message resonates for millions of Americans from all walks of life and every geographic region, who share his vision of a morally based government founded on the principles embodied in our nation's Declaration of Independence. The Republican Presidential candidate received his Ph.D. in Government Affairs from Harvard University, in 1979. He served in the U.S. Foreign Service and on the staff of the National Security Council by President Ronald Reagan in 1983. He was Assistant Secretary of State for International Organization Affairs from 1985 to 1987. Following his tenure with the State Department, Ambassador Keyes was president of Citizens Against Government Waste, where he founded CAGW's National Taxpayer Action Day. His political activism continues to challenge both liberal Democrats and those within his own party who fails to support the essential principles upon which the U.S. was founded. Over the past ten years, Ambassador Keyes has been featured at different times on a daily, syndicated talk radio program and television series. He is the author of two critically acclaimed books, *Masters of the Dream: The Strength and Betrayal of Black American* and *Our Character, Our Future: Reclaiming Amer-*

ica's Moral Destiny. It is my sincere pleasure to welcome Dr. Alan Keyes. Alan, welcome and thank you for joining us today.

Alan Keyes (Keyes)

I am glad to be here. Thank you.

Wright

I'm interested in exploring two subjects with you today that I believe are intrinsically linked, and in which I believe you are uniquely qualified to offer our readers insight. I'm speaking of freedom and leadership. Before we dive into the subject matter though, would you explain how you became interested in cultural issues related to our Constitution?

Keyes

I have always been interested. As a graduate student, I spent a lot of time studying the foundations of America's system of self-government and the ideas that our founders were following when they put together the constitution and the free way of life that we are supposed to enjoy in America. What has struck me most forcefully, over the course of both my studies and experience, is that there is a moral foundation for our way of life. Without which it cannot be sustained. That moral understanding, the principles that are articulated in the Declaration of Independence, is essential if liberty is to be properly understood, properly applied and preserved. It requires a certain character in the people and a willingness to look back to our moral heritage and understand its deep roots in respect for the authority of God and the idea that he is the source of our rights and justice. I believe that a right understanding of our way of life both in a political and constitutional sense requires that you take seriously the challenge of moral character to a free people.

Wright

For those of us who are not history experts, can you explain why our Constitution is unique compared to those of other countries?

Keyes

Our Constitution was a result of a unique, providential moment in human history. I think that there were insights involved that were a consequence both of the Christian heritage of our founders and their respect for the need to apply disciplined reason to the challenges of government. That combination led them to acknowledge certain basic principles that were contrary to their own class and personal interest. You had folks who were land owners and slave owners and were acknowledging given the fact that all human beings are created equal; and that God intends for that equality to be the foundation of the sense of justice in any regime. As a result, government has to be based upon consent and structural around institutions of representation. These were things that they believed a just acknowledgement of Gods principles required. At the time, it went against what would be considered the selfish interest of many of them. When you see the human heart responding to principles of right thinking and justice in spite of deep inclinations of passionate interest, I think one has to acknowledge that there is at work a divine grace.

Wright

In a broad sense, do you see a correlation between our country's recent interpretation and application of the Constitution and the personal lives of individual citizens of the United States?

Keyes

Sadly, I think so. We have been in a period when our understanding of our constitutional life has become very undisciplined. We are not living according to the principles that are reflected in the Constitution. When a great deal of ignorance is combined with manipulation on the part of the elite's in the society it turns us away from the path that the nation was set by our founders and toward a path that could lead to Tierney. That is dictatorship by the few instead of a government of the people, by the people, and for the people. That approach reflects the licentiousness that has become more and more prevalent in the entertainment culture, in the media and in their personal lives of a lot of folks. We are acting as if there are no standards of behavior, no standards of judgment and responsibility. But, if at the end of the day there is no basis for distinguishing between right and wrong in one's personal life, then how is one going to maintain rights that are drawn from a sense that there is a transcended authority who commands respect for these rights? So, I think there is a definite connection between the erosion of a personal moral sense and the erosion of our understanding of the moral principles that underlie our way of life.

Wright

Political commentators argue about the role of government in our lives. Some are proponents of larger, more "active" government. Others, like you, believe less is better. To what extent do you think government can affect an individual citizen's ability to succeed, to reach their goals and fulfill their dreams?

Keyes

I think the government should operate the way our system of traffic lights and the enforcement of traffic laws operate. When you are driving along the road, nobody is dictating to you where you are going. But you do have to respect the rules that allow everybody to use the road in a way that doesn't lead to accidents that would make it impossible for people to get where they were going. I think that's the right understanding of how a free way of life ought to operate. The government is there to help us create an environment that facilitates the ability of individuals and the associations they form. Government cannot substitute for individual effort, responsibility, organization and preparation and should not attempt to do so. There has developed a combination of a mentality of false compassion, which seeks to use the government for all kinds of welfare purposes in substitution for the initiative and responsibility of the individual. At the same time, that sense of compassion leads to a welfare mentality. It also leads to two things: A sense of entitlement, which then can substitute for a sense of personal responsibility and also a willingness to put up with all kinds of dictation and domination in pursuit of the welfare objective. At the end of the day, you end up sacrificing real freedom. I think that the government can be a facilitator. But when it attempts to substitute government action and power for the initiative, discipline and responsibility of individuals, then you get into a situation in which freedom is undermined. And ultimately, I think the results that are produced will mirror the failures of social estates that we have seen in that last century.

Wright

Along with the seriousness of this county, you made an impressive run for the Presidency a few years ago. Few would argue that you won every debate you entered. What kind of leader would you have been as President of the United States? Will you describe the principles by which you would lead this nation?

Keyes

Well, I think that is pretty simple. I have tried in my public life to do what—if I understand him correctly—Lincoln tried to do, which is to apply the principles and insights that are in our Declaration of Independence to the politics and laws and policies of the United States. So, you begin from the premise of God's existence and his authority, you go to the conclusion of the emphasis on human liberty and responsibility and you formulate policies that seek to promote that liberty to preserve the moral foundations that are necessary for that responsibility. Also, to defend in the world a sense of securing from foes and from domestic deterioration the Constitution that allows us to realize these principles. I think that approach allows one to look at a whole range of subjects—economic subjects, foreign policy subjects, and of course, the issues that involve moral judgments and moral challenge issues of our times. It allows one to look at them in a way that will reflect choices that contribute to preserving this constitutional system and the blessings of liberty that it is supposed to entail.

Wright

The recent scandals in corporate America have reminded many Americans that great leaders must be men and women of character. To what do you attribute this failure in leadership and what solutions would you offer a country hungry for stronger leadership?

Keyes

I think the main problem, whether it is in the private sector economic enterprises, is the sense of selfishness, self interest, unbridled from any over arching sense of discipline or responsibility to the higher authority of God. That leads to a situation in which people do what they can get away with. Instead of approaching every situation in terms of what your responsibilities and obligations might be to your family and to the community; you are thinking about how to maximize your own success. If you need to do that at the expense of others, at the expense of moral decency, that is ok as long as you succeed. The notion that somehow success can substitute for moral principle is in all areas of our life hurting people. It also reflects itself in a personal ethic at the sexual level that seeks to use people for sexual pleasure without regard to pro-creation. The mentality whether you are pursuing money or pleasure is the same at the expense of those decent holds that can only be founded upon respect for moral principles and standards of right and wrong. I think we have

seen a lot of that spirit. It is what leads leaders in business to disregard the interest of stockholders and to look for ways around and
through the rules and ethical standards, so that they can maximize
the bottom line come what may. I think that mentality, the unbridled
self-interest, the ramped selfishness, is precisely a problem and is
precisely the result of the destruction of an over arching sense of
moral standards that then applies in all these different areas of life.

Wright

You know that used to bother me to no end, but now I have a 14-
year-old daughter that would argue that she is 15 because her birth-
day is in thirty days. It is very difficult for me to bring out those
principles of character. I keep her in church, but the government is
not helping all that much.

Keyes

Well, I think that is one of the difficulties we face. The first and
most important thing I have discovered as parent is that you cannot
do it alone. By that, I not only mean the partnership between husband and wife and the support needed from family and friends, I
basically mean God. I have discovered in the course of being a parent,
that the situations you face, break your heart. They face you with a
sense of your own limitations and inadequacies. You find yourself
time and time again resorting to prayer and down on your knees
humbled by the sense that your are not adequate to provide the items
that your children need. That leads to your reliance on God. That reliance is perhaps the most important thing we can pass along to our
children. Yet, it is challenged everywhere in our society. You are
taught to rely on money, government, power, science and so forth. All
of these things are pushing themselves forward as a substitute for
ones reliance on Gods will and favor and guidance. I think this is one
of the saddest consequences of the secularization of our entire way of
life. It has resulted and been promoted by people who have a false
understand of what our society is about. They have used arguments
like the separation of church and state to reach conclusions that end
up separating God from every aspect of our society and our culture as
well as our politics.

Wright

Many of our readers are leaders in corporate America, small business, local churches and volunteer organizations. Would you take a

moment and reflect of the leadership positions you have had through the years and share some practical insights that would empower people to be better leaders?

Keyes

I come from a perspective where almost everything I have done has involved efforts to work with and organize people at the grass roots around issues and purposes of common concern. Whether in the economic or the moral realm. In the arena, the most important thing that I have had to both learn and remember is that I was involved in enterprises that were all exercises in voluntary cooperation. The people were attracted to the things I was doing and were accepting the leadership that I could provide. They had come because their hearts were dedicated to a cause and a purpose that we shared. They were in that sense, not just tools or instruments; they were to be respected as folks who represented the very same principles that I was pursuing and wanted to respect. I think that is at the heart of it, the real meaning of self-government. We are people who are working together on a basis of equality, trying to pool our talents and resources. If one is in a position of leadership, it is not so much domination, as it is an effort to bring out different aspects that are contained within all those abilities and talents. I think that is what achieves the best results. None of us can do anything on our own. Leaders in particular have to remember that leadership is really defined in terms of success; in terms of how well you get others to make that contribution. So, you are not out there acting on your own or imposing your will on your own. What I have found over the years is that you have to have a strong sense of where you are going and why you think it is important. As well as what the principles are that govern your judgment. You also have to be willing to listen to people, because you wouldn't have them around you if they didn't represent the abilities, talents, insights, and perspectives that are need to achieve the goal. I think it is quite foolish sometimes that way folks will be blinded by their own sense of what need to be done. You need to look through the eyes of others that you are working with, because they may be seeing things that are vital to your success.

Wright

Some of the things I have listened to recently are just beyond my imagination. Such as: the President asking for 87 billion dollars to send to one purpose. Number one, that is a mind-boggling number that is hard for me to get my mind around. Second, I'm wondering if I have any choice in that matter at all.

Keyes

I think over all, of course we do. We are making choices. We will again in the year 2004. We will decide who goes to the White House, who goes into Congress and who goes to the Senate. A lot of times, I think people are wasting their votes. They are voting for people they don't think are any good. They take a lesser than evil mentality. If you take the choice of evil what you get is evil. And therefore, don't be surprised when it doesn't work out. I think folks need to start deciding what they think is right, look for people who are standing for those things come what may and casting their vote to reflect their heartfelt beliefs about what is right for the country. A failure to do that is explaining a lot of the mediocrity in the leadership right now. That mediocrity comes at the end of the day because people doubt the courage of their own convictions first; that lack of courage is related to a lack of faith. It is an inability to try to figure out what is your duty and leave the rest to God. I think that lack of a sense that God is watching, that he'll take care of it if you do what is right, the lack of that conviction of faith is leading a lot of people to waste their citizenship and do things that in the end put people in office that shouldn't be there while they go away saying, "Well, I didn't have a choice." In plain fact, most of the time, people do have choices. They just don't have the guts to make those choices that reflect their true convictions.

Wright

You served President Ronald Reagan as Ambassador to the United Nations. What kind of leader do you think Reagan was and can we learn from his successes and failures?

Keyes

I think we definitely can. The thing we have to remember though—that has been forgotten because of the great success of his Presidency—is that Ronald Reagan was a man of principal. For a good part of his career, he was willing to fail for the sake of his principals. He was willing to do things that the people in the political reign said, "No, you can't do that, you have to compromise to get elected, you've got to tone this down so you can get into office." He never did. He was willing to spend twenty years in the political wilderness, working with people of similar conviction and principle. Before, at a juncture critical to this country he was finally elevated to the Presidency. He wouldn't have been the man for the job if he had listened to those people who told him to throw away his principles, to compromise his integrity, to give up the things he believed in for the sake of short-term political success. When he got to office the sense that he was somebody who knew who he was, who knew where he stood, who knew in fact what his principles were and who knew that he hadn't come to power for the sake of power was known. He had come to power in order to serve those convictions with respect to limited government, free enterprise, anti-communism, the morals and foundations of society that he had stood for in his public life. It is that sense that he was somebody who came to office with a mission that transcended his own personal ambition or reputation that made him the great President that he was.

Wright

When you consider the party and the people who are in power today, in 2003—I don't want to put you on the spot or talk negatively about any of your friends, I know you are in the republican party—how are they doing do you think? When you consider all the things that you have said about moral character and consciousness of things that is right and wrong. How do you think they are doing generally?

Keyes

I think that in the course of the last several years, we have obviously reached a nadir, in terms of the moral status of political leadership in American life. Bill Clinton represented that nadir, in my personal opinion. I think that we have certainly seen an elevation of standards from that era. In the same time, of course, we have faced a major challenge, which is both a challenge to our security in the form of terrorism and a challenge to our will and resolve, which is a challenge to our moral spirit. I thing the American people have risen to that challenge and they have inspired leaders to come forward and rise to that occasion. We have been able to face this period with a sense of unity and resolve that was reflected in the hearts of the people as they responded to September 11th. A lot of people returned to their understanding that this nation's fate rests ultimately in the hands of God. Therefore, we have to turn to God, ask for his blessings, ask for his guidance and not be ashamed to humble ourselves as a people as we face an era of tremendous danger. Our innocent people are on the front lines of the war that we fight against terrorist who are implementing policies of violence against the innocent in order to achieve their objective. I think in that context we have seen folks rise well to the occasion. We have responded to it with forcefulness and resolve and I hope we will continue to do so. So of course, there are other issues, which have to do with the underlying integrity of the moral foundations with which we face this crisis. Those issues continue to percolate, sometimes satisfactorily, in terms of leadership, sometimes not. I think we are going to need leaders who are willing to think things through in terms of the principles and requirements of moral leadership in a free society and stand where they need to stand in spite of political calculation. We don't see that all the time and I just keep praying they we will see more of it.

Wright

When you consider all the decisions you have made down through the years, in all aspects of your life, has faith played an important role?

Keyes

I think it has played the decisive role. I can't imagine why I would continue and keep going against the odds except for faith in God and the gratitude that he gives me. That is what I pray for and I have been blessed in that regard. It is the sustaining, underlying premise of my life. I think that has been in found the things that I have been able to do in public life. None of it would have any meaning except I deeply believe that God's will is at work in our human affairs. If we can, to the best of our ability, try to discern what he wishes for us to do. Regardless of how it looks to the world we are on the right path.

Wright

Dr. Keyes, you don't know how much I appreciate you taking all this time with me today to share your views on leadership, success and on the principles of our government. It has been a pleasure visiting with you. Thank you so much for taking the time for this inspiring conversation.

Keyes

Thank you.

About The Author

Alan Keyes, candidate for the 1996 and 2000 Republican Party presidential nominations, founder and chairman of the Board of the Declaration Foundation, and former chairman of the Grace Commission influences the public through a variety of media. He is an author and public speaker on a wide range of national and foreign policy issues; an educator; the writer of a weekly nationally distributed column on current affairs; and the host of, *The Alan Keyes Show: America's Wake-up Call*, and a nationally syndicated "call-in" radio talk show. Author of *Our Character, Our Future* and *Masters of the Dream*, Keyes also served as the U.S. Ambassador to the United Nations Social and Economic Council and as the Assistant Secretary of State for International Organizations.

Alan Keyes

www.AlanKeyes.com

Chapter 16

DARRYL C. WALLS

THE INTERVIEW

David E. Wright (Wright)

Darryl C. Walls honed his leadership expertise during his tenure as a highly decorated manager for one of the nation's largest and most respected telecommunications companies, where he developed a team of professionals into his division's top performers. Mr. Walls harnessed his broad knowledge of leadership skills and tactics and his considerable oratory abilities to form MINDS (**M**ental **I**ntensity **N**aturally **D**etermines **S**uccess), a leadership consulting firm specializing in training seminars and motivational speeches. MINDS counts among its clientele, Fortune 500 companies, colleges, major religious organizations and a host of others.

Mr. Walls is a loving father of two and an active participant in his Church and community affairs. He is also co-author of Insight Publishing's *Conversations on Faith*. Darryl, welcome to *Leadership Defined*.

Darryl C. Walls (Walls)

Thank you and good afternoon, David.

Wright

When I say the word leadership, what is the first thing that comes to mind?

Walls

SERVICE.

Wright

Specifically Darryl, how do you authenticate that concept?

Walls

Typically, we associate great leadership with words like communication or accountability, etc. If we study each of these words, we find that ultimately they provide a **_service_** for someone or something. This equation developed by MINDS is a guide to support this concept:

When a leader/person effectively (fill in the trait; i.e. communicates), does someone or something benefit? *If the answer is yes...they provided a **service**.*

For example:

Communication – Leaders, who **effectively** communicate to team members so they **fully** understand, have provided a **_service_** (*remember the definition of **service—work done for others***)! They have provided a service to the team members, a service to the organization, a service to the internal or external customer, and a service to themselves.

Accountability– Your Company advises employees that anyone failing to demonstrate effective accountability behavior will result in a decrease in their rating. You fail and your rating decreases. A service was provided not only for the company (because they need to uphold standards), but was also provided for you because you were addressed on an unhealthy behavior that could increase and be detrimental to your work ethic, monetary benefits, and your employment. It might not be what you like, but what you *need* to effect **change** (key operative term) in you. He (the leader) also provided a service for himself and the other staff members because they can see he's a man of his word and will hold them and himself accountable. (*remember the definition of **service—work done for others***)!

Wright

So am I then to assume that as long as a person provides a service they can become great leaders?

Walls

No. In fact, if we look at two great leaders we can quickly determine just by their names that although they both provided a service to many, only one stands out in terms of a continued *legacy* and global *positive* productivity. The two men I make reference to are Martin Luther King Jr. and Adolph Hitler. Opposite ends of the leader continuum.

King and Hitler possessed the following leader qualities: Communicator, Orator, Strategist, Intelligence, Accountable, Delegates, Vision, Conviction, Passionate, Decisive, Motivator, Inspirer.

The Separations were as follows: King saved lives—Hitler destroyed lives; King had a vision for **all**—Hitler's vision concentrated on "his people" only; King comforted—Hitler terrorized; King stood for peace no matter what—Hitler stood for war; King taught love—Hitler taught hate; King was forgiving—Hitler was unforgiving; King was respected—Hitler was feared; King was approachable—Hitler was irreproachable; King possessed integrity—Hitler did not.

This is why so many people who have the potential of becoming great *"__good__"* leaders never make the cut because they decide to go with the easy route and chose the side that supports their negative behavior (lack of integrity). These types of leaders are so far in the mustard that they can't see how to ketchup (*catch up*), nor are they willing to. They simply fail to challenge the status quo. And as a result, you, your organization, your family, etc. may suffer physically, mentally, and/or spiritually.

In our everyday walk of life, I cannot stress enough, the importance of how frequently and how effectively we must use this "leader tool" of integrity. We have countless opportunities to display our "separation" as leaders (carpenters) in an effort to provide what I call an inter-example (example for others) and an intra-example (example for self). In the workplace, home, church, or otherwise, we have three choices: 1) Do what's right—demonstrate your accountability/incorruptibility (producing a positive environment where others are challenged to raise their bar). 2) Do what's wrong—demonstrate corruptibility (producing a negative environment where others are likely to become infected; unchallenged). 3) Do nothing—demonstrate inaction (producing a **destiny awaits** environment instead of a **destiny seized** environment).

Wright

Give me two examples of individuals who successfully challenged the status quo?

Walls

The first is Warrant Officer Hugh Thomspon, Jr., of the Charlie Company, 11ᵗʰ Brigade, Americal Division in March, 1968.

I just watched a man on television explain in detail what transpired one awful day in March, 1968. Warrant Officer Thompson told the reporters that he arrived on the scene of a bloody massacre that would forever change his life. He bore witness to a massive slaughtering of Vietnamese men, women, children, and babies. He had never seen anything like this before. He said that troops were given orders to kill anyone they encountered because NLF guerillas might be hiding in My Lai. Unfortunately, this was the furthest thing from the truth and resulted in the murder of over 500 innocent people.

Fortunately for the few remaining alive, Warrant Officer Hugh Thompson arrived from his helicopter and confronted the "leaders" (lacking integrity) of the troops and told them he would open fire on them if they continued their attack on the civilians.

Two members of his helicopter crew brandished their weapons at the officers committing the atrocity and were instructed to shoot anyone who interfered. **They were responsible for saving at least eleven (11) lives!** Eleven (11) lives that would be reunited thirty-six (36) years later just because a man, a leader (with integrity), sought to take action and challenge the status quo. As a result, they were awarded the **Soldier's Medal**, the army's highest award for bravery not involving direct contact with the enemy.

On the other side of the world there was another type of struggle brewing in the heart of Newark, New Jersey that would be the catalyst to evoke academic change for the urban child. This brings me to the second example—the 1967 vision of The Chad Schools materializing.

In this bitter lemon turned sweet lemonade scenario, death screamed with a high pitch and the volume and emotions were raised beyond control. This Newark death (as a result of riots) would result in a group of leaders (with integrity) creating an alternative education system for the urban child. They would adopt the name **Chad** because during the time of the riots in Newark, a similar activity of oppression was transpiring in Africa in a place called *The Republic of Chad*. It seemed only proper to join thoughts and concerns under one name...**Chad**. A representative from The Republic of Chad was contacted and came to visit the school; thereby birthing local and international leadership.

The Chad school model was piloted at a local "Y" facility and then relocated to a three family edifice where academic and character building excellence would continue to be the focus. They would establish a new method of teaching that would generate a type of magnet effect in attracting parents to the program because of its tremendous success. So much so that not only would there be an elementary school standing tall and producing high scoring well spoken African American children who found a new respect for themselves and their culture, but the need for growth would cause the leaders to initiate a college preparatory school in the mid nineties. This would be the start of a legacy; the magnitude of which continues to unfold, all because leaders decided to challenge the status quo (and themselves) and take action that supported a tangible vision. Both of these examples provide a look into leader behavior that **"walks the talk"** by challenging the status quo and achieving another level of excellence in character and academia, respectively.

Wright

So how does one become a leader if their personality is more of a follower?

Walls

I think the very first step in dissecting that question would be to clearly define the word follower. If we use MerriamWebster.com to achieve that definition, then we will see that a follower is *"one that follows the opinions or teachings of **another** c: one that imitates **another.**"* Further, we can break this term down into four different categories and find that there is one common denominator. For example: 1) **FOLLOWER**—may apply to people who **attach** themselves either to the person or beliefs of another (an evangelist and his *followers*). 2) **ADHERENT**—suggests a close and persistent **attach**ment (*adherents* to Marxism). 3) **DISCIPLE**—implies a devoted allegiance (or ***attachment***) to the teachings of one chosen as a master (*disciples* of Gandhi). 4) **PARTISAN**—suggests a zealous often prejudiced **attach**ment (*partisans* of the President).

In each of these examples, the words **attach** and **attachment**s are used, or can be used in place of another word to represent the relationship to something and/or someone. As a **disciple**, you attach yourself to the teachings of another. Therefore, as a **follower** you attach yourself to a person and/or their beliefs.

The follower now has the opportunity to be *transformed* into a leader just by committing to learning and taking action on the teachings and behavior of his leader(s) and then effectively teaching another. The follower must also determine if the leader behaviors he is observing are in alignment with his ethics, morals, and values. If they are not, he should decide if he is willing to realign them to his leader's. Finally, he must ask himself if he is strengthening or jeopardizing his character by doing so. If he is not strengthening his character in a positive manner, I think he should seriously rethink his direction.

Wright

So you're saying that our leader's behavior provides examples for us to *"attach"* ourselves to?

Walls

That's exactly right Dave! In fact, they provide examples for us to *"detach"* ourselves from as well. Remember, if you are looking to raise your personal leadership bar, then you are not only seeking out what **to** do but what **not** to do. For instance, if you are always on time getting to work but you observe your boss arriving at work late most of the time, you can either get on the bandwagon and start coming to work late because that is what you observed, or you can decide that your boss has a poor work ethic that you do not want to include in your leadership "**tool belt**."

Wright

What are these tools that you feel prepare and support present and future leaders to lead effectively?

Walls

Dave, when we think of an outstanding contractor or carpenter or handyman the first thing that comes to mind is how great things look when they have completed the task they were asked to execute. But "how they got there" lies in their handy dandy "tool belt" or tools that they used to cut, smooth, measure, plaster, weld, screw, etc.

In leadership development, I offer models and acronyms that are "**tools**" that help to support and enrich the behavior of an individual(s) who desires leadership growth. These tools are designed by other leaders and myself that provide visuals for cognitive learning such as the Situational Leadership model by Dr. Paul Hershey, the DISC model by Carlson Learning Company©, Group Development Assessment© model by Dr. John E. Jones and William L. Bearley Ed. D., the Communication model introduced to me by Dr. Duffy Spencer, the Five Stages of Leadership© model introduced to me by Dr. Ireland, and a host of continued learning materials. Some tools I've developed include the FEAR/STRESS model©, G.O.A.L.S.© acronym, D.I.V.E.R.S.I.T.Y© acronym, and a Leader Personality Authenticator©.

Wright
Darryl, can you explain some of the tools and how they prepare and support leaders?

Walls
Certainly. Let's start with the Situational Leadership® (SL) model by Dr. Hershey; I call it the "Hershey Bar." In using SL it is useful to keep in mind that there is no "one best way" to influence others. Rather, any Leader Behavior may be more or less effective depending on the "Readiness" of the person you are attempting to influence. The model provides a quick reference to assist (the leader) in: 1) Identifying the specific task, job, or activity to be performed. 2) Assess the readiness of the follower for this task. 3) Select the matching behavior to meet performance needs of the follower.

The model categorizes and defines the leader behaviors (**TASK** and **RELATIONSHIP**) as follows:

The **TASK** behavior is to the extent to which the leader engages in defining roles, telling what, how, when, where, and if more than one person, who's to do what in the following: 1) Goal Setting, 2) Organizing, 3) Establishing Time Lines, 4) Directing, and 5) Controlling.

The **RELATIONSHIP** behavior is to the extent to which a leader engages in: 1) Giving Support, 2) Multi-way Communication, 3) Facilitating Interactions, 4) Active Listening, and 5) Providing Feedback.

The model then defines the leader **Decision Styles** as: **S1 (Style 1)** Leader-made decision, **S2 (Style 2)** Leader-made decision with dialog and/or explanation, **S3 (Style 3)** Leader and follower-made decision or follower-made decision with encouragement from leader, **S4 (Style 4)** Follower-made decision.

Finally, the model provides **Developing** and **Regressing Cues** known as the **Follower Readiness.** The Follower Readiness is categorized as: **R1 (Readiness 1)** Unable & Unwilling or Insecure (leader directed), **R2 (Readiness 2)** Unable but Willing or Confident (leader directed), **R3 (Readiness 3)** Able but Unwilling or Insecure (follower directed), **R4 (Readiness 4)** Able & Willing and Confident (follower directed).

And so when a Leader Behavior is used appropriately to fulfill the follower's needs as expressed in their Readiness Level, it is termed a High Probability Match.

Let me give you an example of how I used the SL model and the Group Development Assessment (GDA) model to effect change within my work environment resulting in positive impact.

When I was working for one of the largest communications companies in the world as a team leader, I was moved by the General Manager (mid-year) at the request of my direct supervisor to lead a group that was considered to be the worst in both performance and behavior. The GM charged only my unit with a numeric objective to decrease their payroll errors by 50% by year-end. Typically, this would be considered a "yank" goal.

I performed a one or two-week assessment of the group and determined that based on what appeared to be poor numeric results relative to performance and poor behavior tendencies (skyrocketed absenteeism, no team spirit, etc.) I developed a four-phase plan called Project E.R.A (Error Reduction Attack) to be implemented immediately. I called the group in for a group meeting to discuss my findings and strategies.

I began outlining my expectations of the group based on my findings (which suggested that they were Unable and Unwilling/Insecure). Therefore, their Follower Readiness was Readiness 1 as a group. After explaining my expectations and how the four phase plan would be implemented and monitored I asked them if there were any questions, suggestions, or general feedback (providing inclusion). A response came from one member of the group that emphatically stated, "We don't need to work this plan Darryl. We can do the work." I asked them, "Why haven't you been doing the work?" and they said, "Every time we challenge the supervisors (status quo) our decisions get overturned and we get no support from our direct supervisor (*thus, a need not satisfied*)." This proved to be the pivotal question that would quantum leap the group from a Readiness 1 to a Readiness 3 and from an Orientation Phase to an Open Data Flow

Phase in GDA. It was at this point that I gave strong consideration to the time we had to effect change in their task behaviors (non-personal dimension relating to the task) and their process behaviors (personal/interpersonal dimension related to the process by which the group interacts to get the work done). I opted to take a risk (leader quality) and let them be a part of the decision/planning process (follower and leader made decision). I achieved a "buy-in" from the group and we agreed that: 1) They would perform their duties effectively (numeric objectives clearly defined). 2) I would back their decisions with pre-consultation (not empowered yet). 3) The process would be monitored to see where improvement could be made. 4) If this agreed upon process wasn't trending in the right direction by month end, we would implement the four phase plan. 5) They would provide the behavior that would create the atmosphere for getting the work done. 6) An absence policy was strictly enforced. 7) They would be cognizant of what the mission and vision of the organization was. 8) They would create self-development plans that support the mission and vision of the organization and include a vision for themselves. 9) They would create a name for themselves that best represented their skills and behavior—"The Dream Team." 10) They would create a team mission statement that supported the organization's mission. 11) They would have "venting sessions" bi-weekly to iron out any personal issues among them. 12) Everyone would be required to participate in group meetings. 13) Ground rules for the group meetings would be implemented. 14) Group meetings would be held weekly to track progress unless something emergent arose. 15) They were challenged to dress better then the dress code (optional). 16) They would effect change in other processes and in other parts of the organization. 17) They would receive paid developmental training. 18) Everyone would exhibit a high level of accountability for their actions and adapt a "what more could I have done" approach. 19) Rewards and recognition would be ongoing (very important).

As a result of these and other initiatives put in place, my group ultimately became an **Effective Team**, generating group synergy unlike any other team in the entire state. In fact, we far exceeded the expectations of the General Manager by seizing a 71% reduction in errors where 50% was all that was required. My team was then recognized for Leaders In Excellence accolades (receiving monetary rewards) and a national Excellence Award was achieved by the person I was mentoring to be my successor. To date, my team's achievements are unmatched. There were employees who took positions with my team even though they would be in a lower salary range, but they **wanted** to be a part of *something going somewhere!* This happened because I listened, then took action/risk on my people creating the environment they needed to thrive in. In return, the group took a quantum leap to authenticate themselves as an effective team.

The SL and GDA "leader tools" were used as "environmental and perception" tools that helped to move the people to change their behavior. Each time I (the carpenter, handyman) supported their decisions (sense of empowerment) or explained why their decision couldn't be supported, I created a perception that generated an environment that would produce a positive behavior. Understand that you will **not** get a positive behavior all the time but your follower will be clear about your direction and expectations.

As you begin to put these models to use, you will find that they are intertwined in some way, shape, form, or fashion and it is important to note that SL and GDA can be applied in virtually any environment from blue collar to corporate to non-secular to parenting. In fact, the Center for Leadership Studies developed a Situational Parenting model that is a spin off of Situational Leadership and proves itself to be quite useful in family situations/decisions.

Wright

That is intriguing Darryl. Now tell me something about the DISC model you mentioned?

Walls

Many of the readers have probably received a taste of themselves through this model. If not, I highly recommend it. **DISC®** stands for Dominance – Influence – Steadiness – Conscientiousness. They represent people's Dimensions of Behavior.

Some years ago when I took this Personal Profile assessment. My main behavioral style was classified as Dominance based on the environment I was working in.

My tendencies would include: 1) Getting immediate results 2) Causing action 3) Accepting challenges 4) Making quick decisions 5) Questioning status quo 6) Taking authority 7) Managing trouble 8) Solving problems.

The environment I would most likely desire would include: 1) Power and authority 2) Prestige and challenge 3) Opportunity for individual accomplishments 4) Wide scope of operations 5) Direct answers 6) Opportunity for advancement 7) Freedom from controls and supervision 8) Many new and varied activities.

I would need others who: 1) Weigh pros and cons 2) Calculate risks 3) Use caution 4) Structure a more predicable environment 5) Research facts 6) Deliberate before deciding 7) Recognize the needs of others.

And to be more effective I would need: 1) Difficult assignments 2) To understand that I need people 3) Techniques based on practical experience 4) An occasional shock 5) Identification with a group 6) To verbalize reasons for conclusions 7) An awareness of existing sanctions, 8) To pace self and to relax more.

One of the biggest things that helped my development process was recognizing my dominant personality style. I made a conscious effort to learn how to shift from one personality profile to another to accommodate other personality profiles (people), as needed, which would help to provide the most productive environment possible.

One of my supervisors was a strong "D" style and he put me in charge of training my followers (direct reports), my peers (same job title), and him (higher-up) on the use of these tools (SL-GDA-DISC) and how they can make positive impact on our groups. We have to understand that there is a difference between administering training to your followers as opposed to training your peers in terms of receiving the message. Your training "message" when *"managing down"* may be more readily received simply because you are the follower's perceived "leader" in terms of legitimate power (status) whereas your peers may be inclined or have difficulty with you *"managing side-to-side"* and your supervisor may have difficulty with you *"managing up"* due to the perception of position. For this team-building recipe, three ingredients were a must for me to be most effective in this challenge: 1) Get a buy-in from my supervisor to allow me to put him on the spot at times to make a point 2) Get a buy-in from everyone that we would keep our focus on self-improvement and 3) Ensure it was understood that this was relative to our behaviors not the task.

Subsequently, I created the Leader Personality Authenticator (**leader tool**), which allowed every team member to vote independently and privately (optional privacy) on the perception they had of themselves and of each other. The tallies were populated in a spreadsheet, which generated an exploding pie chart displaying everyone's perceived behaviors. It either authenticated our perception of ourselves (how we felt we behaved relative to our team) or rendered it invalid. It also gave us a visual of how like styles may provide similar

ratings and unlike styles may give much lower or much higher ratings. If a "D" style is rating another "D" style, their perception of each
other will most likely result in the same or lower rating because they
are accustomed to that style in themselves. My boss (high "D") didn't
think of me as a high "D" and I didn't think of him as a high "D."
However, another style (I-S-C) may consider me to be much higher
because to them I may be perceived as overbearing.

After this data was collected, we began to discuss the results
OPENLY and although things were tense, it was clear that we were
heading in the right direction to accomplish our goal. How do we
gauge its clarity? Because we came from an environment where we
did *not* share and when we did, we were *not* OPEN. We then took the
results of the LPA and committed ourselves to monitoring our behaviors. This helped to support the environment we needed to work more
effectively. Again, looking at it from a "carpenter's" perspective, we
used the tool or tools needed to get the work done...effectively.

If a leader has a DISC assessment of each of his followers, he
would be able to delegate more effectively and create more effective
sub-groups because he would know what type of environment the follower would thrive in better. As you go through this process by way of
this leadership tool, you will find that you will begin checking off the
elements of trust and slowly building a foundation for your legacy.

Wright

Darryl would you elaborate on the terms "elements of trust" and
"legacy?"

Walls

During a Coaching and Counseling workshop at AMA in New
York, our instructor opened the discussion by asking us to define
trust and then asked that we provide an antonym for trust. After we
exchanged dialogue for a moment or two, she provided us with a list
of about twenty bullet items that were eye openers for us all and
great references to have.

Some of the elements of trust are: 1) Trust is a feeling. 2) The opposite of trust is **fear**. 3) Trust is not a permanent state. It is in
constant flux between person and person, person and organization,
organization and organization, etc. 4) Trust is a process of building,
creating, discovering, and enriching. Fear is a process of tearing
down; it stops or blocks the building process. 5) When trust is high,
people function well and will devote their energies toward continuing

to function well. 6) When trust is low, people will devote their energies to self-protection and self-defense; not to functioning well. 7) **Risking trust means you're betting on future predictability**.

In the example I mentioned before, my group was advised of the ground rules and what was needed from them to "make things happen" (buy-in). As a result of our commitment, we were able to see many of the elements of trust come to fruition. Again, we took the initiative to not only put this "trust tool" in our leadership tool belt, but to USE IT to provide an environment that would be most productive (we were betting on future predictability). In your workplace, home, or any arena where you are dealing with people, it is incumbent upon you to demonstrate consistently, that you can be trusted and others can trust you. This means that in your emails, meetings, responses, memos, hirings, firings, gestures, tone and rhythm of voice, composure, and all else that embodies you must ooze with the feeling of trust. Remember; if a carpenter takes the time, energy and money to buy and learn how to use a tool for his tool belt and then he NEVER uses it, he might as well have never bought the tool in the first place.

Wright

And legacy, Darryl?

Walls

When I mentioned the term **"legacy"** I am referring to the **five phases or stages of leadership**. Typically, as we go through the growth process of leadership we find that there are five common stages that virtually every leader encounters. I would like to take a minute to define each stage and provide examples of the lives of two non-fiction people in what I believe represent their timeline, and then forecast what might be their final outcome.

Phase 1: Beginning Stage – In this stage, something occurs during your birth and/or formative years that indicate something special about you or in you. **#1 person** – As a child he excelled in music and dramatic reading; when asked what he wanted to be when he grew up he said "a minister." **#2 person** – As a child he watched his mother cut the hair of family members and friends in the basement of their home and he began to do the same.

Phase 2: Confusion Stage – In this stage you begin to discover yourself in an uncertain manner and you continue to examine your inner and outer being. You may question your feelings or "calling" and try to find a "way out" instead of accepting your calling as a leader. **#1 person** – His talents in music and dramatic reading made it difficult to decide what direction to take. In fact, even during his incarceration he excelled with new ideas and material in both music and drama but only in drama did he win an award. **#2 person** – He decides not to go to college to pursue a conventional career. Lack of resources and training forces him to go from location to location to exhibit his innate skill although thirsting to create his "own" business entity. In fact, he has already mapped out the design of what his business will look like when it materializes.

Phase 3: Conviction Stage – The constant echoing of your leadership calling simply overpowers you and secures a seat of precedence in your life's itinerary causing you to develop an action plan to facilitate your vision. **#1 person** – After a job layoff allegedly due to downsizing, he begins thinking about the consistent impact he has had on team members, youth, and audiences during speaking engagements and coaching initiatives, that clearly defined his abilities, who he is and what path he must take...*purpose*. **#2 person** – His father purchases a multi-family dwelling that includes a storefront that could be used as a barbershop and he realizes that his special gift and vision have finally intersected [his calling] and he now acts with a visible fervor that proclaims, "I did it. Now look out!"

Phase 4: Cruising Stage – You have a fixed confidence in your style and gifts that permeate resistance and you have formed alliances of committed people that have your vision and your best interest at heart. Growth of your vision is evidenced and authenticated. This now allows you to begin the selection of your successor(s). **#1 person** – He begins developing programs (*may include music*) that support his mission, vision, and purpose in an effort to create an environment that perpetuates his work or legacy while maintaining a watchful eye as to who might be a viable replacement; or those he has coached carry on his vision without being under his immediate "umbrella." Either way, he is clear in his direction and what tasks those around him must execute. **#2 person** – He is now established as an entrepreneur and outside organizations begin recognizing and rewarding him for his talents and contributions. He is satisfied with his visionary input and constantly seeks to introduce change in his physical environment. He provides direction and encouragement to his team members.

Finally Phase 5: Legacy Stage – In this last stage, you have reached leadership prowess and understand that your time may be limited but you will have touched, mentored and empowered your successor. And again, since these two examples are based on real people who have yet to reach the legacy stage, I am going to provide what I envision as the legacy stage for these two people. **#1 person** – This individual is recognized for his work performed in the urban community, programs developed and literary publications. They are used to continue his legacy. His children or participants in his program(s) express interest in continuing his legacy. His successors begin to modify his process to create an even stronger program that will be used as a model for other institutions to follow. **#2 person** – Additional shops are opened that incorporate a new approach to providing service to its clientele and key employees have been appointed to oversee operations.

So this process gives the leader an outside looking in perspective (gauge) on where he or she is with regards to their life's direction, the impact it has on the lives of others, and the preparation piece in having their legacy (their baton of purpose) continued and taken to another level.

Had I been introduced to this model at an earlier stage in my life, I may have made a more clearly defined decision about the direction of my life and could have shared this "leader tool" with others. In this way, they too would have been challenged to **seize their destiny** as opposed to **waiting for destiny** to materialize.

You may find that there is something that keeps gnawing at you. **It's your PURPOSE!** One way of knowing is that you ENJOY doing it and feel a sense of WORTH. Sometimes in an effort to fool ourselves we talk ourselves out of our purpose or we get involved in things that may be honorable or good causes but they only serve as a band-aid to the gnawing effect you feel inside. As soon as you get up-*you think about it*, while you're in the car or on the train heading to work-*you talk about it*, while at work or at lunch-*you envision it*, on your way home or just before bed-*you pray about it*, and while you sleep-*you dream about it*. If you are currently part of the hustle and bustle that life brings in your workplace, the importance of this model can certainly help you to make some difficult decisions or decisions you've been putting *way, way, way* down on your priority list. It may in fact tell you that you need to be somewhere else, doing something else that makes you happy and provides you the environment to be more productive both at work and at home.

The #2 example is a gentleman by the name of Gregory Thompson II – owner of a community business known as GTI². He styles my hair (or what's left of it-smile). More importantly, he is and has been focused on his vision since his early teens and as a result, he has secured the respect of his peers and is looked upon as one of the leaders in the salon industry locally.

Wright

Now would you share a couple of your personal tools?

Walls

In my first book featuring Dr. Robert H. Schuller, I talked about three options a person has as they process FEAR or STRESS. Fight, Flight, or Freeze. I call this F³. I developed a FEAR/STRESS model to illustrate how they can impact our behavior. In my model I demonstrate the following: **The first slide** - Represents the constant flow of traffic between the three dynamics: *Environment – Perception - Behavior*. These three elements work together in an ever-evolving manner (infinity symbol ∞). **The second slide** – Represents the visual we now begin to develop as a result of this constant flow of elements (eyeglasses). **The third slide** – Represents how we begin to complete ourselves relative to the perception we accept as being real. Our reality (body figure). **The fourth slide** – Represents the internal combustion that initially happens due to the impact or introduction of FEAR or STRESS; our vision can become blurred relative to making decisions, rendering us destabilized or moving us to a state of withdrawal, aggression, or rationaLIESing things away although we know we are not behaving with integrity (blocked or distorted vision/behavior).

Fear can be a good thing, just as failure assists leaders in developing their character. It is my belief that those of us that feel we don't have any fears may miss something crucial in the decision and team building process. A leader who truly thinks failure is not part of their future is sadly mistaken. One of the ways I determine how well I'm managing my fear and stress is by the amount of time it takes me to recover from its introduction. The leader needs to process this fear or stress in a way that says, "A setback...is a setup...for a comeback" and then begin using the other tools to create the environment that diffuses the fear or stress.

Wright

How does a leader combat withdrawal, aggression, and rationaLIESing by his people?

Walls

In one word...ENVIRONMENT!! We all have needs and when they are not satisfied, people have a tendency to behave negatively or regress. Yes, even the best employee/person. You want to immediately find out what the issue is that is creating this change in behavior so you can focus on a resolve. If the request is something that you can implement, then do it; if it does not go against the policies or the integrity of the company or relationship. If it does, it is incumbent upon you as a leader to explain that it does and that their input, skills, and positive behavior are needed to help facilitate that process.

Good behavior unaddressed leads to bad behavior. Bad behavior unaddressed leads to worse behavior. Therefore, you want to recognize your people effectively and discipline (seeking to teach) them appropriately. Effective recognition is not saying, "Wow, you did a great job Wanda!" It is being specific about the compliment so they are laser clear about what exactly it is that they did a great job at. For instance, "Wanda, the approach you took in rearranging the PowerPoint presentation resulted in unanimous support by our clients. We definitely want you on our next project. Thank you for your assistance!" Or, if it is about their behavior you might say, "The way you greeted our customers today provided a productive climate for today's meeting. Please continue to be an example for each of us to follow." So be sure to take a minute to celebrate both mini and major accomplishments!

Wright

So what about the person who you cannot satisfy?

Walls

There will be some people you cannot reach...period. If you know you have followed the right steps and they still haven't come around, I have a saying that one of my mentors shared with me that addresses the probable outcome:

"If you don't come to work _fired_ with enthusiasm...you'll be **fired** with enthusiasm!"

I am not saying that if you can't fix it, it can't be repaired. However, I am saying that if you have done what you can, using the resources you have available without jeopardizing the integrity of the organization, and provided them time to change their behavior, it may be the only recourse.

Wright

Can anyone lead?

Walls

I firmly believe that everyone is equipped with a leader tool belt from birth. I didn't say we are all born leaders! NOT TRUE! It is whether we choose to begin filling our tool belt with positive and effective "good" tools and then putting them to "good" use that makes the difference. We must be cognizant of the impact they have on potential followers and aware of our leader limitations. In other words, one might be an awesome leader when leading a group of ten to one hundred people. However, no sooner than he attempts to lead a group of one thousand does he find myself becoming ineffective as a leader. We must be able to determine our cap and obligate ourselves to honor it. Recognize that you can't do everything yourself. Recognize that you can't win **every** time. Recognize that you must delegate responsibilities in an effort to build your legacy and teach others to take the initiative to do the same. Otherwise you will not reach your fullest potential, subject yourself to burnout, and negatively impact those you serve and those who want to support your mission.

Wright

What are some things you would recommend to someone to focus on if they were seeking to lead or find themselves in a leadership role?

Walls

Build your "A." L.I.S.T.© (Accountability, Legacy, Integrity, Service, and Trust). This would represent my recipe for a positive environment and positive leadership.

Wright

Why make the distinction between integrity and trust?

Walls

I feel integrity relates to the overall principles (high moral standards) of a person (how one should behave) whereas trust relates to the person's feelings about something or someone. Dictionary.com tells us that: 1) **Integrity - possession of firm principles:** the quality of possessing and steadfastly adhering to high moral principles or professional standards. 2) **Trust - position of**

obligation: the position of somebody who is expected by others to behave responsibly or honorably

And so an executive of a company would have a position of obligation. This would not preclude him from having a low integrity bar. If you examine the big companies that failed recently, or were ripped off by their leaders, it was due to the high trust (others' expectations) but low integrity of the leader. Therefore, integrity breeds exponential trust and that trust breeds an exponentially good environment to work in.

Wright

So, management versus leadership. Where do you stand?

Walls

Well, I believe a manager may know how to perform a task himself or even explain a concept to a person or group of people, but a leader will be able to teach it and encourage movement within his people's behaviors. In other words, a manager leans on the task behaviors (what has to be done) of his people while the leader focuses on the process behaviors (behaviors that support the task), vision...transformational leadership.

Here are some descriptive ways to see the difference between a manager and a leader. A manager does things right, while a leader does the right things. A manager develops skills, but a leader encourages the behavior to support those skills. A manager plays by the rules, but a leader questions why the rules were created in the first place. A manager goes along with the status quo while a leader questions the status quo. And one of my favorite differences between a manager and a leader has to do with how they view people. A manager is concerned about the work, but a leader is concerned about the people doing the work. A manager tells the troops to "Go straight ahead," while a leader climbs the tree and says, "We're going the wrong way." A manager is concerned with the present, while a leader has a clear vision of the future. A manager has boxed thoughts, while a leader thinks outside of the "outside of the box." A manager is comfortable working with groups, while a leader transforms groups into teams. A manager wins some or loses some, while a leader understands that some are rained out. A manager enjoys the comfort zone, while a leader is a change insurgent. A manager is intrapersonal, while a leader is interpersonal. A manager is scientific, while a leader defies science. A manager sticks to procedures, while a leader knows when to cut the red tape. A manager is unsure of how to respond to the unexpected, while a leader revels in it.

I stand on the leadership side of the fence Dave, because it has been and continues to be my experience that in order to move people and effect change, leadership must be the focal point...the integral part of the solution; quite frankly, any solution. It is the service piece that works for me.

Wright

Any final thoughts you want to share?

Walls

I would like to leave our readers with some motivating and challenging words that have guided me over the course of my life and helped to inspire me.

"The ultimate measure of a man is not where he stands in moments of comfort and convenience, but where he stands at times of challenge and controversy."

Dr. Martin Luther King Jr.

"On the plains of hesitation bleach the bones of countless millions who, on the threshold of victory, sat down to wait, and in waiting, died."

William Moulton Marston

"In the absence of leadership, people will walk to a mirage and drink the sand."

Michael J. Fox

"Power is only important as an instrument for service to the powerless."

Lech Walesa

"The road to excellence has little traffic."

Unknown

"Focus on how you can vs. why you can't."

Unknown

"Leadership is the art of accomplishing more than the science of management says is possible."

General Colin Powell

"Leaders are teachers; but not all teachers are leaders."
Briner & Pritchard

"Trust but verify."
JL Scott

"Wonderful wonderful!"
Dr. Harry S. Wright

"Don't say can't, say difficult!"
D. Christopher and Amara Walls

Wright

What an inspiring conversation on Leadership. Today we have been talking to Darryl C. Walls. Darryl is the founder of MINDS, a leadership consulting firm specializing in training seminars and motivational speeches. Thank you Darryl for taking your time to share your insights with us today on *Leadership Defined*.

Walls

Take care Dave, and again thank you for this opportunity to share my thoughts on such an ever-evolving topic...LEADERSHIP.

Some Final Thoughts

After years and years of study by scholars, writers, and experts who have explored the dynamics of leadership and tried to explain what leadership is, we are as close to defining leadership as we are close to achieving world peace. There will probably be a litany of theories, models, thoughts, research, and definitions found across the globe to suggest that leadership is influence, personality, an outcome of group process, and even a particular focus on effort and attention. Maybe, just maybe, we should not exhaust our energies in defining what leadership is...but forge forth with fervor and pour our strengths, souls, and spirits, into teaching our present and future leaders what leadership is **not...**

Leadership is not forgetting that the position you hold should not have a hold on you. Leadership is not forgetting to be receptive to change for growth. Leadership is not forgetting to challenge the status quo without disrespecting it. Leadership is not forgetting to communicate effectively to those you lead. Leadership is not forgetting to apologize when you don't. Leadership is not forgetting to raise your integrity and accountability bars. Leadership is not forgetting to be giving. Leadership is not forgetting to keep your self-esteem high. Leadership is not forgetting to increase trust in your environment. Leadership is not forgetting to surround yourself with positive people. Leadership is not forgetting that the comfort zone is the danger zone. Leadership is not forgetting that the times of challenge and controversy will mold you one way or the other. Leadership is not forgetting to thank, reward, and recognize those who have helped you. Leadership is not forgetting the sacrifices of your ancestors. Leadership is not forgetting that all leaders must be teachers. Leadership is not forgetting to teach others good morals, values, ethics, and beliefs. Leadership is not forgetting that you are an example to someone. Leadership is not forgetting that when you make decisions, the decisions make you. Leadership is not forgetting that when you get what you want, you might not want what you get. Leadership is not forgetting that as a leader you still have to follow someone. Leadership is not forgetting that we all are born with leader tool belts, but we have to put leader tools in them and then make a choice to put them to "good" use. Leadership is not forgetting that the closer you get to the top, the lonelier it may be. Leadership is not forgetting that just because you work or live in the basement, doesn't mean you have to have a basement mentality. Leadership is not forgetting what leadership is not. Leadership is not forgetting that leadership is service.

About The Author

Darryl C. **Walls**, an accomplished student and progenitor of contemporary leadership philosophy, is CEO of MINDS (**M**ental **I**ntensity **N**aturally **D**etermines **S**uccess), a leadership consulting firm specializing in training seminars and motivational speeches. As a highly decorated Fortune 500 team leader, Mr. Walls applied cutting edge leadership theory in a challenging business environment with spectacular results. His teams were recognized with consecutive National Leaders in Excellence honors and Exceptional Contribution Awards. Mr. Walls established MINDS as a platform to champion the leadership insights borne of his unique and diverse experiences. MINDS counts among its clientele, Fortune 500 companies, colleges, major religious organizations and a host of others. A gifted and powerful orator, Mr. Walls has been invited to make countless appearances at national conferences and other venues and has achieved professional member recognition at the National Speakers Association and the International Speakers Network. He has been awarded a Mayoral Citation from the City of New York and has received national awards, certificates, trophies and honors for his talents.

Dedicated to the memory and legacy of my teacher, my leader, and most importantly a man of God, MY FATHER Deacon Joseph Milton Walls.

Darryl C. Walls, MBA

CEO, MINDS

Leadership Consultants

Phone: 973.675.3467

Fax: 973.414.9245

Email: dcwminds@verizon.net

www.darrylwalls.com

Chapter 17

DR. WES SIME

THE INTERVIEW

David E. Wright (Wright)

Dr. Wes Sime is committed to the mission of "Identifying Leadership Potential at a Very Early Age and Nurturing it to the Fullest." He has always been and innovative pioneer in every aspect of his personal and professional life. Coming from hardy Scandinavian background, Wes lives his life to the fullest just like his father, his grandfather and his great, great grandfather Johann who emigrated from Norway in the midst of a famine. He had no money so he sold his farm and booked passage for his family of six to sail for America. Leaving his homeland with very little money took tremendous courage and leadership. Getting his family to follow and to be optimistic about the future had to be a very difficult task requiring unusual personality traits.

Those same unique personality traits were passed down to Grandfather Olaf J. Sime who homesteaded land in Iowa and raised his family of eight children through the depression. Just after WW II he started the first John Deere implement business in Minnesota to obtain some labor saving equipment for his own farming when two of his sons returned from fighting the war in Europe. He must have had a grand vision about modern ways of farming, because he kept the business going even when his neighbors could not afford tractors. "O. J. Sime & Sons Equipment" became the first business in the community willing to take horses in trade in order to sell tractors.

Dr. Sime has taken many risks and broken new ground in his career as well. During the 1960s when tractors, cars, and modern appliances were making hard work a thing of the past, people simply wanted more labor saving devices (and easy jobs) while becoming enamored with television. Exercise and hard work were quickly replaced by sedentary living and the "Good Life." Therefore when Wes and others like Dr. Ken Cooper discovered the health benefits of hard work and exercise, the average Joe "Q" public guy scorned those ideas and continued the over-eating and under-activity lifestyle. Still he persisted, finding that the only substitute for hard work in the modern labor-free world was jogging, bicycling and climbing mountains.

Advocating for the health and well-being benefits of exercise, Wes lead an expedition of 13 year-old kids to the top of Mt Rainer in blizzard conditions and to the bottom of the Grand Canyon in desert heat. He watched them mature amidst the hardships and toil growing up as young men and women because they had endured, they had conquered and they had developed close personal bonds of friendship and camaraderie along the way. Dr. Sime also worked with daring cardiologists who risked their careers taking recent heart patients through rigorous exercise programs to stimulate the development of new vessels where there had previously been blockages. Some could have died in either of those courageous adventures, but the risk was worth the potential for ultimate gain. Dr. Sime is a leader who is willing to go against the grain and against public opinion to do what is right when it needs to be done. He has written numerous research articles, multiple chapters in scientific publications and his own book titled: *Making Do Out of Doo Doo: Lessons in Life for Health, Hardiness and Fitness.* Dr. Sime, welcome to *Leadership Defined.*

Wes Sime (Sime)

Thank you, David.

Wright

Dr. Sime, as you consider the path you took to get you where you are today, who were some of the people who inspired or helped you in your younger day?

Sime

My father obviously and both my parents were great role models as the struggles on the farm in the post-depression years were excellent learning venues for adapting to hardships with creative solutions. Later my coaches were the strongest role models who inspired me to seek and achieve higher and higher aspirations.

Leadership is about building relationships. I was on a panel at the Western Academy of Management with Richard Riorden, former Mayor of Los Angeles in the Spring of 2003. In the middle of his comments he stopped abruptly and asked me, "Dr. Sime who are some of the greatest role models you remember inspiring you to reach the heights of great accomplishments throughout your life." For a moment I was dumb-founded, not expecting such a direct question. Then it flashed before my eyes like a banner on the TV screen—it was the coaches in my youth sports that inspired me. The first person that impacted my life was a football coach in 7th grade. He pitted me in a one-on one tackling drill with the biggest lineman on the team. When the dust settled and we got back on our feet, he praised our efforts extensively and inspired us to try harder next time. I did try harder, because I was hungry for the encouragement and the recognition. When game day rolled around I remember hearing that my parents cringed and could hardly keep their eyes open as the littlest guy on the team was sent out onto the field at the end of the game, much like "Rudy" in the movie about Notre Dame football.

That football coach, and the others to follow in basketball, baseball, track, gymnastics, and volleyball were there every day pushing me to try harder, encouraging me when I fell down, praising my few accomplishments and nourishing my need for attention. Surely they were even more critical at times than my parents or my teachers in expecting a higher level of performance. Because I was accustomed to hard work and loved hitting the baseball or scoring the touchdown, I usually worked harder and invested more than my peers. Maybe because I was never the most talented and certainly never was totally fulfilled in those athletic accomplishments, I just kept striving to find new training and conditioning methods. I was inspired so much by those coaches that I would do almost anything just for their encouragement, their stories, their instruction. Obviously the feeling of camaraderie and acceptance that goes into playing for a team and for a coach is a great inspiration for leadership. Now I have taken the leadership role and the baton feels different from day to day. Most of the time, it is a very good feeling to be carrying the leadership load, but other times the baton seems very heavy and even hot, hot, hot—like I should just drop it and leave.

Wright

What, in your opinion, are some of the most important habits that an effective leader must develop?

Sime

Patience, prudence, goal setting, carrying out consequences and of course, leadership by doing and sharing the opportunities with followers are the most important, in my opinion.

Leaders have to think outside the box regularly, not just once in a while. To be creative and open-minded about solutions never previously considered I have to make it a habit to try something new. In order to do that effectively, I feel that I want to listen to lots of different opinions and glean the best insight from diverse sources. Some of these ideas will transform into viable, profitable innovations, of course, if not today then perhaps tomorrow.

When I was just 10 years old my father was building a new feeding system to mix corn silage and ground shell corn from two silo's together with supplements to get it all mixed thoroughly and carried by augers to feed lots in two different directions. When he asked me how I thought the system should be built, I was astonished, never imagining that my ideas would be helpful. Some 30 or more years later when I returned home to visit family farm, I still marvel at the feeding operation that he and I built with my ideas included. I never dreamed that some of my ideas as a ten year old would eventually come to pass and have a lasting impact. In the years since that time I have often gotten great ideas from my sisters, my wife and my daughter as well as from many of my students that have helped immensely with routine problem-solving. These would never have come to surface if I had not learned to ask for suggestions. This I learned from my father who probably learned it from his father (and the generations that preceded him) to seek input from many and digest it into something productive. That gesture to delegate some of the decisions on the farm gave me a tremendous boost in confidence that I could contribute and that I was a valued part of the family business.

Wright

Could you give our readers some insight into what makes people respond and keep on doing superior work?

Sime

Affirmation makes people feel valued so they will go the extra mile for you. Let people know which specific things they do that are important to you and to the business or the profession. However, be cautious and prudent, because it is not sufficient to give blanket accolades that do not have salience and are not believable. If an employee or a subordinate in any venue (family or volunteer effort) gets a compliment for something he/she knows is only a very ordinary product or may be even "poorly done," then the effect of the insincere compliment becomes counter-productive. In order to dispense rewards appropriately and productively, the leader has to invest the time and effort necessary to know the project and to evaluate the true display of talent and great effort. Unfortunately, not many leaders are willing to make those sacrifices of time and effort to identify accomplishments that deserve reward and encouragement.

In order to gain respect from subordinates, it is important to be willing to do everything that you might expect from others. My mother used to get angry with Dad because he would give the hired man and I tough dirty jobs and then leave for town to make important decisions like negotiating the purchase of some new piece of equipment to make our jobs easier. She did not see the times when he would come back later and lend a hand when I could not keep up with the machine or was too tired to finish the job. I always respected him for his willingness to climb the hill along side me, but I came to appreciate my mother's admonition about earning the respect from the people who are doing work for you. No greater opportunity for gaining respect can be had than to find the leader who is willing to get down in the trenches to labor and suffer a bit with the salaried employees who are the ones that do the necessary and sometimes unpleasant work that makes the operation successful. This applies to white-collar sales and marketing units as well as common laborers who get dirt under their fingernails. The corporate leader who is willing to lead by example and to find out how tough it is to make the sale under these difficult economic conditions is going to be admired and followed enthusiastically by the best and the brightest in the work force.

Wright

How does one successfully gain the trust and respect of others, which seems to motivate and drive people toward excellence?

Sime

Make others trust and respect you by living up to your commitments. A few years ago I was faced with a tough consulting assignment involving a group of steel workers who were on the graveyard shift. I had to interview them about the stress in their jobs and find out how to improve working conditions. I could have asked them to stick around after their shift ended at 7:00 am for another hour or two to let me work with them at my convenience and their sacrifice of personal time, but instead I chose to arrive at the steel plant at 2:00 am, just before they were due to have a lunch break. I asked the "lead man" (not supervisor) to show me the fabricating system. I just observed and asked questions about how the machinery worked and what productivity problems existed. The steelworkers in overalls and steel-toed boots were so surprised to see a management level person showing interest in their jobs that by the time I was ready to interview them over lunch they were individually scrambling to see who got to go first. I earned their respect with very little extra effort and a sincere interest in what they were good at in their jobs. The loss of sleep that night was well worth it and is a constant reminder to me of what to do next time to be sincere and authentically interested in the client's real needs.

Wright

Could you give me an important key to keeping employees satisfied and working towards organizational goals.

Sime

Keep everyone informed of the progress, the prospects and the future. When I took the hit along with 30 others who were optioned out for loss of job or early retirement, I was angry and really upset that my employer valued my efforts so little that they would hide their intentions and then take a cowardly route to ending a productive career in my work environment. My initial reaction was to protest and to lobby for re-consideration and I did that for several months. Fortunately I had some grace period to fight the battle, but it was to no avail. I know that I still have grounds for age discrimination and unlawful termination of contract, but I choose not to fight in court, as the acrimony and extended hostility are not worth it to my health and that of my family. Now several months later, I am finding that, like so many other losses I have experienced over the years, that I will be much better off because of the hardship and unfair treatment than I was before it all happened. Fortunately, I had some forewarning. I had an alternative plan. I was prepared to face the turbulent waters. I had built my ark even years previously.

Wright

Delegation of duties seems to be one of the hardest things leaders do. How do you handle delegation?

Sime

Teach them how to do it—then stand aside. If you let another person learn from your insight while also giving them the flexibility to use their own ingenuity, they will become wiser, more skilled and accomplished producers toward your mission. Consider making the person a partner in your efforts. There is not much greater satisfaction in life than to be able to celebrate the successes and commiserate the occasional failures with a partner (or partners) who shares the same vision and dedication to the task. Then it matters not who profits more or who gets ahead further because it is a team effort and we all win no matter what the score is.

Wright

Many leaders, manager and supervisors that I have interviewed in the past few years have given me several methods of motivating their people. What have you found to be the best method to insure that you get the best out of people as well as finding their hidden talents?

Sime

Reward the good things, "catch 'em doing it right." I have found that when I lavish praise, attention, and occasional monetary benefit upon my subordinates for accomplishments that are well done, I have greater chance of discovering new strengths in them. Then I have to back away, be patient and watch what happens. We may have to repeat the rewards or withhold them from time to time; we may have to step in and re-direct when there is inadequate performance, but we must always look for the opportunity to encourage and support at irregular intervals and with unexpected variable rewards. In so doing, the person will gradually begin to praise and reward him or herself without depending upon you. The "irregularity" element of this reinforcement process makes it unexpected and therefore intrinsic rewards will gradually take over for the extrinsic rewards they have been expecting over time.

Occasionally, I have the opportunity to work with kids who have been in trouble with the law and are court ordered into counseling. With one particularly bright but stubborn young man, I struggled for months to get him to let go of the "chip on his shoulder" that compelled him to be defiant to authority (police officers, teachers, parents were the bad guys to him). One day I had inadvertently double booked two clients in the same slot on my appointment schedule. Delrick was there waiting when I was supposed to see three other little kids who needed my time because of a crisis. I contemplated sending Delrick home (which he would have thought was great), but instead I opted to get permission of parents and then bring him in with me as I talked to the three young kids whose father had abandoned them in a nasty divorce. Delrick's parents had also divorced many years earlier and his anger at authority was likely related to that abandonment issue as well.

The outcome of bringing Delrick into the session with those three young kids cannot be measured adequately in dollars or lives saved. Delrick became an inspirational role model for the kids because he loved art and racing cars and would draw neat pictures featuring each kid's first name in a fancy artistic caricature. With some prompting on my part, the kids would ask Delrick tough questions about parents, and jail time and drug/alcohol use, to which he would answer candidly and more responsibly like a parent than the rebellious kid that he had been previously. Delrick has now graduated from high school and just might go on to become an artistic design specialist for a NASCAR racing team some day. Delrick is a better young man today because he accepted the challenge and was rewarded by the enthusiastic appreciation he received from the kids. I am a better counselor today because I tried a different approach—and it worked.

Wright

Many employees that I talk to are angry and confused about the process of down-sizing which results in more work for them with the same pay. How do you approach this problem?

Sime

Allow time and opportunity for rest, refueling and recreation. Everyone needs a certain amount of flextime, autonomy to decide when the job needs to be done and how it can best be done. Job sharing, alternating work responsibility, compressed work schedules, and time off for good behavior are all important rewards to the valued employee. Most conscientious employees gradually become just a little like the infamous "workaholic." It may not be intentional, but if you love your work and you care about the quality of the output, it is natural to put in longer hours and to be dedicated to the job even during leisure hours with family. My wife is quick to point out to me when I have been late for dinner or when I have missed an important family event because of my sense of "need" to be at the office committed to the task at hand. It goes along with having a strong "work ethic." Finding a balance between dedication to the work at hand and spending time alone or with family for rejuvenation is not easy. It is not being lazy or decadent to take a break from a monotonous task or to leave work early for a recreational event; after all, the word is "recreation" of one's inner resources, and innovative thought patterns.

Just today I got an email from a composer of film scores living in Los Angeles who had been seeking new ways of developing creativity in his work. He had just read the Reader's Digest article on Understanding Your Brain Power (April, 2004) featuring my work with golfers. He said he was intrigued about the description of elite athletes being able to perform beyond their usual ability when they learned how to "get into the zone" using neurofeedback to shape and condition brainwaves to be more attentive and well focused on the task at hand. Resilience to distraction and the enhanced ability to muster creative energy could help this professional bring out the best in his ability as a composer. I am excited about this and other similar prospects, as they are a reflection of the intuition and persistence that it took to make this technology a reality in the business of performance enhancement, whether it is in academics, in sports, on stage in music, in business decisions or in the creative arts.

Wright

As a leader, how much autonomy do you tend to give your people to get the job done?

Sime

People like to be entrusted with responsibility and given a chance to succeed or struggle. Thus, I think it is important to pick the tasks carefully in accordance with the ability of the individual, monitor closely at first, but then let out the rope a little further each time given credit and kudos where appropriate.

Avoid overseeing the project in too much detail. Lay out what needs to be done and get out of the way. Ken Blanchard says in his book, *The Leadership Pill* that "People will think for themselves when you quit doing it for them." Occasionally I work with parents who are frustrated by the difficulty their children have in finding an area of interest, a major in college or a career that is satisfying and rewarding. The irony is that it all starts with the kids in elementary school on up through high school when parents feel the need to push their kids into activities and help them succeed.

Parents who sit at the table every night and sometimes do the homework for their kids are not doing them any favor, of course. That does not mean parents don't have a responsibility to be there. In fact, a parent who studies or does work at the same table with the child who is rankling about the need to do homework is more likely to be setting a good role model. He or she can just be there to prompt an idea, to coax a little creativity and to coach the child into a successful experience. Too many parents have done it all for their kids and then wonder why they have no initiative for themselves when they grow up.

Wright

How much of your personal style in business do you think rubs off on your management team and influences others in your company?

Sime

Being a leader is about being truly authentic. That is, being "real, not fake" to the people around you. You don't have to be in an important position or have power designated in order to be a leader. It is how others respond to your actions, thoughts, and opinions in any circumstance or environment. Do others seem to like what you do and try to emulate it at times? If so, then you are a leader. Throughout my career, I have found too many colleagues who were afraid to voice an opinion, especially contradictory opinions. Sometimes it has been contagious. I watched a department deteriorate over a period of years until it was finally eliminated because one person behaved in a "toxic" manner. Unfortunately this person was smart enough to use the mission of the organization as his platform to put others down and to enhance his own vested interest. The rest of us failed to confront and to challenge the disparaging language he was putting out soon enough to save the sinking ship. We all went down with it because of the short-term lack of courage to take on the battle and to show reasonable leadership. I regret not having learned this lesson earlier in my career, but it is burned into my brain indelibly from this time forward.

Successful organizations are both smart and healthy. But it is easier to strive for being smarter (having more technological skills, more intellectual resources) than it is to ensure there is healthy interaction and synchrony from within. It takes a leader personally invested in the outcome who will open up to allow his/her persona to shape the culture of the organization. For example, Patrick Lencionni, author of the Four Obsessions of an Extra-Ordinary Executive cited his description of an ideal CEO of a technological consulting company in the Bay Area. The persona of this executive was that of being humble, hungry and smart (in that order). Everyone he hired was evaluated by himself (and other employees) according to those criteria. Because he was so open about his values, his mission, his role and his responsibility, it gradually became contagious so that everyone in the company adopted a similar style or one that was complimentary to the CEO's style. Not that they were clones but that their personalities were like an open book—no politics, no hidden agenda—just a clear message to a highly cohesive group that tended to "over-communicate" to subordinates and to reinforce high quality work on a daily basis.

In that Bay Area (Silicon Valley) organization, roles were clarified/re-clarified and performance evaluations were held quarterly, not by the usual annual reviews. Core values were elicited from within the organization, not laid upon them from outside sources. While the CEO and key staff were an "open book" as to who they were and what they represented, each employee also went out of their way to get to know the personal history of everyone of their "direct report" subordinates.

Wright

What about a leader's strengths and weaknesses?

Sime

Authentic leaders recognize their own strengths and weaknesses. Authentic leaders are constantly seeking to grow, refusing to compromise themselves. This is difficult behavior to emulate if you have grown up in the Midwest where Garrison Keilor's message about the families who are "Minnesota Nice" rings true and hits too close to home...It is very difficult to push others to reach for a higher goal if you are not showing them the way by stepping out around and moving ahead of them as you go along the way. The unwritten rule in the community and the family where I grew up was to be careful not to offend anyone and try to be as humble as possible.

Sometimes that humility has helped me immensely to gain the respect of peers and subordinates whom I held in high regard. However, when it came to dealing with my administrators and managers who made the decisions about my future, I know that I was far too reticent. I would have likely been much more successful and true to myself if had I unleashed a blistering tirade of criticisms and/or disgruntlement over the direction the department was taking, over gradually dwindling resources and questionable policies regarding opportunities.

Wright

It seems that many CEO's in the immediate past have worked only for the big money, made as little change as possible, and covered themselves when it came to stockholder's meetings. How does this compare to the great leaders you know who seem to thrive on risk and new directions?

Sime

Great leaders have the courage to risk to take on new ventures. Mediocre leaders are not always willing to make the old business practices obsolete, especially when they are still very profitable. In the book, *Authentic Leadership,* by Bill George, former chair of Medtronic, I learned about going for the unknown in making acquisitions. Just a year ago I had open-heart surgery for a rare genetic obstruction that could have been fatal. The surgeon was able to do the delicate and life threatening surgery without having to stop my heart. It is a new procedure called "beating heart" surgery, made possible by a Medtronic suction device and it preserves brain function because the heart does not have to be stopped which would temporarily reduce blood flow to critical areas of the brain.

Ironically, I discovered that, Bill George had to encourage, and maybe even coerce, his staff to abandon a very profitable part of the company that produced the heart/lung machine for "heart stopping" procedures in order to risk the viability of the newer "beating heart" procedure. I am delighted they did and I believe that Medtronics are now larger and more profitable because Bill George had the courage to go for the unknown potential of the future rather than hang on to the sure profit for today. Furthermore I am grateful because my brain cells were likely spared a great deal of damage that would have occurred if my heart surgery had occurred under the old "heart stoppage" procedure. I probably would not be writing this material, due to a partially damaged brain from the older "heart stoppage" procedure, were it not for the efforts of Bill George and his courageous research team.

Wright

Could you talk to our readers about the importance of mission that seems to be a positive characteristic of great leaders?

Sime

Great leaders are motivated by mission, not money—values, not ego. Great leaders learn to connect to others from the heart, not ever relying on a fake persona. Determine what is your calling in life; what will be your passion. What kind of legacy do you want to leave? I read the story recently about the man whose father died and at the funeral amidst his family and friends, who needed strength and support, his business partner said to him, "With your father gone now, perhaps it is time that you stepped up to the front pew." Wow, what powerful words those are for some of us in the sandwich generation with aging parents and sometimes needy adult children. Why is it that we sometimes hesitate to step up to the front pew while other valued family members or colleagues are still around to make the important decisions?

Is it now time for you to step up to the "front pew" and take the opportunity to make a difference in the lives of many, many people around you? Fortunately it is not always necessary and perhaps it is inappropriate to simply wait patiently for grandparents, parents and esteemed colleagues to age and retire before starting to take over new responsibilities and embrace risks on new adventures.

Bill George also shared a wonderful scenario of Medtonics contribution to the leadership of our country. Stymied by the restriction of the FDA, Medtronics and the threats posed by lots of other companies, Bill George was not able to get the new Medtronics products tested and evaluated for safety quickly and judiciously. Many months and sometimes years would go by before the FDA would come down with a decision and often it would be stifling and restrictive. Eventually Bill felt so desperate about the viability of his company and about the needs of many medical patients that he went PUBLIC—he made a scene and eventually testified before Congress. And much to his surprise he was successful in the bid and FDA has made a revolutionary turn around.

It is no small coincidence that our Vice President, Dick Cheney, is alive, well and in a crucial leadership role because Medtronics had the valuable portable defibrillator to be used by surgeons to repair his heart... The FDA has since been reformed and now makes much more expedient and judiciously appropriate decisions about health patent issues.

Ironically however, Medtronics is not our all-time favorite among all of the health care companies. One of their other product developments is an electronic stimulant device that supposedly controls the constant tremor effects among Parkinson's Disease patients. It was touted as the miracle cure for the agonizing effects of Parkinson's, but in practice it has proven to have many side-effects and limited utility for most patients in addition to being very expensive and causing very high risk of surgical complications. I am pleased to say that an alternative medicine approach that defies the odds of success in cases of debilitating health care disease is currently being tested by a team of researchers including one of my colleagues in San Diego California.

Lisa Tatyrn is a master's level neurophysiologist who understands brain function very well. She has been doing neurofeedback with a variety of difficult medical cases for several years. Recently she stumbled onto a protocol that has proven successful in reducing the majority of tremor in most of the Parkinson's patients she has encountered. NIMH research trials are now underway and Lisa is among the group carrying out the study at a national level using her "home-grown," simple and unsophisticated procedures. Ironically her strategies are very similar to those described in the Reader's Digest article titled "Understanding Your Brain" for the purpose of enhancing performance in school children and in athletes whose focus and concentration must be shaped into disciplined patterns for ideal outcomes in learning math or in winning medals. Courageous, "out of the box" thinking is the mark of a great leader in medical care as well.

Wright

Do you have any last thoughts or insights you can share with our readers?

Sime

I would be remiss if I did not give appropriate credit to the work of Donald O. Clifton, the founder of Selection Research Institute and the Chair of the SRI-Gallop International Research and Education Center. He is the co-author of the book, *Now Discover Your Strengths* and the inspiration for another book by his business partners titled, *First, Break All the Rules* by Buckingham and Coffman. These two publications represent a lifetime of work in the area of quality leadership. The premise of the work is that managers, who try to make their employees fit the mold of the ideal worker thus trying to get better at skills un-natural to them, are making a big mistake. One of Don Clifton's essential legacy's is that he made it popular and proper to identify the employees strengths more so than their weaknesses and to shape each employee's working assignment so as to capitalize upon those strengths and to improve even further on the strengths of the individual for the betterment of both employee and institution.

While the corporate model of leadership gets the most attention because of the immediate need for productivity and success, there is another model of leadership development that deserves our consideration. Don Clifton's vision for leadership extended also into the schools and the identification of kids who have great un-tapped leadership potential. With insight and funding support from Clifton, the Nebraska Human Resources Research Foundation, Inc was developed about 20 years ago. It has quietly been operating as a leadership entity that matches first year college students with elementary school children in a quasi-educational mentoring environment that lasts for at least four years.

The college students are carefully selected and guided with coursework designed to enhance their mentoring skills aimed toward effective leadership. The elementary kids who are paired one-on-one with the college students are similarly selected carefully based upon special kinds of traits that are not ordinarily identified as leadership talents. That is, the children who are selected must be recommended to the NHRI program by a knowledgeable teacher who has noticed a special quality of caring and sensitivity. It is not the brightest, most intelligent youngsters, nor the ones who organize teams on the playground, but rather the kid who welcomes in a stranger to the class and offers to befriend a needy child, thus exhibiting the far-reaching insight to perhaps make "world peace" decades down the road.

As I think about the potential for NHRI, I am reminded of Delrick, the angry mis-guided young adult who found inspiration and pride in his own life when he was given the chance to help three young boys deal with their parent's divorce. In the same way that Delrick got his life together by helping others, there was another trans-generational mentoring experience that prepared him to carry out this important though impromptu role. One year prior, I found a lonely senior citizen (a former military man in law enforcement) whose life became more fulfilled when he was asked to share words of wisdom with Delrick about that "chip on his shoulder" and how important it was to respect authority and find satisfaction without causing trouble. I think the ultimate message of caring does get passed on. Isn't it interesting how generation gaps that separate us, can also bring us closer together, when the leadership model has a chance to be proactive and creative.

Funding to expand these programs to a nationwide level would be in the best interest of all of us, for our children may be the ones who will benefit the most from this kind of grass-roots leadership potential. Interested persons who wish to learn more about the mentoring leadership program of the Nebraska Human Resources Institute can find more information at www.NHRI.org.

Wright

Dr. Sime, I want to thank you for taking this time with me today. Dr. Sime has also co-authored another book titled, *Making Do out of Doo Doo: Lessons in Life for Health, Hardiness and Fitness.* Thank you for sharing your stories and insight on leadership.

Sime

Thank you, David.

Some Final Thoughts

Great leaders build close trusting relationships; they are very authentic (like an open book) and very dependable in meeting deadlines while fulfilling responsibilities without complaint. Effective leaders look forward to new challenges and are willing to take risks in order to be innovative, thus thinking "outside the box" to accomplish dedicated missions based upon remarkable values including: achievement, autonomy, honesty, loyalty, morality and wisdom. They have embraced occasional moments of failure and welcomed feedback from both friends and critics to be used in revamping to become stronger and more successful in the next venture. They have sought the insight of many role models throughout their careers in each case drawing knowledge and experience from the "difference-makers" in life who have developed wisdom of the ages by listening and reacting. Great listeners watch the speaker carefully and absorb the content of a conversation without interruption; then they integrate the essence of it with other gems of insight offered up to help create new concepts.

The most deserving leaders have earned legitimacy with their expertise and with their access to critical information thus developing power. Less deserving "wanna be" leaders try to rely on coercive power or the reference given by others who may or may not be unbiased in giving recommendation thereof. Great leaders are "difference-makers" who hung around remarkable people that shaped them like potters who add a little clay to the statue of the man or woman but he/she remains receptive to new ideas throughout his or her career. Those who lead by example often share influence with associates because no one can lead in a vacuum. Sharing the burden of leadership is illustrated by geese flying in the inverted "V" formation. They fly in a rotation where birds with fresh wings slide forward to take over the load of breaking through the wind periodically. Similarly, the most productive groups or organizations welcome the contribution of many rather than depend upon the power of one.

About The Author

Dr. Wes Sime is exceptionally well qualified having two Masters Degrees and two Ph.D's, yet he is as down to earth and personable as your best friend and neighbor. Dr. Sime is certified in Stress Management and Biofeedback for his clinical and consulting work and also in Sport Psychology wherein he has worked with notables including Tom Osborne and Nebraska Football Players, the Kansas City Royals Baseball Players, Payne Stewart and many other professional golfers. Among his current Leadership Roles, Dr. Sime is Chairman of the International Stress Management Association-USA and Clinical Director of Affiliates Family, and Individual Counseling Associates. Wes Sime is an outstanding, dynamic and entertaining speaker who has shared the podium with Walter Cronkite and Nido Qubein. His powerful message touches the heart and delivers practical punch in stress coping and peak performance for all audiences including executives, sales, professionals, families and aspiring, talented youth wherein he inspires great leadership development.

Dr. Wes Sime

University of Nebraska-Lincoln

Lincoln, Nebraska 68588-0234

Email: WSime@unl.edu

www.unl.edu/stress/mgmt/

Chapter 18

SHARON MCGEE

THE INTERVIEW

David E. Wright (Wright)

Today we are talking to Sharon McGee. As a long time president and CEO of a successful mechanical construction firm in Austin, Texas, Sharon has spent many a day down in the trenches doing what it takes to satisfy her own demand that every customer be 100% satisfied with the work performed by her company. Sharon entertains the audiences with relevant educational and hilarious real life stories from her years of hands on down in the trenches experiences. As an international marathoner, a mother, a nana, a Red Cross volunteer, a woman of great faith, and a lady of charm, she will leave your audience with a renewed sense of confidence that they too can achieve 100% customer satisfaction and have fun while doing so. When you think of Sharon, you think of someone who lives life in the 480-volt zone. Her zest is contagious to everyone who meets her. Although putting in a 12-hour day on a regular basis, she still finds time to balance her life with family, friends, and other activities such as giving her time and resources back to the community. Sharon was awarded Outstanding Volunteer by the United Way in 2000, and was named Hero of 2003 by Central Texas for her work with the American Red Cross. Sharon McGee, welcome to *Leadership Defined.*

Sharon McGee (McGee)
Thank you.

Wright
Who is Sharon McGee? Could you give us some background?

McGee
Well, Sharon McGee is often called the human energizer bunny, and that's totally correct. I live life in the 480-volt zone, and if you are in the business that I am, 480 volts defines high voltage, producing great results with total efficiency in record time—always. And what I love to do is to be able to affirm others at all times, and if they need help and encouragement to build themselves up, that's what I love doing.

Wright
It shows you my grasp of the electrical world when I call it 480 V.

McGee
That's okay. If I had spelled out volt (v) you would have understood it. However, in the construction business, it is known just as that. It is either 110v, 220v or 480 volts, which is the maximum consumable voltage. And I chose to live my life, and am blessed to live life in the 480v-high voltage/energy zone.

Wright
A lot of people actually consider the purpose of life. Have you done it? If you have, what do you feel your purpose in life is?

McGee
David, my purpose in life is to be able to touch the lives of others, one person at a time. I am blessed with a contagious zest for life and others feel this when I am around them. Therefore, I love being able to lift up and affirm others and to highly motivate them so whatever they think they can't do, I can make sure that they can. What I love about the 480-volt process is being able to make their light shine for the world to see.

Wright
What has been your greatest achievement so far?

McGee

Everything I do is a great achievement because I put my all in everything I touch. I give credit where credit is due, which is God. All things I do, I do because of Him. One of the most important achievements in my life would be the fact that I have gained great respect as a female in a male dominant industry, being a mechanical contractor in Austin, Texas and across the United States. In reality, how I achieved this respect was to work as a partner with males on the job site. I am their friend, not a foe, and I use the same port-a-potty! This is a big thing when I arrive on a jobsite. You see, when I claim "from the trenches," I mean just this. I hang ductwork, change out compressors and do what others do. I will never ask anyone to do something I have not done myself. So, when I arrive on jobsites, men think I am going to have a pink port-a-potty delivered there, which just isn't the case. My employees think it is really cool when I work with them in the field—they understand we are equal and that my business wouldn't be in existence without the great labor force I have. Is it hard? No, I am just myself. Sometimes, I do have to work a little harder to prove myself, but I am not afraid of hard work.

Wright

I have a very close friend in North Carolina who recently was featured on the *Better Homes and Gardens*. The person has owned a construction company for almost 30 years, and builds houses for the super rich. I asked her, "What was your greatest achievement?" She said, "Doing all I've done in 30 years and being a woman." I had never thought of it before, but in a male dominated industry, you probably have to work twice as hard as a man, wouldn't you?

McGee

I think in the beginning you have to work harder to prove your expertise, just as in the military. This is what I did. I worked really hard and everyone very soon learned my business and personal ethics. However, this isn't any different than I would of done in a female retail world. My work ethics are just as my daddy taught me; you don't get anything in life unless you work for it.

Wright

When you say one person can make a difference, one person at a time, what do you mean by that?

McGee

Can I tell you a little story?

Wright

Sure!

McGee

I've always believed that one person can make a difference. I had an employee that needed to talk after 9/11, so we sat down and we talked. He couldn't understand why 9/11 had happened, so I pushed everything aside and said, "Let's stop and make sure that we understand this." To me the greatest thing about leadership is listening. It's about being an influence. It's not standing up in front of a room to teach. After I sat there and helped him try to understand 9/11 and what happened, three weeks later he died of an aneurysm at 36 years old. So the following year, in his honor and in honor of 9/11—I was probably one of the very first people that did a tribute to 9/11—as I was running, I asked God to help me decide how I could make sure that everybody knew that we were still praying for them. I purchased 3200 flags and my staff and I personalized them to each family. I delivered them to all the sights where the terrorist activities took place. I took 2600 of them with me to New York and ran the New York Marathon; they now sit in the homes of the family members. This is what I mean by one person can make a difference. As long as fear doesn't stop you, when you have an instinct or you want to touch somebody's life, just go for it. Just do it. It is all about the small things in life. It's not about the big things. When I did the flags, I didn't put a name or telephone number on them; I didn't want to be contacted because I just wanted everybody to know that we're still thinking about them, and we're still praying for them.

God is my pilot. I am just the co-pilot. Sometimes I try to take over the controls, but I let Him have it back because He gets my attention. But on this particular day about six months ago, I got a call from a man that said, "Is this the Sharon McGee that loves flags?" I said, "Well, yes," not knowing who this is. I'm very patriotic. I love the flag and the symbol for it. I'm symbolic. So he said, "I just want you to know that I'm the dad of a man that was killed at the World Trade Center, and your flag was given to me through the Red Cross. They helped us get this flag. It's in our centerpiece. Every morning we pray, and your flag is a memorial to our son every day of our lives. Thank you!" Isn't that wonderful?

Wright

That is wonderful! So what type of leadership skills do you use in running a mechanical company?

McGee

I absolutely use the servant leadership. I was blessed early on with a great mentor, and that mentor taught me long ago that you, yourself, as a leader, need to be on the bottom of the totem pole, and you lift everybody else up skyward. Whatever you need to do to make sure they achieve what they need to. What you give, you'll get in return. From my aspect of the mechanical company, I absolutely lead this company under servant leadership where I'm at in the role of command, or chain of command, as far as on an organizational chart, I'm at the bottom. It is my belief that I am the foot soldier that helps others not just stare up the steps, but step up the stairs to success! I want to make sure that happens.

Wright

Interesting!

McGee

As a company, we fluctuate from 50 to 100 employees. We're definitely family, and in that particular case in the construction business. Some have it a lot better, some have it a lot worse, but we average about nine to ten years as far as an average year that people stay here. That's a long time in a construction business for being in business for 28 years.

Wright

What do you mean when you say "customer service from the trenches?"

McGee

Well, I touched on that just a little while ago meaning that I get down in there and do it as well, not asking anybody to do something I wouldn't have already done. And it's kind of like the way I believe in business ethics, which there's not any, it's living by the golden rule. How would I want to be treated in this situation? So I train people that work for me to put themselves in the position of the customer; treat them how they would want to be treated. So, customer service from the trenches is getting down there and doing it. I do customer surveys myself, saying, "Hi, I'm Sharon McGee, owner of RM Mechanical. I'd like to know how my service technician did as he visited your house today." You know, they are number one, that just says a lot to not only the customer, but to our technician. It keeps everybody on check. It's a neat thing. Plus I love talking to people.

Wright

I've often heard people like Zig Ziegler, Cabot Roberts, and people like that, some of the guys that have been around for many, many years, say if you help enough people be successful, you'll be successful. How do you help? How do you personally help others to become successful?

McGee

The number one most important thing is listening. I help people be successful by wondering into their offices and talking to them. I get to know them, get to know their hearts. And sometimes I think that if you look across the country and you read different books, maybe that is or isn't the type of leadership role or management role that you should do, but to me, managing and leadership are two different things. I would much rather be a leader. I help others become successful by listening number one, and helping them achieve their goals, especially from a training aspect. I'm an instructor and I'm a trainer for a lot of different things that affect OSHA. I am a certified trainer for Maximum Impact Speaking. The most important thing is that it's all about listening.

Wright

Let's talk about passion for a second. I've noted that most successful people, and I would certainly put you in that category, are always passionate about something. What are you passionate about?

McGee

That is a tough question to answer. In fact, I asked a couple of people that I am close to, my close friends, mentors and husband, "What am I passionate about?" The answer back was this: anything you put your hands on. I don't do anything that I'm not passionate about, whether it be writing a story, staying at the job, going to a jobsite, teaching OSHA, teaching leadership or changing my granddaughter's diaper. I'm passionate about doing anything I do right the first time. I have this incredible heart the size of Texas.

Sometimes that gets in my way, but whatever it is, whatever I'm doing, I'm passionate about it.

Wright

I hesitate to ask this question, but it's always interesting to find out. Do you have any regrets? And if so, what are they?

McGee

I would mention two. One being that the gift that I have been given, which is the ability to really connect with people. I believe that I have had this all my life, but I also believe that earlier on in my 20s, I was in a state of denial. The regret is that I wish I would have used the talents that God gave me earlier on as my kids were little. They see it as they are adults, but I just think that sometimes you're just so busy building yourself that you forget that it's already *there*. I just didn't tap into the resources that were already there. In addition, I think a regret that everybody has is that sometimes you put those material items like going to school, getting where you need to be, in front of your family. I think I have probably missed quality family time.

Wright

I think it's Ecclesiastics where it says that there's a time...

McGee

Oh, you're awesome! I love it!

Wright

As you said that, I was wondering if she had started sooner, would she be as passionate? Then, I thought to myself, "I doubt it." One probably gets the passion because they waited. You may have had it all those years but waiting as long as you did, that's probably what makes you so passionate about it.

McGee

There's a time and there's a season for all things under God. When I was raising my children, I would get frustrated because I knew they had the ability to do some things they didn't feel confident to do. God would tell me this is their life and when they are ready, they will understand their worth. He's going to impress upon my kids, so don't force their learning—just be an influence. Regardless of their age, your kids do watch and model after what their parents do. My parents are very important role models to me. My mom used to run, and whether she had a tough day or not, you would never know because she always had a positive attitude. They both worked very hard and provided for our family. I learned great lessons from both of them. I praise God for my parents.

Wright

You have alluded to your faith a few times in this conversation. What role has spirituality played in your life?

McGee

To me, just the acknowledgement of where we came from, and who created what our purpose is, and that God created us is number one. Religion and spirituality are two different things. In my role, I think they go together. With religion, you believe in God and you know who created you. Spirituality to me is also the form of being spiritual, having that human compassion to be able to have this high on life. Everybody always asks me, "What are you on? What are you taking?" My response to them every single time is, "I'm high on life," or "I'm high on God," that is truly the truth. Spirituality is how I flow through the losses or highs, flow through a marathon of highs, flow through life. The human compassion forum is if somebody is crying, just cry with them. If somebody is happy, I'm going to be happy with them. I'm going to hug. I'm going to touch. It's all of those forms of spirituality that all credit goes to God because He created it all.

Wright

How important is being physically fit to you when it comes to being a role model? If you're a marathon runner, you must really be physically fit.

McGee

Well, I think it's important. I believe in walking the talk that you state. That is a person can walk the walk and talk the talk, and we've all heard that. I believe that you have to walk your talk. Therefore, I believe that leadership is influence. That's it. Just influence. I believe that if people look up to me as a leader, they're going to see me from a spiritual aspect, to a physical aspect, and to a success, and that just goes on to the next part of what success means to me. To me, being physically fit as being a role model, or even in your personal life, is critical because you have to feed your mind. You have to feed your body important things, meaning exercise. You've got to invigorate it. Whenever I go out on a run and come back, I am the most creative person in the world. In fact, my secretaries always say, "Oh my gosh, she's on a run again," because whenever I come back they know something's going to come off the computer.

Wright

What does success mean to you? It has so many definitions I've heard, but I'm always interested in the individual definition.

McGee

What does it mean to me? It's about the little things. It means doing the best that we can with what we have. We think success is this huge, grand, spectacular, once in a lifetime happening in our life, but to me, success is the little things in life every day. If you lose that one particular pound that you wanted to lose, or if you completed that report that you needed to get done. We see success every day in our lives, and we fail to look at it as success, so therefore we don't celebrate it. To me, if we would realize that every day we achieve success in our lives by doing something that we want to accomplish with what we set forth, then to me, you have succeeded. So therefore, it creates an inner peace and self-worth in yourself. That's to me success. Success is not about money.

Wright

Do you set goals?

McGee

Absolutely! Daily, quarterly, yearly, they are on Excel. I put plans and purposes and actions underneath how to achieve them, then I go back to them. The biggest, greatest thing about setting goals is being flexible. That's why it's always so important to go back to them and analyze them, and think about whether or not you are going to be able to do them? Absolutely, I set goals. Daily goals, quarterly goals, yearly goals. That is how I run my mechanical business, as well.

Wright

I had a brilliant man back in the '70s teach me a real lesson about goal setting. After I studied goal setting for a couple of years, I think the most important thing he said to me was what you just stated, but he put it a different way. He said, "When setting goals and writing your goals down, always use a pencil."

McGee

Yes, exactly. That is good.

Wright

Flexibility was his bi-line.

McGee

Don't you agree with that? You have to be flexible.

Wright

Oh, yes. Well, there are so many outside forces over which you have no control over, but most of the time when I really got into goal setting, for many years, I would put on my judicial robe before I made my goals and judged myself too harshly. But after I found out that flexibility was important in goal setting, it was a lot easier for me. The more goals I had, the happier I was.

McGee

That's exactly right. If we set the little goals and we are able to achieve something every day that's where personal happiness comes from. I know that one of my five-year goals was to run the Iron Man at 45. Of course, I have the marathon thing down because I have ran 18 marathons, but last year I did the biking. I can't remember how many miles the biking part is to that. This year I am working on the swimming, which I just don't like, but there are things that you have to achieve to get to the big picture. And if my big picture is to do the Iron Man, I have to do all three. This will be a struggle with my goal this year. One of the other things that I wanted to do is sky dive, which I plan to do that next Sunday. I also want to fly a helicopter. I do a lot of leadership training in the military at Fort Rucker, Alabama, so they've given me the opportunity. Every time I go down there to each class, they allow me to visit the helicopter trainer.

Wright

Oh, I'm beginning to feel sorry for your husband.

McGee

Oh, I know. It's funny you say that because when I leave classes, whether I'm talking about real life experiences or wrapping a duct jack around an oak tree, they all want to say, "Can I get your husband's address so I can send him a sympathy card?"

Wright

I was thinking about getting him a prayer partner. It would be more long term.

McGee

There we go. That is so neat. Gosh, you're awesome. That's incredible.

Wright

You talked about business ethics a few minutes ago. Could you tell me what you mean?

McGee

Sure, living by the golden rule. I even teach a course on that. I also encourage you to have great mentors as well. It's really about how you live your life, and asking yourself how do I want to be treated. It is not only business, or your personal life, it's in both. It's how would you want to be treated if you were in that same situation. That is what I believe ethics are.

Wright

You know it's strange to me that so many people that are really, really high up in the business circles that were role models, we thought, and their business ethics in the past year or two have just dropped them down. Many of them going to prison. How do you explain that? I mean, how do you get that kind of success making 8, 10 million dollars a year running a company, and then just walk right on by when an ethical question arises?

McGee

A couple of years ago when a couple of things happened in our own industry, here in Austin, involving other mechanical companies, one of the things that I was asked in a media question was, "What keeps you from involving yourself in activities or doing things that maybe other companies do?" And you know I didn't have a textbook, I didn't have a college prepared answer. All I said was, "As long as I can sleep at night, that's all that matters to me. Because if I have done something wrong, you know what? The good Lord is not going to let me sleep at night. I know that whenever I leave this office and I go home to go to bed, put my head on that pillow at night, I know that I can go to sleep and soundly sleep all night long because I have taken care of my people, my customers and my community. That's ethics. That's good ethics, the ability to be able to sleep at night, peacefully. Those people that have done things wrong to people, especially people's finances, which creates a tough future, they can't sleep at night. They probably have to have something to help them sleep. I can't even imagine that.

Wright

Well, what an interesting conversation. Your management style is simple, as far as I'm concerned, and one to which I adhere. I remember Paul Meyer told me many, many years ago that, he said, "If you consider yourself a leader and you look around and no one is following you, you're only out for a walk."

McGee

Whenever I teach for OSHA across the United States, I always began at 9:00 in the morning, and I always say you're not going to care how much I know until you know how much I care. In fact, I marketed the softer side of OSHA. We have *fun*, but it really gets down to the real life stories and the fact that people care. The fact that I care is what impresses people, not my knowledge, not my education, not the fact that I own a mechanical business, because anybody can do that, but it's that I care.

Wright

Interesting. Today we have been talking to Sharon McGee, president and CEO of a successful mechanical construction firm in Texas. But as we've heard today, she has spent many a day down in the trenches doing what it takes so that every customer might be 100% satisfied, which is a tremendous goal in itself. I just wish I were one of Sharon's customers. Thank you so much for being with us today, Sharon, on *Leadership Defined*.

McGee

Thank you so much, sir. It was a great conversation, and it's awesome to be able to talk about God in a conversation.

I aspire to the philosophy of servant leadership—whereby our first concern is to serve others, not the bottom line. In this posture, what matters most is how much we care, not how much we know. It is walking the golden rule and standing firm for integrity.

We must always remember. It is not through lectures, threats or a lofty title that a leader inspires; it is by example. We cannot bellow orders down into the trenches if we want respect. Trust is won trudging in the mud with your team—everyone working hard at what they do best. Leadership is partnership. It is everyone involved and in tune with the big picture. It is, what do you think? What are your ideas for getting the job done? Shall we get started?

If every person on the team feels essential and valued, an extraordinary spirit of camaraderie can result—not unlike that experienced when people come together to shore up the banks of a gorging river. In such an atmosphere, mundane tasks seem less mundane. Enthusiasm prevails. Pride in the work thrives. And all pull together to share in achieving such goals as 100% customer satisfaction or an impossible deadline. Forever gone is the 'that's not my job" attitude; and, in its place, a workforce of three or twenty or hundreds who give their all and feel accountable.

Leadership is greeting each day with a desire to serve, and giving thanks at night for being part of a team willing and eager to do the work—heart and soul engaged.

About The Author

Sharon McGee brings 20 years of experience of serving The Team of R.M. Mechanical, Inc.—a multi million-dollar corporation, in the role of President/CEO. Sharon has spent many a day down in the trenches doing what it takes to satisfy her own demand that every customer be 100% satisfied. With her extensive background as a Certified Safety and Health Official and Leadership Instructor, Sharon is successful in creating a fun and interesting learning environment and delivers a dynamic inspirational and motivational training to her audience. Her zest is contagious to everyone who meets her. When you think of Sharon, you think of someone who lives life in the 480-volt zone.

Sharon McGee

International Center for Leadership Excellence

3312 Duke Road

Austin, Texas 78724

Phone: 512.517.1583

Fax: 512.928.2920

Email: Sharon@sharonmcgee.com

www.sharonmcgee.com

Chapter 19

DON W. HOOPER, PH.D.

THE INTERVIEW

David E. Wright (Wright)

The Center For Quality Leadership (CQL) is a consulting firm engaged in a broad range of services for public and private entities including management and performance reviews, organizational studies, program design/delivery services and leadership development training. *CQL* is committed to assisting clients with the planning required to focus available resources on effective performance. Clients include school districts, private companies, law firms, charter schools and associations.

Dr. Hooper, its founder, has over 33 years of experience in public education including serving 25 years as superintendent of schools. He was named as Texas Superintendent of the Year in 1995. Don, welcome to *Leadership Defined*!

Don Hooper (Hooper)

Thanks, David. Good to be here.

Wright

Tell me, what is the concept of executive stewardship?

Hooper

Basically, David, the concept of executive stewardship is that you do not have to choose between leadership and management. Really, executive stewardship is the effective and proper use of both leadership and management skills at their appropriate times. Some say organizations in America are over-managed and under-led. Such debate raises this question: What is the real difference between leadership and management?

Some individuals in organizational management take pride in their efficient management of resources. Others take pride in their leadership ability to work effectively with people. All might agree that efficiency means doing things right, while effectiveness means doing the right thing.

I believe excellence occurs when we do the right things right. Efficiency denotes left-brain activity, involving concrete sequential thinking, while effectiveness denotes right-brain activity involving creativity and vision. From this, one could conclude things should be managed and people should be led. After all, if an organization is to produce excellence, it must take all inputs and transform them into outputs.

This transformation function may be production oriented (involving materials, methods, and equipment), service oriented (involving people, processes, and organizational culture), or task oriented (involving time and the assignment of work). In all cases, however, inputs generate the activities to be performed. Those activities are divided between management and leadership.

One must know how and when to manage things and to lead people. The ability to manage or lead appropriately is known as "executive stewardship."

Executive stewardship suggests a dichotomy of the leadership/management functions. Executives contribute to the performance of the organization, while stewards manage another's property or other affairs. These definitions imply a sense of trust and service to others, in contrast to the role of executive, which has a dictatorial connotation. Effective leadership/management, i.e. "executive stewardship" is a whole-brain activity.

This same dichotomy also exists in the respective functions of the left and right hemispheres of the brain. The left side is responsible for the concrete sequential and logical functions of the brain whereas the right side is responsible for the sensitive, intuitive functions.

People sometimes are characterized by their dominant cognitive functions as "left-brained" or "right-brained." Where such polarity exists, one sees either a narrow-minded bureaucrat or a scatter-brained poet. This may also be the genesis of the belief that one must be either a manager or a leader, but cannot nor should not be both.

However, effective executive stewardship is a whole-brain activity. The left side of the brain is dominant in the management function because management is a function imposed on things, such as the procedural knowledge of finance.

On the other hand, the right side of the brain dominates when the leadership function engages because leadership involves people, not things. Without sensitivity, one cannot be an effective consensus builder. Team building activities, motivational and inspirational activities and judgments of fairness and equity are important leadership skills.

Executive stewardship manifests whole-brain activity. The left hemisphere commences when the management of things is necessary, and the right hemisphere commences when leadership is called for. This is the practice of executive stewardship. The executive steward engages both hemispheres in collaboration to articulate and accomplish the organizational mission.

Now with the recognition that probably management has a lot to do with control which has a lot to do with the left hemisphere of our brain where the things are very linear, and leadership is that creative aspect that has to do with the human spirit, and it's pretty much in the dominant right hemisphere of the brain. So the idea is that you don't have to choose because in fact, God created each of us with a whole brain. In other words whole brain thinking then enables us through the concept of executive stewardship not to have to choose between both leadership and management but to choose appropriately the effective use of those skill sets, as they are needed.

Wright

So while most others that I have talked to would differentiate one from the other and literally imply that you can't be both, you are saying that is possible?

Hooper

I'm saying that it is very possible, and in fact, the way that most of us truly operate. You may become frustrated trying to decide if you are a manager or a leader. The truth is you can be both and should hone your skills in each area. Our natural behavior tendency may cause us to categorize ourselves as either a leader or a manager, but people of all personality behaviors can lead and manage by practicing executive stewardship.

Each one of us has a more comfortable style and while our personalities are unique, we still fall into general categories. We may try to find our natural dominant style, but it is easy to see what we are not the most comfortable with as opposed to being able to articulate what we are comfortable with. The reason for this is that there are about four types of personalities that most of the psychological tests would put each of us into those four types.

Throughout history people have attempted to explain the differences in people. The earliest efforts were found in astrology; where it was believed that the alignment of the heavens influenced the formation of behavior. Even today many enjoy reading their horoscope and some even believe in this concept of 12 signs in four groupings symbolized by Earth, Air, Fire and Water. Among the ancients Hippocrates espoused a belief that there were four temperaments – Choleric, Phlegmatic, Sanguine and Melancholy. It was his belief that personality was shaped by Blood, Phlegm, Black Bile and Yellow Bile.

In the early part of the twentieth century psychologist Carl Jung suggested that there exist "Psychological Types" where he described the four types as the Intuitor, Thinker, Feeler and Sensor. Jung ushered in the modern concepts on behavioral differences of which there are more than a dozen. Still most models can be simplified into only four categories of grouping behaviors. Modern brain researchers tell us that both the right and left sides of the human brain have a cerebral hemisphere and a limbic hemisphere, each with its own special function. While it is generally agreed that we have each of the four parts in each one of us, there seems to be a dominance of one or the other followed by secondary and tertiary tendencies in the other three categories.

A person's observable external behaviors characterize their predictable different styles manifested regardless of their internal differences. Tony Alessandra, a well-known business consultant categorizes these into two major dimensions of behavior—Supportingness and Directness. Supportingness is the readiness and willingness with which a person expresses emotions and enters into and develops relationships. There are open supporting people and there are self-contained controlling people. The open supporting people tend to be and "open book" and greet people with a warm handshake. They are willing to share and discuss almost any matter openly. Individuals who resonate with this tendency may view themselves as "leaders." Self-contained, controlling people take a while to show their openness and warmth. The second dimension or directness is where many managers feel they must reside. These people like to know just where a conversation is leading and avoid chitchat. They want to get to the bottom line quickly. Time is of great importance to these people. Prompt dealings are a must. They are rational, logical individuals who expect timely results within a structured environment. Because of the demands of the job, many "managers" fall into the latter category.

Directness is the other dimension of behavior. It manifests itself in the way in which a person deals with information or situations. This dimension has direct and indirect people at opposite ends of its scale. Direct people are fast-paced, assertive, forceful, competitive, controlling, outspoken, talkative, and dominant. The world to them is either black or white with no middle ground or gray area. They speak with authority and conviction and are risk-takers with a propensity for making it happen yesterday if not before. Ready, fire; aim would be an accurate description of this type of thinker. Some think this is a charismatic style of leadership with a hard-line management approach. Their counter part on the directness scale, the indirect people, are slow-paced, unassertive, compliant, quiet and cooperative and take deliberate action. They don't like to rock the boat, are more cautious, supportive, and are better listeners. While they take a roundabout approach, they still go step by step in reaching a conclusion or an objective. These individuals feel that they are providing stable, solid leadership while managing assets cautiously.

In summary, the supporting continuum ranges from guarded controlling behavior to self-disclosure that is ready and willing to outwardly show thoughts and feelings. The direct continuum ranges from risk taking and assertiveness to caution and a need to follow established rules and policies. It is possible to be a successful executive steward regardless of where an individual falls on this continuum.

As you've heard a number of different authors say, you manage things and you lead people. So the idea here is people who are going to accomplish something usually have to have resources. Many times those resources include things. So a leader still needs management. As a manager, you can take care of a lot of things, but if they're never used properly to accomplish some worthwhile goal, then that's a real waste. So you need both leadership and management. And every individual has within them the capability to do each.

Wright

So what is leadership excellence?

Hooper

Leadership excellence is part of the quality movement. You've heard the term "performance excellence," which basically means that you're using both efficiency and effectiveness. I think it was Peter Drucker who first of all said that a simple definition for each of those would be that efficiency is doing things right, but effectiveness is doing the right thing. However, excellence is when you're doing the right thing and you're doing it in the most right way. So "leadership excellence" supports the concept of executive stewardship, which indicates that you must lead using resources appropriately with a high level of quality, hence producing excellence. Performance excellence has a lot to do with the ISO standards and the continuous improvement of things regarding management skills.

In fact, some people used to call it total quality management (TQM). While some still refer to TQM, many refer to the same thing as business improvement process. W. Edwards Demming, developed a 14-point philosophy of quality, and Joseph Juran, a contemporary of Demming talked about the way to build a strategic intent using continuous improvement. While neither of them intended for a movement to be established known as TQM, in the quality initiative movement, people came up with the term total quality management or TQM as a nomenclature. Terminology continues to evolve and concepts such as continuous improvement, performance excellence and leadership excellence emerge.

What I'm saying is that leadership excellence goes beyond performance excellence by considering the concept of how you can use your mind for a much higher level of thinking, a much more effective way of thinking. The concept of executive stewardship which emphasizes tapping into each person's inherent leadership ability to create and innovate coupled with their management ability to focus that innovation for accomplishment is one that should have great currency.

Wright

You have said that leadership is first about character, then about courage and competence. Could you enlighten us a little bit? Tell our readers what you meant by that.

Hooper

Well, after I had written that, it occurred to me that you could have evil leaders as well as good leaders. So if leadership is the capability of having influence over someone to accomplish some particular task or goal, then you have to consider the motive for the influence in order to determine if the influence is for good or evil. Some motives are for the greater good, and some are for selfish gain. An indicator of how one carries responsibility can illuminate their character and therefore predict if they are a good leader or an evil leader. Whether a leader is evil or good they may each have skills, capabilities, and values. Good leaders who are focused on a good greater than themselves have a sense of ethics and mores to serve others. Evil leaders may live by some self-determined set of norms, but the result serves only them even though they may say otherwise. So while both live by a set of norms, one is focused on service to others and the other is focused on selfishness.

Leadership is an affair of the heart, which deals with the mind, the body, and the soul of individuals. Leadership deals with the things people are willing to stake their life on. Good leadership deals with ethical values and moral decisions. Leadership competencies include such things as human relationships skills, technical skills, conceptual visualization skills, decision making skills, problem identification skills, problem solving skills, implementation of determined goals and strategies, evaluation of results, strategic planning, goal setting, communicating, motivating, delegating, enabling/empowering, and being aware and able to correctly use organizational dynamics, and group dynamics.

Management competencies include some of the leadership skills, but also include human resource management, materials management, legal compliance, time management, business process management, policy management, and implementation of strategics identified and selected during the leadership function.

When a person determines to lead someone, they are doing so from a set of values and ethics. These values and ethics are either learned through experience or have been taught to the leader in both formal and informal ways. These values and ethics determine whether a person will act responsibly in a mature fashion or irresponsibly. It has been said that the line between immaturity and maturity is crossed when a person stops saying, "It got lost," and begins to assume responsibility and says, "I lost it." Indeed, being accountable by understanding and accepting the role our choices play in the things that happen is a crucial sign of emotional and moral maturity. That's why responsibility is one of the main pillars of good character. A good "respons-I-bility" enables a good "respons-A-bility." In other words, good character gives one the ability to serve unselfishly and well.

To further explain the balance between leadership and management with regard to executive stewardship one must understand the relationship between authority, responsibility and accountability. Authority is an executive function while responsibility and accountability are stewardship functions. I must also clarify that the term executive, in this context, does not mean a position. It does mean a person who performs executive functions such as being a thinker, a problem identifier/solver, a decision maker, a learning leader, a competent role model, and a person who is not afraid of taking a measured and calculated risk. This person can be a catalyst for action. The stewardship part of the definition indicates service based on a balance of power that is purpose driven according to previously agreed upon principles that have been learned and discussed with the people working closest together. A person of strong character focused with a purpose for the greater good understands how and when it is appropriate to use leadership power.

There are five forms of leadership power. Three of them are given by the organization in a formal way and carry with them authority and some responsibility. Two of them come from within a person and are related to choices that person makes for him or herself and carry with them responsibility with or without the accompanying of authority. All five carry with them the need for accountability.

They are: 1) Legitimate (given by the organization) 2) Reward (given by the organization) 3) Coercive (given by the organization) 4)Expert (individually gifted or acquired) 5) Referent (individually gifted or acquired).

Legitimate power is given by the organization because of a position in the hierarchy. Examples would be like the president of a company, the chief financial officer of a company, a manager or supervisor over a particular division, or in the public school setting a teacher, principal, administrator or superintendent. Usually granted along with this power is the authority to use reward power. Reward power is based on the ability to control and administer rewards to others (i.e. money, promotions, praise). The third type of power, which is given formally by an organization, is coercive power: This power is based on the authority and ability to use punishment on others. Examples include giving reprimands, issuing letters of termination, handing out demotions and the like. These actions are usually for noncompliance with orders or directives.

Two other types of power are not granted by the organization, but are usually acquired from within the character of an individual. These two are expert power and referent power. Expert power is derived from some special ability, skills, or knowledge exhibited by the individual. And, while training and development may be offered by the organization, it is still up to the individual to develop expertise over time. This requires discipline and purpose. The second type of power, not necessarily granted by the organization is referent power, which is based on a certain appeal or attractiveness of one person to another, or based on a person's connections or relationship with another powerful individual. Relationships and reputations are developed over time and are fragile. They must be nurtured in order to yield the right type of power appropriately. People of strong moral courage and good character acquire these last two types of power because of their stewardship attitudes and the accompanying trust, which accrues, to them because of this.

So, executive stewardship blends the classical management functions of planning, organizing, commanding, coordinating, and controlling with the classical leadership functions of motivating employees, influencing employees to perform, forming effective groups, and working with and through people to improve job performance. An executive steward is a person who engages both hemispheres of their brain to creatively lead when appropriate and to exercise control when appropriate choosing both leadership and management skills when appropriate.

The real measure of executive stewardship is a person's judicious use of authority, responsibility and accountability. Authority, which is the power or right to command and allocate resources may be delegated and implies an executive strategy. Responsibility, which is an obligation to account for the achievement of goals, the efficient use of resources, and the adherence to organizational plans, procedures, and rules may be shared, but not delegated and implies a stewardship strategy. Accountability, which is the reporting of what took place, implies an obligation, liability, or responsibility and implies a stewardship role and like responsibility is character based.

Again, executive stewardship is the ability to manage or lead appropriately by creating a balance between management skills and leadership skills while exercising authority, responsibility and accountability effectively.

The benefits of accepting responsibility far outweigh the short-lived advantages of refusing to do so. No one makes anyone's life better by avoiding responsibility. In fact, irresponsibility can be a form of self-imposed servitude to circumstances and other people—a "losers limp" victim mentality easily develops and that person continually looks for someone or something to blame for the outcome of things they don't like. Or in some cases responsibility (or blame) may be shifted to other people for the selfish gain of an individual in power.

Responsibility is a matter of character, which sometimes requires us to do things that are unpleasant or even frightening. Responsibility is primarily about our ability to positively respond to circumstances, to choose the attitudes and habits of thought, which lead to actions and reactions that shape our lives in a more desirable direction over time. It is a concept of power that puts us in control of making choices, which ultimately lead to our destiny. The full impact of this can only be understood and appreciated when we begin to be accountable, responsible and self-reliant. Responsible people not only depend on themselves, but also show others that they can be depended on. This breeds trust, and trust is a key that opens many doors to be able to lead people both by example and in formal leadership roles.

Good leaders handle trust responsibly, while evil or poor leaders may handle trust irresponsibly and indeed may deceive and violate trust. Character determines if an individual will be trustworthy or not and therefore responsible or not. That is why I say leadership, and for that matter, management is a matter of character. Therefore the concept of executive stewardship also implies character as well as competence and courage.

Let's look back down through history at some of the known evil leaders. For example, Hitler, during the middle part of the last century, was a very evil, powerful leader in one sense in that he told a lie early enough and often enough that people soon began to believe the lie for the truth and was able to lead a nation to do some great atrocities. The values that he chose to form his character determined a direction where he exerted his influence for leadership to spark a world war with the forces of evil battling against the forces of good. On the other hand, history is also completed with any number of individuals who are of a good character, a good leadership role model.

Today we find ourselves, in our modern day global society, and definitely here in the United States of America with questions of character where ethics come to bear. Are you going to use your character in a high ethical manner to provide leadership in a very positive and a very good direction that's going to benefit individuals or are you going to be of a shady character that you're going to exert your influence and/or leadership to accomplish some things that may not be of the highest ethical methods? So there's where I say leadership and management, indeed executive stewardship really does start with character. Now this is not to say that there are perfect individuals out there, for we all know that there are none. So everyone has, to use an old trite expression, "feet of clay." However, most of us would try very hard to always be very ethical in what we do, and try to exert our energy and our influence and our leadership to do things that are positive and things that are correct, things that are effective, meaning things that are right.

Wright

So, how do you define leadership?

Hooper

Well, I don't think that there is a commonly accepted good definition for it, but I'm going to give you one. But it's probably just in line with a thousand others. One of the co-authors of this anthology, I believe, said you couldn't define leadership because there are so many different definitions to it. But to me, at its root, leadership is the ability to exert influence over yourself and/or others to accomplish something worthwhile.

Wright

What examples have you seen of leadership being exhibited in informal rather than formal roles?

Hooper

Well, I think that first of all you have to understand that at any given time anyone can be a leader and that at any given time people who are leaders are also followers. And of course, there are formal leadership roles as well as informal leadership roles and in any situation, whether you're in a formal role or an informal role, the opportunity to lead informally presents itself. But I've seen even children lead adults because under the basic definition of leadership they had brought to bear some influence to cause someone to do something that is worthwhile. Now, perhaps a child can see something through their eyes that we, due to our conditioning, and our experience, just have overlooked and yet it's right there in front of us. So having been an educator for 30 + years, 33 years, 25 years as a school superintendent, there were many instances where I would see young people of any age bringing to bear good influence for some worthwhile things, and then that episode passed. So just on an episode-by-episode basis, I came to understand a definition of leadership, which is the ability to bring influence to cause people to do something. Hopefully something worthwhile.

Wright

So if you were making a speech this month to graduates of college level, or for that matter graduates of the high school level, what would you tell them that it takes to be a leader?

Hooper

I think what it takes to be a leader is to certainly understand who you are and who you are not, but to place no limits on your own thinking and your own capabilities, not to be an individual who's so puffed up with your own importance, but an individual who realizes that there are opportunities to serve. When you see those opportunities, when you see that there is a need, when anybody can say or do something, yet nobody decides to do it, and somebody should do it, you need to be that somebody. You need to be that individual who is courageous enough to emerge with the thought, and with the idea, and express it because you never know when someone else is just sitting there saying, "Why doesn't someone say something?" You be that someone.

Wright

What do you think is the best, leadership or management?

Hooper

Well in the concept of executive stewardship, you have to look at the situation to asses what is needed at the time. Do you need to lead? If so, lead. And that's usually as in the situation where people are involved. Or do you need to manage, which is the situation where there are some resources other than human resources that need to be wisely used. Also there is the implication of stewardship for taking care of someone else's material in a good manner. So you're asking me what's the best, leadership or management. That depends on whether you are presenting me with something where I'm going to need to deal with people and I'm going to need to get people to do something. If so, then leadership is better than management. And let me give you an example of what I'm talking about. I know of an administrator one time that was elevated to a position of an area superintendent. And in that role, they were so concerned about employees taking advantage of the system that they've sent out an e-mail that if you're going to be gone from your workstation more than 45 minutes, e-mail me and tell me where and why. Now you see that's an example of management because that's an example of control.

Wright

Right.

Hooper

In this case, the use of management is a total abuse of discretion. It's a total abuse of power, and it treats the direct reports as individuals who cannot be trusted. In my opinion, a leader would have not even worried about that. A leader would have trusted that if you collectively have a clarifying vision, you've set goals and developed the plans to go and accomplish those goals and you're going to receive regular reports back of the progress; you don't need to know where people are every 45 minutes. It might be okay if they had a cup of coffee or that they went to get a haircut or to run a personal errand and get their mind cleared of that because you know we all have the same 24 hours and people do have families, and they do have other things going on in their lives, so they've got to attend to their needs before they can be able to attend to your needs. And when you're in a leadership role or position, sometimes you're strong and sometimes you are weak, and sometimes you've got to regain your strength through taking care of some other types of needs. And in the process, I have seen employees come up with some of the most creative ideas that you could possibly imagine because they were outside their normal setting. And then when you get into creativity, you get into innovation, it's the piecing together of things that don't seem to be related whatsoever that sometimes creates the most creative approach.

So that's an example of someone trying to manage people rather than to lead people. Now if it were a situation to where you had some limited resources, say for example we have 100 reams of paper to finish the school year, and so I need to know that your use of paper is for the highest priority. Here are some priorities we think paper should be used for. If you need to use paper outside that priority, contact me and let's discuss it. You see, that's an example there where you are managing, but you're also leading in the management process. So it's a resource, i.e. in this case paper, that would need to be managed, but the individuals who are using that don't need to have their creativity, their innovative spirit, their work spirit stifled because you've focused too much on that resource. And so that is why I say you have to lead or you have to manage depending upon the situation.

Wright

My mother retired from the school system in Tennessee after many years and I got to watch as a very young boy for years and years the administrations of several different schools. And I was always fascinated with the politics of all of it. Where does politics fit in with leadership?

Hooper

Well, clearly it fits in. I always told my university classes that it takes at least three people to have politics, and let me discuss this concept of three here for just a moment. If you have two people, they can either agree or disagree and they are either going to get along together or they're not going to get along together or they will kind of negotiate their way through what they need to do. And one is as equal to the other unless there is a clearly dominate role or some other arrangement that one is, by agreement, going to set aside and subordinate their thoughts, their feelings, their concerns, or reactions to the other. But when you get three people together, you begin to get little jealousies and you begin to see some elements of power develop that don't exist in a twosome because any two people can get together and decide to go against the third person. And in fact, when there are three people, especially if they are all somewhat equal in position power, and resource power, and character power, and charismatic power, on any given situation they're not all going to see things exactly alike. So one might determine that they could influence the other against the third, and that little triangle can morph and change over time depending on different situations. That's why I say that the magic minimum for politics is three. Now, if you move beyond that to where now you have four people or five people based on the permutations and combinations makes mathematically understand to be much greater and much different. So whenever you find yourself in a situation where there are at least three people, politics at that moment exist.

Wright

So politics is always going to be a part of that.

Hooper

It's always going to be a part of it. And then what you have to note is whether or not this person who is in a leadership role, who begins to exert influence can have influence over a significant number of people to reach the required number for a go ahead. Sometimes that's a simple majority and sometimes that's a two-thirds majority.

Wright

How do you know when it's time for a leadership change in formal leadership roles?

Hooper

Well, that's a really tough question to answer. First of all, my basic philosophy is that any leader should be the first to determine it, meaning that they should have their senses so attuned to those individuals who they have the privilege to lead, that they can simply know, and they should take themselves out rather than waiting for some other outside force. Now that would be true in most instances. It's not true in every case. For example, when by rule of government you have an individual who's either elected or appointed in that formal role and has a term that they were appointed for or elected for, they need to serve out that entire term, and they need to exert that leadership in whatever ways that they are capable of doing during the entire term. Because the way our form of government works, to use an old expression and I wish I could remember who said it and I don't, perhaps you do, "The mills of the gods grind exceeding slow but they grind exceedingly fine."

Wright

I've forgotten as well.

Hooper

Yes, but almost all of us understand what I'm talking about. For example any president of the United States whether they serve a four year term, or if they are elected to serve two terms and it's eight years, has their time during history to make a leadership impact whether the majority of people by the time that their term was midway to half over, liked it or not.

Wright

Well, we're in a situation now where the president finds himself like all presidents before him, you go halfway through your term and then you have to almost quit governing and start politicking again to be elected for the second term. It's kind of a futile situation for the presidents, is it not?

Hooper

Well, in a way it is, and with the way it is for the President of the United States, that's exactly true. But let's look also at say Churchill during World War II. He was a leader whose time came public, and England needed him. The world needed him. The United States needed him. And he exerted his influence very capably through his time and while his entire early career prepared him for that time, his ability to continue to serve effectively passed. And when that time passed, people didn't desire his leadership and his leadership style so it was time for a change because the crisis for which he was needed had passed. Now, I don't remember whether Churchill was removed by the processes that unfold in their proper timeframes or whether he stepped down or exactly what, but let me say that his highest and best time for leadership had passed. Let's also examine a CEO of a company or let's take a school superintendent, a school principle, a minister, anyone serving in those various formal leadership role capacities where it's not as crucial to the outcome of the country like the President of the United States or Prime Minister of Great Britain or something of that nature, and let's just talk about that for a moment. I know in my own situation as a superintendent of schools, I would see superintendents take jobs and leave jobs at various times for various reasons.

Sometimes under their own power and motivation and sometimes they were asked to leave. And that's the context in which I'm saying that a minister or a CEO of a company or in the case of the superintendent of schools, CEO of that educational enterprise, they need to

have their senses so tuned to the needs of those whom they are privileged to lead that they do not exceed a useful term in that role. Many
times their appointments are a rolling term. For example, you may
have a five year contract that's annually renewable, so you always
have five years out in front of you, and maybe you stay in that role
10, 12, 15 years, you're going to reach a point in time that your ability
to influence wanes.

So therefore, your leadership capacity and capability in that setting wanes, and that's what I mean by you should have your senses so
in tune that you measure that. You may want to benchmark it with a
few trusted confidants. And then you have also the leadership, the
character, and the courage to take yourself out of that situation. Put
yourself in a new situation where you can be more effective again. So
I just think it needs to be freshened up from time to time. So in the
presidency of the United States, we do that with four-year terms. In
governorships we do it with a certain number of terms, same thing
with senators, House of Representatives, that sort of thing. I'm not
necessarily saying term limitation; I'm not trying to get into that political philosophy here. But what I am trying to say though is that
power comes with leadership, and one of the most difficult things for
people to handle is power.

Wright

Right.

Hooper

So you can be in a role and keep yourself in that role well beyond
the time you should actually be in that role to be the most effective
for the people you're trying to lead. A prime example of that could be
a dictator or even a career politician whose constituency is disenfran-
chised and lets the inertia of the incumbency leave that person in
power too long and for whatever number of reasons they don't remove
them or they don't remove themselves, then the situation becomes
stagnant.

Wright

That's really interesting to me. I hope you can give us some insight
on that. Is it possible to only lead yourself? Or just what exactly is
personal leadership?

Hooper

Well, personal leadership is the most difficult leadership. And the reason is because there's always going to be a gap in our know-how and our do-how. In other words, we may know what we should do, but we cannot make ourselves do it. Or we don't make ourselves do it.

Wright

You must be talking about my weight.

Hooper

Ah, that's the example that comes frequently and quickly to each of our minds. It could be what we eat, what we do as a hobby, or you know anything that we over do. Yet at the same time, I may be an overweight doctor, but you come to me for health advice, and I give you that advice and exert influence over you in ways that you, because I'm a figure on authority, will follow what I say even though I won't follow what I say. So I think personal leadership is very difficult thing, but it's also at the very heart of what true leadership is all about. For example, back to the concept of character, you know we said that you had to have character and then you have to have some confidence, and you have to have some courage. The deepest innermost thoughts that we have, and the things that we allow into our mind to guide and steer our own deep personal thoughts which are the development of our character makes personal leadership one of the most difficult ones. You can fool some of the people all the time, all the people some of the time, but you can't fool anybody all the time. And the first person we try to fool is ourselves, and yet when we're very, very honest, we can't fool ourselves. Unfortunately that's so. Personal leadership is important. The same things are there about influence and the way you influence yourself is the environment you place yourself in, the material that you allow yourself to be exposed to, the things that your mind is fed with or not fed with, your own personal practice, the habits that we develop, all of those come to bear in personal leadership. And so personal leadership is very, very important, and truly the best public leaders that we know of over time leads themselves first and probably are the hardest on themselves and need to be.

Wright

Well, what an interesting conversation. I've learned a lot about leadership. It's always been a fascinating topic for me anyway. Today we've been talking to Don W. Hooper, PhD., who is the CEO of the Center for Quality Leadership in Sugar Land, Texas, and as we have found out today, knows a lot about this leadership thing. Don, thank you so much for taking this much of your time to talk to us on *Leadership Defined*.

Hooper

Certainly, David, I enjoyed it.

About The Author

The Center For Quality Leadership (CQL) is a consulting firm engaged in a broad range of services for public and private entities including management and performance reviews, organizational studies, program design/delivery services and leadership development training. *CQL* is committed to assisting clients with the planning required to focus available resources on effective performance. Clients include school districts, private companies, law firms, charter schools and associations.

Dr. Hooper, its founder, has over 33 years of experience in public education including serving 25 years as superintendent of schools. He was named as Texas Superintendent of the Year in 1995.

Don W. Hooper, Ph.D.

President

The Center for Quality Leadership, Inc.

75 The Oval Street

Sugar Land, Texas 77479

FAX: 281.265.9773

Email: dhooper@CQL.net

www.CQL.net

Chapter 20

PATRICIA BALL, CSP, CPAE

THE INTERVIEW

David E. Wright (Wright)

Patricia is a CSP and CPAE. She is president of Corporation Communications. She served as president of the National Speakers Association and served as International President of the International Federation for Professional Speakers. Patricia is a Certified Speaking Professional, communication specialist, a keynoter, diversity trainer, author, and presentation skills coach. A graduate of Washington University, she has been on the lecture platform since 1972, speaking nationally and internationally. Patricia has helped thousands of executives, sales people, and others achieve greater success in their personal and professional lives through the dramatic impact of her workshops and lectures. In 1994, she was inducted into the Council of Peers Award For Excellence Hall of Fame, the Oscar of the speaking profession. Less than 120 people worldwide have received this honor, and only 25 women have received this award. Patricia has received intensive training in diversity and gender issues from the Copeland Griggs Institute in California. Patricia Ball, welcome to *Leadership Defined*!

Patricia Ball (Ball)

Thank you. It's great to be here.

Wright

Patricia, your credentials are incredible. Will you tell our readers a little bit about your background, and how you chose the speaking and training industry?

Ball

The speaking and training industry actually chose me. I began as a dance instructor, many years ago. I had my own dance studio at age 16, my first leadership role, and had 14 years of dance training by then. I ran the dance studio for three years, two of which were during my first two years of college at Washington University. Then, while in college, and thereafter, I studied communications, speech and theater. After college I became a professional actor doing commercials and one-woman shows and plays. About 10 years after doing all of that, I put together a series of one-woman shows, because I felt it was very important to be able to control my own destiny. In a sense, I was doing my own casting, instead of waiting for the phone to ring. In 1972, I was selected to be in a speakers' showcase, even though what I did at that time was acting. I took some pieces from my theatrical one-woman shows and showcased them. A meeting planner came up afterwards and was very complimentary. He said I was talented and he enjoyed the showcase. He would like for me to speak to his employees, but they were interested in not only entertainment, but they wanted to know what I could do to help them learn. Of course, I do have a degree in communications and theater and speech. So, I told him that I could put together a communications program for his company. He was excited about that. I was equally excited because I could see the vision and the new direction toward which that was leading me. This is how my speaking and training career began, and I have been at it ever since.

Wright

And doing it very well, I might add.

Ball

Thank you very much.

Wright

I've watched your successful career for many years. You've trained leadership groups, and you've led your own company. Looking at leadership issues from both sides, what do most executives struggle with in their quest for becoming better leaders?

Ball

Really, it boils down to the field in which I teach, communications. It boils down to the executive making an appropriate connection with people. Many executives I've been in contact with lack a strong dose of empathy. They do everything they think is right, but they lack that connective tissue, that ability to put yourself in the other person's shoes, to read between the lines, read what's not being said. So to me, one of the most important attributes of the leader is empathy and good communication skills, understanding executive communications between them and their employees.

Wright

The focus of your presentations seems to be communications. Since great leaders say that communication is such a vital part of leadership, how would you suggest people in leadership positions hone their communication skills?

Ball

First of all, I'm a strong believer in hands-on training, reading communications books, attending seminars, and getting private coaching, if necessary. I am a presentation skills coach and I firmly believe being able to present effectively is necessary for executives. Being able to speak well is such an important business skill. Then, after studying, you need to practice it. You need to think about your audience members, which, in the case of the leader, are the customers and employees with whom they come in contact. If you can figure out the customers' needs and wants and you understand the needs and wants of your organization, if you can mesh those together, you will be a very effective leader. Leaders need to learn the skills of listening. Listening is one of the most important skills. A lot of leaders know how to speak well, but they don't know how to listen well. They need to learn how to use silence. They know how to put words together, but silence is a wonderful technique. Being silent allows you to hear what the other person has to say. People are afraid of silence, so they will rush in to fill in the space, which, in turn, gives you additional information. You need to be able to read non-verbal clues, or what the other person is saying that they may not be putting into words. You need to be sensitive to the needs of other people. You need to be a good questioner as well as a good listener. You certainly need to be knowledgeable about your field, your products, your services, and people in general. A lot of skills that are necessary there.

Wright

Someone told me recently that the end result of most communication is misunderstanding. When I asked him why, he said that people don't communicate anymore. They just take turns talking.

Ball

My daughter once said something that was profound. Of course, we all have profound daughters and sons sometimes, don't we? But she said, "What did you say, Mom? I didn't hear you because I had my answer running." Isn't that true of so many of us?

Wright

I've done that before.

Ball

Truly, we're thinking about what we're going to say next, and therefore, we don't hear what has been said to us. Effective listening is *re*acting to what's going on around you and to what the other person has said.

Wright

You're the author of *Straight Talk Is More than Words, Persuasive Communications: The Key to Achieving Your Goals.* Could you tell our readers a little bit about the book, and why you wrote it?

Ball

I'll answer the second part of that question first, if I may. I wrote the book because I have a fascination with straight talk. In my opinion, *straight* talk means *power communications. Power* is a fascinating word. It has both negative meanings and positive meanings. It can mean manipulation and control, some of the negative kinds of things that we think of when we think of power. In my book, I only use it in a positive way. I tried to think of all the ways in which it's important for us to communicate effectively with other people, or be a straight talker. The premise of the book is based on an analogy of a play. I start out with the Shakespeare quote, "All the world's a stage. All the men and women are merely players. They have their exits and entrances, and one man in his time plays many parts," I believe that's true. I think that we are continually playing a part. We are a different person as a leader than we are perhaps in our personal life, than we are with our children, than we are with our friends. Many of the same traits may still be there. When I say playing a role, I don't mean acting; I mean using some of the communication skills in my book. The first thing that I explore in the book is understanding yourself. This gets into some inner or internal tools of power, some inner kinds of strength. Then, I discuss some external tools of power and that looks at necessary verbal skills, non-verbal skills, behavioral skills, and understanding the other gender. That's certainly an important tool in today's world. I also look at conflict situations, understanding meetings, and how to get the most out of meetings, and how to be more persuasive in meetings. I have four chapters— that's a lot of chapters in the book—on speaking skills, because I believe it's such an important business skill. Not only does it give you exposure, but it also gives you confidence that carries over into other areas of your life. And then finally, the final couple of chapters have to do with image and dress, or what I call the dress rehearsal, which is putting it all together and making it work for you.

Wright

In your book, you write about the problem of misunderstandings between genders. If you were advising the leader of a company or an organization, how would you suggest this problem be addressed to ensure better communication between men and women?

Ball

It's important to understand men and women are indeed different from each other. For a long time we tried to pretend we were all the same, and it didn't matter as long as you treated everybody the same. That approach simply doesn't work in today's world. A good leader will learn to recognize and respect the other gender's style because there are communication style differences. In a sense, the leader needs to become an androgynous manager. He or she should use the strength that works best in any given situation. For example, if you're a woman dealing with a man, speaking of verbal skills, men are often better at statistics. They are more interested in succinct direct talk that cuts to the chase. Knowing that is the preferred communication style of men, if you adapt that style when you're dealing with them, you'll be more effective. It doesn't mean you become a man. All it means is that you begin to use what works best in the given situation. You might end up using a traditionally female style in one situation, and a traditionally male style in another situation.

Wright

Sometimes my wife comes in and says things like, "Guess who I saw today?" And I'll say, "Who did you see?" And she says, "Well, I was walking down the hall there at the mall, and I was wearing my red dress..." And I'm thinking, "Get to the point!"

Ball

Women often do waffle or elaborate about the point. Many women don't get directly to it. This is where we need to be very careful. You can't stereotype and you can't generalize. When I say women do this and men do this, I certainly don't mean all women or all men. There are many exceptions across the board. But patterns of behavior do exist. If we can learn to recognize those patterns, it can be beneficial.

Wright

That is right. You know many people use the terms management and leadership interchangeably. Do you think there's a difference between the two? If so, could you point out some of the differences for us?

Ball

I believe there's a very strong difference. Years ago, I read an article from *The Harvard Business Review* by a professor from Harvard. He felt that the two words were not interchangeable. I don't necessarily agree. If business managers fail to consider the importance of leadership dynamics, then all they end up doing is managing "things" and people, but they will not be taking the group anywhere. Managers need more leadership skills than management skills. You can hire a manager, but you need leadership skills. I think the most important trait that differentiates leaders from managers, is vision. Leaders have long-range goals and vision, and they know how to empower others to follow that vision and those goals. Managers have the job of putting all the resources at hand—people and materials, etc.— together to achieve those long-range goals and develop a system that will help achieve them. Another example is managers often manage things. Leaders manage people.

Wright

Patricia, you have written extensively about diversity in the work place. A few years ago, diversity meant black and white. Today every conceivable culture is a part of America's workforce. I would think that leaders would need to understand diversity issues. So, where do they go to get this information?

Ball

I have a number of books in my library, and I pulled a few that I thought would be good sources for the person beginning to be extremely interested in diversity. One is called, *Beyond Race and Gender* and it's by R. Roosevelt Thomas. It's an excellent book. Then, there's another called *Bridging Cultural Barriers for Corporate Success,* by Saundra Thiederman, Ph.D. Another example is, *The Diversity Advantage,* by Lenora Billings-Harris. And finally, Catherine Fyock has written a book called; *America's Workforce Is Coming of Age.* This one has to do with the aging workforce in America, but it's also very interesting and relevant. Any of these would be an excellent start for anyone who doesn't have a beginning knowledge of diversity. I think what's more important than what diversity is, is what it is not, because you pointed out one of the most important factors. People sometimes think of diversity as being a black and white issue or a race and gender issue. It is not that. It is about respecting all differences and that can mean age, physical disabilities, flex time, lifestyle related concerns, and sexual orientation. It's not about the exclusion of white males. That's another misconception. It used to be in the workplace that the white male was expected to understand and respect everybody else, but when you think about it, the white male is part of that diversity. Certainly a 55-year-old white male manager, for example, has different needs and wants of a 30-year-old white male manager. You need to understand and respect those differences and be able to deal with them. It's really about creating a culture that enables all employees to contribute their full potential. It's not about focusing on differences of groups. It *is* about a diversity of ideas and human potential. Here's a definition that works for me: Diversity is the full utilization of all human resource potential.

Wright

That is great.

Ball

There's an outdated approach that no longer works, and people are still using this approach, but it doesn't work. It used to be years and years ago, that managers felt people needed to be assimilated into the workplace into the main stream. We all needed to be like everybody else. That was the era when women looked like men. They wore the male ties and the male looking suits. Now the approach is to respect and understand all differences. People are coming into the workplace and they're saying, "Yes, I want to work with you towards your goal. I'm excited about it, but I want you to respect and understand the differences I bring to the workplace." So it's a totally different arena, and the effective manager will work to understand those differences.

I will give you a couple of examples. If you were a manager and had an Asian male working for you and were considering him for a promotion, if he were a traditional Asian male (This is where you need to be careful about stereotyping. You need to understand, pay attention and observe, so that you don't make a mistake that way.), typically he will not want to tout his own abilities. He will not want to talk to you about his excellent traits. He will talk about the fact that his team did this, and his division did that. You need to be an astute manager to be able to read between the lines and figure out what *he* personally contributed to the team and to the division.

If you had an Indian woman, for example, who worked in your office and she drew a design of a widget (assuming you made widgets) and you held up that design in the office and said, "Isn't it wonderful? Look what she did!" Typically, if she were raised in the traditional Indian culture, this would be a poor way to deal with the situation, because she would be embarrassed by the attention. She might not come back to work the next day. She might even quit. In the Indian culture, it's not appropriate to have attention brought to yourself in that manner.

So a manager would need to know that. A better way of dealing with that particular scenario would be to write up a nice letter to go in her file, so that when promotion time came around, that would be taken into consideration. Diversity is a very complex kind of thing where a great deal of knowledge is needed. And diversity, of course, goes to thinking globally as well. During my presidential year in the National Speakers Association, I was extremely proud of the fact that a vision of mine—one that I had as long as I can remember—came to pass. We formed the International Federation for Professional Speakers during my presidential year of National Speakers Association. I have long felt that the world's a very small place and the world can learn from professional speakers around the globe. So that's another part of diversity.

Wright

It's far reaching, a lot farther reaching than you suspect on the surface. Most of the successful leaders I've interviewed tell me that they could not have made it without the help of others. Who in your life has been a mentor to you and helped you to become a successful leader?

Ball

That's an excellent question, and there are many, many people. But the first one that comes to mind is my dad. He was an encourager from as far back as I can remember. I think I mentioned to you, earlier in the interview, that I started dance lessons at age two. In his mind and he said this to everyone that he met, I was the most fantastic dancer that had ever existed on the earth. He constantly promoted my abilities. If there was something I couldn't do, he never let me believe that I was incapable of doing it or that it wasn't within my grasp if I wanted it badly enough. He has helped me in every way throughout my life to reach my full potential. Another one that comes to mind is my husband of more years that I care to mention here. Because of his background, he has been tremendously helpful in my career as well as in my life. He is a psychologist, Dr. Kenneth Ball. He was also president of a successful international company for 16 years.

So of course, those two skills, practical management as well as theoretical, were very helpful to me in my Presidential year of National Speakers Association, in my work, and in my life. I had a challenging year as President of National Speakers Association. I inherited a Board that was divided and filled with outspoken personalities. The Executive Vice President resigned the day before our first out-of-country conference held in Bermuda. And as a leader, I had to learn some very important skills. I had to find somebody to take the place of the Executive Vice President very quickly, and I did. I also learned that I had to communicate to many different kinds of groups. Once again there's that word. It was important for me to bring the past presidents in and have meetings with them, so they understood the dynamics of what was happening. Of course, we met with the Board a number of times and with the NSA staff, so that they didn't feel left adrift. There were many things that happened, and it turns out that the National Speakers Association is going in an excellent direction these days.

The last person that comes to mind that acted as a mentor to me was the founder of the National Speakers Association, Cavett Robert. He is no longer living. He passed away about two years ago. He made you believe that anyone who had done anything at all could be phenomenally successful. I was excited by his vision of what the National Speakers Association and the speaking profession could become. I was excited about how he connected with speakers in the organization and got other people excited. That's my definition of a leader. He had a vision. He had a goal. He was able to get people to follow that vision and goal. He talked about having a bigger pie. Rather than everybody getting a piece of the pie, we just needed to make a bigger pie. I was also flattered because—this is sort of amusing sideline—he used to call me "Wonder Woman." I had a passing resemblance to the woman that played Wonder Woman years ago, Linda Carter. Every time he saw me, he said, "Here comes Wonder Woman!"

Wright

He was a fine man. He encouraged me years ago, and I'll never forget him for doing that. We feel that leaders seem to believe in themselves. They seem to draw from some inner strength that others seem to either lack or not use properly. You have written extensively about inner strength. Will you tell our readers how to develop and use inner strength?

Ball

I believe it is something that develops over a long time. It has to do with self-esteem. My definition of self-esteem is simply liking yourself, accepting yourself for who and what you are at that moment in time. Self-esteem comes about not only through positive experiences, but also in being able to handle failure, learning from those failures and being strengthened by them. It also has to do with a strong development of understanding ourselves and realistically judging ourselves, whether experiencing success or failure. It is being honest with ourselves about our performance. When I have an excellent program, it's not necessarily the audience that tells me I was excellent, although it is frequently. When I have a program that I don't think is up to my usual standards, it's not necessarily the audience that tells me that either. I know within myself, when I'm doing the best I can to the best of my ability and when I'm not. That's really what it's about. It's about accepting that failure or challenge to be better and moving forward. It is really about choice. We make choices every day, all day long. We choose to find life a series of problems or exciting challenges. We choose to find people interesting or boring. We choose to be the best-informed, most attractive people we can be, or we choose to give up and blame others. There is a fascinating premise that I talk about sometimes in my programs. It is that the mind—our mind—doesn't really know the difference between truth and fiction. It believes anything we tell it. So if we put a negative thought in there, for example, "You're going to forget everything about this speech. You're not going to remember it. You'll draw a blank." The mind immediately says, "Oh, okay. That's what you want me to do." And it follows the dictate and forgets and draws a blank. So if you constantly feed your mind positive thoughts, like "Yes, I didn't do that as well as I could, but watch this next time!" you will continually move forward. It's a wonderful way to build that inner strength.

Wright

You know our book, *Leadership Defined*, is designed to help people to consider and become better leaders in their work, civic organizations, families, churches, and other endeavors simply because leaders, such as you, took the time to bottom line some of the qualities of leadership. Will you give us some of the characteristics that make leaders great, those things that they seem to have in common?

Ball

There are so many and it's fascinating to read all the books on leadership. Of course, yours is going to be at the top of the list.

Wright

We certainly hope so.

Ball

The first one that I think comes to mind is empathy. Empathy is the ability to connect with people, to read people well and understand people, to have excellent communication skills, and the ability to communicate concerns, and to communicate your vision and your goal. Being able to walk the talk is certainly a significant factor. In other words, being an excellent role model yourself, not just talking about it, but also doing the things that you talk about. Persistence is an important characteristic. Effective leaders that I've known are extremely focused. They are persistent. They are goal oriented. They all have a vision. Many are future oriented. They don't simply observe the now, but they analyze trends and they look to see what that might mean for a future day. They have a great thirst for knowledge. They read everything they can get their hands on. Effective leaders are risk takers. They are not afraid of risks. They will examine what might be the outcome and the consequences of that risk and see how they can reduce the difficulty of taking that risk, but they are risk takers. Most leaders that I know have a consistently positive attitude. That doesn't mean they never get down, but they are constantly thinking positively. They have a strong sense of self, confidence and self worth. And finally, most effective leaders that I know are assertive. That's a word that's gotten a bad rap over the years, because a lot of people think assertiveness means aggressiveness. It doesn't. It simply means standing up for what you think is right.

Wright

My last question goes to your main focus in the speaking and training business. Knowing that communication is so important to be successful, happy, and fulfilled life, could you share with our readers what they can do to be better communicators of their ideas, dreams and goals so that other people will want to help them succeed?

Ball

I think first and foremost they need to focus on becoming excellent listeners, using active listening, paying attention to other people, watching their non-verbal behavior, repeating what the other says, giving them your undying attention, so they feel a sense of self worth. You need to learn to be a good observer. Concentrate on getting your cues from others through their body language, their silence, their tone of voice, their speed of speech, etc. You need to become a straight talker. Take the shortest route to get the message across. Eliminate what I call "waffle words." These are words like "you know," and "whatever." You hear that a lot today. And phrases like, "it's only my opinion," and "I don't know much about this, but." All of those words and phrases rob your speech of power. You need to be brief with your speech. You need to learn to use silence. And finally, you need to use what I call the "speech of positive intent." This means that, if you expect a successful outcome, you'll unconsciously choose straight-talking phrases. You'll choose those correct phrases because you expect to succeed. For example, instead of "I'm only the secretary," you might say, "I'm the administrative assistant and I handle such and such." Instead of using the phrase "I'll have to check on that for you," substitute the phrase "I'll be happy to check on that." I'm sure you can hear the difference. It's a positive phraseology. Being a successful communicator really boils down to continual learning. Never stop learning. Never stop trying new things. Never be discouraged when something doesn't work.

Wright

Well, what an exciting conversation. I learned a lot today, Patricia.

Ball

Thank you for the nice comments.

Wright

I could listen to you all day long. My business would be much better I'm sure. Today we have been talking to Patricia Ball, CSP, CPAE. She is the President of Corporate Communications. She has helped thousands of executives, sales people, and others achieve greater success in their personal and their professional lives through the dramatic impact of her workshops and lectures, and as we have found out today, knows a lot about what she is talking about. Thank you so much, Patricia, for being with us today on *Leadership Defined*.

Ball

It's been my pleasure.

About The Author

PATRICIA BALL, CSP, CPAE, is president of Corporate Communications. She served as a past national president of the National Speakers Association and a past International President of the International Federation for Professional Speakers. Patricia is a Certified Speaking Professional, communications specialist, keynoter, diversity trainer, author, and presentation skills coach. A graduate of Washington University, she has been on the lecture platform since 1972, speaking nationally and internationally. Patricia has helped thousands of executives, salespeople and others achieve greater success in their personal and professional lives through the dramatic impact of her workshops and lectures.

In 1994, she was inducted into the CPAE (Council of Peers Award for Excellence) Speaker Hall of Fame—the "Oscar" of the speaking profession. Less than 120 people worldwide have received this honor, and (in NSA's 26-year history) only 25 women were so recognized with both CSP and CPAE. Patricia has received intensive training in diversity and gender issues from the Copeland Griggs Institute in California.

Her superb talent for customizing programs to meet organizational needs has become her recognized trademark, and has earned her the title of "The Speaker With the Dramatic Impact!" Patricia has a best-selling audio album called Honing Your Presentation Skills, and is the author of the book, Straight Talk Is More Than Words, which deals with how to be more persuasive and convincing.

Patricia Ball, CSP, CPAE

14312 Quiet Meadow Ct. E.

Chesterfield, Missouri 63017

Phone: 314) 514-2455

Email: PatABall@aol.com

Chapter 21

JOANNE G. SUJANSKY, PH.D., CSP

THE INTERVIEW

David E. Wright (Wright)

Today we are talking to Dr. Joanne Sujansky. She has over 25 years of experience helping leaders increase productivity and profitability and inspire loyalty. Joanne has worked with numerous organizations including AT&T Corporation, IBM, and GlaxoSmithKline. She is a leadership expert, an international keynote speaker and founder of KEYGroup, a training and assessment company focused on leadership development. A member of the National Speakers Association, she holds their highest earned designation—Certified Speaking Professional. Joanne is also the author of numerous books on leadership, change, and retention. Joanne, welcome to *Leadership Defined*!

Dr. Joanne Sujansky (Sujansky)

Thank you, David. It's great to talk to you.

Wright

What early experiences helped you to lead?

Sujansky

Well, you know, David, it's very interesting. When I think back, probably as young as seven or eight years old, I honestly remember noticing people and how they made things happen—like looking at people who were in charge and how they got things done. I was fascinated by family members who were "take charge" people. We know that children are curious about things. Although I couldn't have named it at the time, I think I was just very curious about leaders or, as I would have called it then, the people who got things done and took charge. The first time I remember moving into a leadership position was in the fourth grade. My fourth grade teacher was more inviting and more empowering than previous ones; I liked him a lot and felt comfortable trying things. So I started taking on more responsibilities, whereas I remember in the earlier grades, first, second, and third, being somewhat afraid of my teachers, which is pretty sad. But in fourth grade, I started to feel more confident. And I think as a first born in a family that didn't have a lot of money, I somehow knew early that whatever I wanted to be, or whatever I wanted to have, it would be up to me to make it happen. And, so, I was quick to take the lead, quick to take on responsibilities.

Wright

You know I've talked to some of the world's greatest minds on leadership in the last two or three years. You're the only one that's ever gone back that far.

Sujansky

I guess that is going back awhile.

Wright

And I thought perhaps I was crazy because I felt the same way back in those early years. I always wondered why all the other kids looked to me to get things going. And, you know, you do kind of look around and wonder why people don't do what they're supposed to without a little help, you know?

Sujansky

That is right.

Wright

What do you mean by the words "unlock the leader within" when you talk about leadership?

Sujansky

I use the term a lot in my speeches and in my writing because I believe that everyone has more leadership within themselves than they may know or than they may let out. They know it's there and some people just don't use it. And I like to focus on unlocking that potential, sort of unlocking their leadership power and helping them unlock potential in other people.

Wright

So is that something that the individual does rather than something that a teacher or a mentor might do, or can it be a combination of both?

Sujansky

I think it's a combination of both. I think the right environment needs to be created, just like my fourth grade teacher provided the kind of culture that allowed me to step forth. We need other leaders around us who inspire us to pull more from ourselves. Besides the right environment, I think we need to make our own decisions to continually develop ourselves. We may have an improvement or development plan for being better able to do our accounting, our strategic planning or any one of our job tasks. Just the same, if we aspire to leadership positions, we need to be planning ways to grow and develop as leaders.

Wright

So how did you become an expert in leadership?

Sujansky

As I mentioned before, my interest in leadership began early in my life. There were also leadership positions that I held that really had an impact on me. If you can believe this, when I was a senior in college, I was student teaching and completing my senior year, and I was asked to fill a position to manage a dormitory of 400 females. Two hundred of them were involved in sororities and 200 were freshmen. I learned a lot in that job about getting things done through and with others. It was challenging. I also started my business at age 30.

I was president of National Association for Training & Development at 35, probably the youngest national president of the association. So, first, it was my early experiences in leadership, and what I learned from those. For the most part, I am currently dealing with the leadership in organizations in my speaking or consulting. So I am observing and coaching leaders all of the time. Besides my academic studies, I also make it a point to pick up any book or article I see on leadership to challenge myself, to read, and to think. I'll pick up something on TV or in the paper. It's really been my passion. So I think that I work at it. I try to master it.

Wright

I'm fascinated when I read about leadership about the things that others might call funny or even mundane. I remember a man telling me many, many years ago that if you were walking through a field and saw a turtle sitting up on a fence post, you can bet he didn't get up there by himself. And you know, I've thought about that for years and years. It speaks so much to leadership, which leads to my next question. From your experience, what criteria or characteristics help leaders to succeed?

Sujansky

I think that a leader needs to be focused, and I mean beyond figuring out where he or she is going. I mean that day-to-day stuff of watching distractions and really being clear about where you're going and what you are doing. You need to see it in your head. So I think focus is critical. I think really strong leaders don't just create or implement change—they propel change. And I think that is clearly a necessary characteristic. I also think that leaders need to understand differences in people. They invite those differences to the table in their corporations and then they really allow people to use those differences. Amazing things happen because instead of "doing more with less," like most of us have to think about, it ends up as "doing more with more." Those are just some things that come to my mind right away.

Wright

Do you think that there are characteristics that also make up leaders, or do leaders all have the same characteristics?

Sujansky

When I think about really powerful leaders and also those who have been valuable in my life, I see tremendous differences. And you know, David, you hit a hot button with me there because one of the things I think is even at a young age, kids get the idea that a leader is a naturally extroverted person, a real charismatic type. Some are, but some have a very different style, which still attracts followers and allows the job to get done. Leaders need to be focused to propel change by looking ahead and helping people get there and they need to understand the concept of "going slow to go fast" with people. Those are the things you learn and hone. Sure, it helps if you're a little bit smart to begin with because you pick up information quickly, information that you can use. Certainly it helps if you're interpersonally skilled because then people can perhaps trust you more or they learn more about you faster. But I really think that all of us are very different in our leadership styles, and if we're getting the job done and people are respected along the way, we're making the impact in our association and in our corporations that we have to make. I founded KEYGroup 24 years ago. Now Dr. Jan Ferri-Reed runs the day-to-day operation and has for the last few years. I see very big differences in our styles, but I think we're both equally effective as leaders.

Wright

I've talked to one of the most gentle men I've ever talked to who most consider to be a strong leader. He's Truett Cathy, the founder and CEO of Chick-Fil-A, and he doesn't come across to me as a leader that would be screaming and hollering and getting people behind him. I think he leads and people just love him because he's just so kind, and he's so knowledgeable.

Sujansky

You have people who are a little bit more excitable and you also have those who are very quiet, strong and peaceful in their leadership style. The thing to evaluate is, are they getting the job done? Are they making the impact? And as they go along that journey, are people respected and interested in staying with the organization and inspired to be with that leader? You take a look at the leader by taking a look at his or her followers.

Wright

What are a few mistakes that leaders consistently make?

Sujansky

That's an easy question for me because I just wrote an article on the "Seven Mistakes Leaders Make." I will give you a few of those.

Wright

Oh, good!

Sujansky

I think that we don't put enough importance sometimes on building trust. Building trust takes time. It means doing what you tell people you're going to do, keeping confidences, getting a job done, telling employees things first, or telling your family something first before you tell others so that the most important people to be informed are the first to hear it. Developing trust needs to be foremost. I'm not sure enough leaders pay enough early attention to it. I'd also say that there's not enough empowering or enabling others to act. I don't think we do enough to give people the authority and then the support to really get the job done. I think the strongest leaders are people who, in fact, help others act because they can't do it all themselves. They recognize that they can't be doing everything and they trust that they have people who are *able* to get the job done. Strong leaders also recognize that people are only *able* to get the job done when they have the information, the resources, the skills, and the authority to do it. I also think that fun has been removed from the workplace at a lot of places. By that, I mean the ability to celebrate, to bring joy back into the workplace, to really look at any small success and realize that celebration should happen. It doesn't have to be a big party, but it has to be recognition, maybe taking some time to ring some bells and cheer and know that something great just happened. I think leaders forget to celebrate.

Wright

What do employees in corporations expect from their leaders?

Sujansky

My first response is that they expect to be led. When you ask people why they leave, and retention research supports this, almost always one of the top three or four reasons has to do with them feeling that their leadership was not strong enough, honest enough or ethical enough. They want to be led. They want to know that they are involved in an effort where people are clear about where they're going. They want to be part of shaping and sharing that vision, but they do want to be led. I also think that people want to have clear expectations. They want to know what you want from them. I've worked for people that didn't really know what they expected of me. I've occasionally worked for clients who can't define what they want from me. I think people have a need to know and a right to know what's expected of them. They also need feedback. Sometimes we give little feedback to our star performers because we think that the star performer functions without us, but I think everyone needs feedback. It's not just praise I'm talking about; I'm talking about real feedback. Feedback like, "This is where we stand this month," or "As a result of what you did, this happened." People need yardsticks to measure their performance and individual contribution. Regardless of what kind of workplace it is, they want to grow and they want to be marketable. If they come to you and you're the leader, and they don't feel like they're growing or they don't feel like they could get an even better job with you or someone else, I think they feel cheated. I also think that they want a life. They want a balance of personal and work time and this holds you more responsible. The hours that some of my client companies work, it just burns people out. If you strike a work-life balance, you're going to get a higher level of creativity. You're going to get more from people if you understand that they want a life, and if you show them yourself how to have one. Follow worklife balance principles yourself and model what you expect from others. The retention studies that I've conducted, and the others that I have read, suggest that when these things aren't in place, people go away. Sometimes, they even go away to jobs that don't pay as well if other things like worklife balance, promotional opportunity and feedback are there.

Wright

I've got a close friend who has a very responsible job in a large corporation. On occasion we go out to dinner with a group of people, we try to do it once a week. He's always or almost always absent and it's because of his work. He's salaried so he works about 80 hours a week. He's always on call, and I can see the wear and tear on both him and his family. He's in his late 40s and I wonder how long this will go on before he either dies or just gives up on the job.

Sujansky

You're so right about that, David. One of the things I say is that a type "A" personality, that leader who expects constant drive of themselves and of everyone else, needs to understand that they and others do burn out. People become less creative and work becomes drudgery. But I'll say for that real type "A" who says well, we have to get things done, well, fine—just recognize the signals of burnout. You're going to be hiring someone else if this continues. Sometimes I get calls for team building sessions to start at 6:30 or 7:00 a.m. in work places where the work day normally starts at 8:30. So I push for, "Well, why are we doing that?" "We have to fit it in. We have to fit it in." So the day starts earlier, and the day goes later, just to fit it in. When people are at that level and there are no breaks, creativity drops dramatically. Enjoyment of work drops dramatically. So if you can't straighten up for any other reason, straighten up because it's going to hurt productivity, not help it.

Wright

Now that I've got an expert, I've got a question that ... it's not beside the point, but it's just an interest area for me. I once attended a leadership conference many years ago with this national company, a very interesting conference. They were trying to define for us the difference between leaders and followers. And I came away from that three day meeting kind of joyful finding out, at least through their eyes, that there wasn't a lot of difference. And I go back to it when you said people want to be led. The leaders chose leadership, the followers chose to follow, and both liked their jobs.

Sujansky

Right.

Wright

Do you think that's true?

Sujansky

Oh, I do think that's true. I think there's a real skill set to being a follower. I mean, I think that the word itself sometimes conjures up some negative thinking for people, but there are skills to being a follower. First of all, knowing who you should be following, whether it is a community activity or the workplace that we're talking about, you need to select the work that hooks you to a responsible, dynamic leader. Being a follower requires a lot of team skills. And if a leader is doing his or her job right, then the follower has occasional leadership responsibility. It's more of a shared environment when the leadership is really effective. So a good follower still needs to exercise good leadership skills, all those skills we talked about before like being able to propel change, being able to hold the people accountable, coaching others and modeling the behavior you expect from others. So your follower needs some of the same skill sets as the leader, but most importantly, he or she is consciously choosing that role. However, if a person is in a followership role, not ever in charge, not ever responsible, something is wrong with how the leader is leading.

Wright

Well, Paul Myer, who was the founder and CEO of the Success Motivation Institute in Waco, Texas, once told me in the middle '70s, "David, if you think you're a leader and you look around and no one is following you, you're just out for a walk."

Sujansky

Right! That's right.

Wright

So I guess it's important for both leaders and followers to lead. What do you suggest for growing and developing leaders, those of us who really are thinking, "Boy, I've got the qualities and the characteristics, and this might be something I'm interested in."? So how do you just develop these kinds of leadership skills on your own?

Sujansky

I think you said a key word, and that is when a person has "interest" in leadership they usually have the motivation to develop more skills. So I would say to a person wanting to exercise more leadership, look first at your skills set. Get some help in trying to identify where you already might be strong and then put a development plan together to get some of the other things that you need. But interest is primary. For me, I was first curious about leadership, and then I had the motivation to develop the skills. I also think that when someone's in your corporation already, that you might want to look for business assignments that help him or her to develop leadership skill. If I'm interested in leadership and I'm inside the corporation, I need to talk to my boss or some other key players to get the solid leadership experience that I need. I would also look for a mentor formally or informally who could coach me. I would also want to provide some of that coaching and mentoring to other future leaders as well. You know, David, my early examples in my life of leadership, I can clearly remember the autocrats, the people who yelled to get their way. It's sort of disappointing for me to have to tell you that some of my early teachers were like that, the old tales of rulers on the knuckle, or grading artwork or terrifying you to silence. That's really sad to think about, but there is a difference in the style of people who are participative. Participative people typically coach and mentor. Those diehard autocrats don't do that, and they are still out there! So I would say if I'm looking for development for myself, find some mentors. I'd find some people who will coach and work with me.

Wright

Let me go back to something that you said a few minutes ago when you were talking. You said you had just written an article about seven mistakes leaders make. The first was building trust. I mean the examples are rampant especially in the last two or three years where CEOs and people in offices of high authority have not done a really good job in building trust—and have not been trustworthy. I think back to my mother who taught me from a pretty good leadership manual, and she always said that the truth will make you free. Why do people not grasp this simple concept?

Sujansky

Maybe they lose sight of the real reason for what they are doing. You know there is a corporate plan. There's a reason for the existence of that corporation or association or government agency. There's a reason that it's there, and the vision and the mission and everything needs to be shaped around that. And I think that some of these folks lose sight of the corporate goal and abuse the power that they have for what might be personal self gain, ignoring the needs and desires of others. It's a little bit crazy to me how easily this sometimes happens. And although I have been described as a person who's pretty influential and can be charismatic, I know that charisma can be abused because you can influence people and sort of coerce them to do things they shouldn't be doing. That's another reason why followership is so important because we have to keep the leader doing the right thing. The good follower gives the kind of feedback to leaders that says, "I don't think so." And says, "I don't think so" pretty strongly so that the leader is not influenced to go in the wrong direction.

Wright

So our readers who are considering leadership roles and taking on leadership roles, when should they begin? When should their development begin?

Sujansky

I know this may make you chuckle, but I actually did a little leadership course in a preschool environment. And, I've spoken to third through sixth graders, although I'm not a youth group speaker as my primary focus. I'm sure it's clear from the comments I've made already, but I really believe that leadership starts at three or four years of age when kids are in nursery school. Each day each person has a leadership role—David or Joanne is in charge of the mats or deciding the game to be played. Those are really important things to start really early. I have three kids and my youngest one is in sixth grade now. Last year I spoke to her fifth grade class about leadership. I had a ball! So I say as parents, grandparents, aunts, and uncles, whatever we can do early to begin leadership development, make it happen. If I'm already a young adult or a teenager, I would find the experiences in school, church, or community and get feedback from other leaders. David, to ask the question, "How'd I do while I chaired that committee?" is something I think some of us don't think to ask or might be afraid to ask. I ask it constantly. I annoy people, and it's not because I want praise. Actually, at this point in my life, I want correction. I know I can always do better at any time that I hold a leadership role. So I would say if you're trying to develop your leadership skill, take a leadership role. Get some good feedback. Try some things differently. Try new things in an environment that's safe and purposeful, but try new things. We also need to recognize that leadership development needs to start in the home and in the preschool environment when kids understand that we share our toys and everyone has responsibility and accountability.

Wright

Like almost everything else in life, parents sure do have a power over children to teach them leadership skills, don't they?

Sujansky

Sure, and parents are the first leaders that children see. They see who really is in charge of the household. Is this really a shared situation, or does dad tend to make certain decisions and mom makes the other ones? And uh-oh, watch when grandma comes. Everything changes. The kids watch that leadership shift.

Wright

Someone told me recently the reason that grandparents and children get along so well is they have a common enemy.

Sujansky

I think that's probably true.

Wright

What an interesting conversation. Well, I really do appreciate the time that you've spent with us here today, and as always, it's such a pleasure talking to you.

Sujansky

Thank you, David, so much.

Wright

Today we have been talking to Dr. Joanne Sujansky, leadership expert, who has over 25 years experience helping leaders increase growth and profitability by creating and sustaining what she calls a "vibrant entrepreneurial organization." She is a member of the National Speakers Association and she holds their highest earned designation. And even though she didn't say it, I think there are only 300-400 hundred of this team worldwide. Thank you so much for being with us, Joanne.

Sujansky

Thank you, David. Have a great day.

Some Final Thoughts

I believe that one of the key priorities of leaders is to execute a vision in the marketplace so that growth and profitability can be achieved and sustained. For this to happen, organizations must be capable of high performance. High performing organizations consistently out-perform their rivals because a vibrant entrepreneurial character fuels employees to respond to marketplace pressures. I have devoted my professional career to helping leaders create workplaces where people are challenged to grow the business, make it more profitable and to be the best they can be. In these organizations leaders are able to develop and retain people by creating a business environment that:

- Supports and expects high productivity while reducing stress.

This is the opposite of what most businesses are experiencing in the workplace today. Downsizing and the maximization of resources, both human and technical, have created destructive workplace environments where productivity is compromised.

- Encourages and permits loyalty.

People who are loyal proactively look for ways to build and improve their organization's future. Leaders who create trust and the right environment permit loyalty to emerge.

- Enables people to take personal risk and allows them the freedom to be accountable.

Vibrant Entrepreneurial Organizations encourage people to take measured risks so that gains can be made and the vision of the business can be advanced.

- Produces a winning tradition.

Success breeds more success and people who become accustomed to winning want to keep on winning. It is these principles that will propel organizations to the forefront of the competitive marketplace, sustaining long-term growth and profitability.

- Elevates communication to an art form.

Communication goes far beyond sending out emails at the right time or holding employee forums on critical issues (although these tools may well be valuable). It means that leaders make sure that people understand and buy into major change initiatives—after all, real change is voluntary—and that, in turn, employees make their voices heard.

About The Author

Dr. Joanne Sujansky has over 25 years of experience helping leaders increase organizational growth and profitability by creating and sustaining what she calls a "vibrant entrepreneurial organization." Joanne has worked with numerous organizations including AT&T Corporation, IBM, and GlaxoSmithKline. She is an international keynote speaker and founder of KEYGroup, a training and assessment company focused on leadership development. A member of the National Speakers Association, she holds their highest earned designation, Certified Speaking Professional. Joanne is the author of numerous books on leadership, change and retention.

Joanne G. Sujansky, Ph.D., CSP

CEO

KEYGroup

1800 Sainte Claire Plaza

1121 Boyce Road

Pittsburgh, Pennsylvania 15241-3918

Phone: 724.942.7900

Email: jsujansky@keygrp.com

www.joannesujansky.com

www.keygrp.com

Chapter 22

STAN CRAIG

THE INTERVIEW

David E. Wright (Wright)

Today we are speaking with Stan Craig. After 27 years with Merrill Lynch, Stan retired as First Vice President and Senior Director of the Office of Investment Performance. He began his company, Legacy Leadership, in 2001. He is also a partner in PSB Training, training financial professionals in marketing and client service. Stan has spoken around the world for such groups as the Canadian Conference on the Environment, the National Governors Conference, the United Nations Conference on the Environment, and the Social Investment Forum. His leadership presentations include a number of Fortune 500 companies as well as small businesses. Prior to his joining Merrill Lynch, he was a pastor in Canada and Kentucky. He and his wife, Gloria, live in Southport, NC. His new book, *Legacy Leadership; The Four Roles of Legendary Leaders,* will be published next year. Stan, welcome to *Leadership Defined!*

Stan Craig (Craig)

Thank you, David. It's a pleasure to talk with you.

Wright

Stan, your title, *Legacy Leadership, the Four Roles of Legendary Leaders,* is really interesting. But before we go there, let's start with the basics. How would you define leadership?

Craig

A classic definition of a leader is one person influencing others to accomplish a mutually agreed upon goal that satisfies the needs of both the leader and the group. Leadership is the act of leading. Those definitions sound pretty simple, but the actual act of leading is not as simple as it sounds.

Wright

Do you believe, then, that leadership is difficult?

Craig

I do, and the evidence is all around us. We've all watched leaders in every field fail in their leadership responsibilities and waste the human resources that every organization relies on. When leaders fail, it deprives employees, investors and the public of their enthusiasm and trust. As a result, cynicism plagues many corporations, churches and religious institutions, our health care and educational systems, and even non-profit organizations. Recently both the Red Cross and the United Way were involved in scandals.

We look for leaders to inspire and motivate us to become better at what we do. But what we've often found is leaders who are more interested in what they get instead of what they give. There are leaders who act as if the public trust and corporate accounts were personal funds where they could withdraw any amount they chose, with total disregard of the consequences. John Dillinger and Al Capone would be embarrassed to be such small-time crooks compared with the massive theft and dishonesty so prevalent today.

Wright

It seems there is more being written about leaders today than ever before, but very little of it is positive. Why do you think that is?

Craig

We have politicians, few real statesmen. We have well paid CEOs, but there are very few true business leaders. We have ecclesiastical and religious authorities, but not many leading with deep faith and a passionate commitment to the people or the institution they serve.

Wright

So your suggestion to heal this epidemic of leadership failure is the understanding and application of your four roles of legendary leadership?

Craig

I think it's one of the workable responses to the problem. Being a leader is a gift. When you lead a group, an organization or a business, it calls for your very best. You cannot take that responsibility lightly, and you cannot, as Indiana Jones said in *Raiders of the Lost Arc,* "figure it out as you go." That usually leads to moving from one crisis to another. The problem is too many leaders are doing just that. When a person takes a position of responsibility, he or she must become a student of leadership. These four legendary roles have a lot to teach us about leading.

Wright

So tell me about these four legendary roles and where they come from.

Craig

The four legendary roles are Monarch, Warrior, Priest and Servant. Their origins are in our history, legends, and myths. Nearly every culture has examples of leaders who represent the best of each role. The challenge facing each leader is to combine the best in all four. The absence of any one of these roles runs the risk of harming his or her future and placing a dark cloud over the future of the organization.

I have been studying leadership over the last 30 years and learned there is no single leadership style or leadership role that fits every leader or every situation. No matter where I served, in management or sales, churches or civic groups, there was one constant—each leader had different strengths and weaknesses. Some were far more successful than others. But each leader, often without knowing it, took on at least one of these four roles.

In studying historic and contemporary literature on leadership, four distinct roles stand out. While the name varies (visionary, innovator, coach), the roles seem to be consistent. But in all of my research over the years, I could find no uncomplicated and easy-to-recall method to teach leadership. So these roles come from trying to find a simple way to explain and teach what's required to be an effective leader.

Wright

I'm really intrigued. Tell me more about these roles.

Craig

The first is the role of Monarch. That's the king or queen, the person in charge. The strength required of this role is vision. We all grew up with stories of famous kings and queens, King Arthur and Queen Victoria or Queen Elizabeth. In this country our Monarch is our president. Every organization has someone assigned that role—a leader with a vision, a clear concept of what he or she wants to accomplish. This role, the Monarch role, has two responsibilities—decision making and empowering others. This legendary role answers the most significant questions for any organization: "What is our purpose?" "What are we doing?" "Where are we going?" In Louis Carroll's Alice in Wonderland, Alice met the Cheshire cat and she asked, "Which road do I take?" The cat replied, "Where do you want to go?" When Alice answered, "I don't know," the cat replied, "Then it doesn't really matter which road you take."

The Monarch values others in formulating the vision but takes full responsibility for the decisions that are made. Every elected official in every organization assumes this role. We've also seen the weaknesses when this is the only role a leader is willing to assume. Conceit, inability to listen, arrogance, placing blame, and a false sense of self-importance are just a few of the weaknesses that need to be offset by adding the roles of Priest and Servant.

In the ancient history of Israel the people cried out for a king, a visible leader who could fulfill their nation's hopes and dreams. However, the first king, Saul, fell victim to his own weaknesses. He ended with a legacy of shame and dishonor because he didn't exercise the Priest and Servant roles. His successor, King David, learned from Saul's mistakes, but then King David forgot what it meant to be a Servant when his own lust and self-interest took over.

The second legendary role is the role of a Warrior. We grew up hearing the legends of Joan of Arc, Ulysses S. Grant and Dwight Eisenhower, leaders who have shaped our understanding of what it is to take action—even to the point of sacrifice. The Warrior role requires "the strength to act." What value is a vision unless a leader is capable of translating that vision into a plan of action? The Warrior role answers the second question a leader must answer: "How do we get this done?" Every organization wants to know—"What are we going to do? What's the plan?" It's the Warrior role that answers these questions. The characteristics of a Warrior are courage, stamina, and a focus on teamwork. It is a strategic role of loyalty, of commitment, of self sacrifice. But this role has famous flaws as well—bullying, bluster, overconfidence and self-promotion. As Boris Yeltsin said, "You can build a throne of bayonets, but you cannot sit on it."

When you think about a Warrior-leader, coaches come to mind. John Wooden and Lou Holtz, legendary coaches and Warrior-leaders, added the strengths of Servant and Priest to their coaching and are regarded as the very best in their field. Both believed in developing more than athletic ability in their players and organizations, and both sacrificed victories in order to live by the principles they taught. That's far different from the cheating, scandals, and poor behavior, by both coaches and players, seen on and off the field in recent years.

Ironically, the role that is most lived out in the business community is the Warrior role. But Warriors without wisdom, humility and compassion can be a danger to themselves and others. Legacy Leadership completes the Warrior role by adding these often disregarded virtues.

The third role is that of a Priest, a teacher or advocate. This is the role of wisdom, ethics and communication. It's a legendary role that understands history, traditions, beliefs, and the core values of the organization. It can explain clearly and completely why something needs to be done. Answering the "Why?" question is on every leader's agenda. As Nido Qubein, prominent author and speaker, says, "It's more important to know why something must be done than how to do it." When we know why, we can figure out how. The characteristics of this role are strong personal values, honesty, wisdom, integrity, consistency in behavior and an unwavering commitment to truth in speech and action. The shortcomings of this role come from being self-righteous or manipulative, having feelings of superiority, relying on situational ethics instead of holding steadfast the organization's strengths, values and traditions.

Winston Churchill and Franklin Roosevelt remind us of the value we all place on this Priestly role of wisdom, ethics and communication. They used the written and spoken word as no others in our time to make values and traditions worth dying for. They understood that when a leader can answer the "why?" question, individuals and nations can be moved to act with courage and conviction. As Nido said, we can figure out what to do when we understand why we're expected to do it.

The last legendary role is the role of a Servant. This role has the strength of involvement, empathy and compassion. It adds the qualities of patience, encouragement, and humility. One of the major characteristics of the Servant role is the focus on others. This role emphasizes how significant others are in the success of the organization or business and answers another key question that every leader must answer: "Who is going to do this?" Every organization must have an understanding of who is going to take the task to completion. The Servant-leader answers, "Come, let us do this together." The Servant-leader strengthens and encourages others by his or her participation and service. That's what makes these leaders legendary. The weaknesses in this role are fear, timidity, laziness, thoughtlessness, and being judgmental or critical. When you add the qualities of the Monarch and the Warrior, the Servant-leader become much more influential.

Servant-leadership is practiced every day in our communities. Think of all the volunteer hours given in your local community. Think of those who work with little or no pay simply because they want to serve. Business leaders sometimes find it difficult to embrace Servant-leadership and that is a real mistake. Marriott Corporation went from a single root beer stand in Washington D.C. to become one of the largest hotel chains in the world and recently acquired the prestigious Ritz Carlton Hotels. It is a real pleasure to visit one of their properties. One of the things you notice very quickly is that when you make a request the response is always, "It's my pleasure." That's what service is all about—putting the focus where it belongs—on meeting needs of others in a gracious manner. Walt Disney created a whole new business—"Theme Parks," and called his employees "cast members," playing for the applause of their audience. Nearly every guest comments on the service at Disney properties. It has now become legendary.

From automobile companies to telecommunications and leisure industries, we're being told that "this company provides excellent service." It is amazing how significant Servant-leadership is to businesses, and how few leaders are willing to assume the role of Servant.

These four roles—the Monarch, the Warrior, the Priest, and the Servant are legendary roles. They began early in human experience and yet still continue to capture our attention today. What has been missing is linking these roles together into a single model. It is the combination of these roles that balances leadership strength and leadership weakness to create a positive legacy.

Wright

So how do you combine these legendary roles? They seem as though they are opposites in some instances. For example, the Servant-King.

Craig

The King and the Servant do sound as though they are at the opposite ends of the spectrum, but that does not mean conflict. Think of a compass. A compass provides direction and confirmation of a journey with four unique and distinctive points. But it's only when all four points are recognized that the complete picture emerges to point the way. Each of these roles, like the points on a compass, can guide leaders as they chart their course to reach their goals. As the leaders become more familiar with each role, they begin to see how each adds a specific sense of self-correction and guidance. A Servant-King is a very powerful leader—someone who can share a vision, make decisions, and participate with a sense of humility and compassion. A Servant-King does not say, "My way or the highway," but, "Come, let us do this together." That's a powerful kind of leader.

Wright

So what you're saying is that a Legacy Leader must have the attributes reflected in each of these four roles.

Craig

That's exactly right. When you look at the list of leadership failures that we've seen recently, each one can be clearly understood as a failure to fulfill one of those four legendary roles. And if you look at the track record of successful leaders, you're going to find that the combination of all four roles was instrumental in their successes. Just as a compass can help you find your bearings, these four roles point the way back when a leader is off course.

Wright

Can you give me an example of a contemporary leader who corrected his or her course and created a positive legacy?

Craig

I sure can. My wife, Gloria, and I were living in New York when Rudolph Giuliani was mayor. He did not become a Legacy Leader until the end of his term of office. As mayor of the largest city in the United States, he was clearly a Monarch. He shared his vision, made decisions, and empowered others. He also assumed the Warrior role with relish, fighting crime and corruption, as well as taking on the political process. The problem is a Warrior-King can become a tyrant and a bully.

Even when he added the Priestly role, which he sometimes did—communicating to New Yorkers the history traditions and values that their city stood for—he still could have missed a positive legacy. The roles of Monarch-Warrior-Priest can create leaders who act as if they are the only source of truth. Too often those leaders become self-righteous and dictatorial, and that's what happened to Giuliani when he forgot the Servant role. In his second term, he was almost run out of New York. He had alienated his base by his widely publicized affair. When challenged, his response to his wife and supporters was simply to give orders. The police and the public were up in arms over the shooting of apparently innocent victims, and his handling of the torture of a man in police custody (also found to be innocent) caused more problems. His reputation, crafted over years of success, was in tatters.

Giuliani lost the support both of public employees and minorities in New York by ignoring their concerns and refusing their requests to meet with them. The press and public had grown weary of him, his affair and his attitude. He was ending his term and quite possibly his public life as a leader with most of his constituents saying, "Good riddance."

And then on 9-11 all of that changed. On September 11, 2001, Rudolph Giuliani became a Legacy Leader when he took on the legendary role of a Servant. All of a sudden compassion that he never seemed to show, humility that he never displayed became evident. He was moved to servanthood. He was there. He was everywhere. He was tireless and selfless, serving all the citizens of New York. He continually expressed a "Come, let us..." attitude, and he identified with every member of the community. He embraced the role of the Servant and, as he did, he not only found his own way, but led New York in a new way that encouraged and inspired our whole nation. Giuliani left a legacy that's going to be remembered with pride and gratitude by adding the role of Servant when it was most needed.

Wright

I didn't remember all of the history, but he certainly is seen as a Legendary Leader now. Do you have any other examples of Legacy Leaders? What about in the business community? Surely, they are not all negative stories.

Craig

They are not, and that's really good news. There are really more good stories than bad. For every "chainsaw" Al Dunlop of Scott Paper and Ken Lay of Enron there are many positive Legacy Leaders to talk about, both historic and contemporary. David Needum, who founded Jet Blue, and Jim Senegal of Costco are just two of many new leaders who are already creating a positive legacy by putting all four of these roles into play. They both had compelling visions of the kind of businesses they wanted to create. They acted with courage to carry out their visions. No one thought another low-cost airline like Jet Blue could succeed, or that Costco could compete with all the other warehouse stores that followed in its wake. Their leadership invigorated their employees and created loyalty in their customers. Both of these men participate in their organizations at every level.

Wright

Stan, why do you believe there are not more positive stories in the news today?

Craig

I probably sound old fashioned, but I think there are a lot of leaders who are adrift. We're living in a world of Monarchs and Warriors who want the rewards but abdicate responsibility. For Ken Lay to say that he had no idea what was going on in his company suggests that he was either incompetent or incapable of telling the truth. Too many leaders have forgotten the morals, values, and traditions that a Priestly leader relies on and have missed the importance of the Servant role.

What Tom Brokaw called "the greatest generation," (the '40s and '50s) was built on sacrifice and service. But the '60s and '70s brought about a new generation whose motto seemed to be WIFM—"what's in it for me?" In the '80s and the '90s the focus became the acquisition of wealth at all cost. The "get all you can because you deserve it" philosophy is widely-accepted and comes with a high price. Self-interest has won over self-control, and, in some places, has become accepted as a new way of doing things. The idea of "creating shareholder value" became a mask that hid the underlying motive of "feathering my own nest." Most of those people talking about creating shareholder value were officers of the company, the shareholders with the largest positions. When self-gratification, status, and position become more important than service, every organization and every institution suffers without understanding why.

Wright

Many people believe it's always been like that, that nothing has really changed over the years. Has it always been that way?

Craig

When corporations began in this country, they were created to serve the public need. Most of the charters of corporations specify their intention to meet the needs of society.

There have been times when corporations strayed from their charters and this seems to be one of those times. When the stock market began to take off in the mid-'80s, leaders began to talk about leading for the benefit of their shareholders. What was not said was that the benefit to the shareholders sometimes came at the expense of the firm's employees and clients. When the Servant role was laid aside in favor of a new marketing plan or business model created around getting more instead of giving more, corporations began to lose their soul. But some have realized it and are leading their corporations back to their original purpose.

In the mid-1800's Pfizer was created as a chemical company. At the start of the 20th Century it became a healing company. Since that time Pfizer and other companies began to focus on the process and the profit. Today Pfizer's leader, Hank McKinnell, is putting the healing focus back into the heart of the company.

It's difficult to convince the public that your services and products are of value when all you want to discuss is the value of your stock. When the leadership of companies begin to talk about their passion, their vision, their plan of action that will fulfill the company's purpose and values for all the stakeholders, when they roll up their sleeves and make changes on behalf of their clients and employees, then society will pay attention and so will investors. It is quality products and quality service that drive earnings. It is committed employees who believe in what they're doing and the firms' ability to make a difference that creates quality products and service.

Corporations are finally beginning to discover that good corporate governance makes good economic sense. And that's all about having the right leadership in place. The old Warrior model of "follow me; we are going up that hill," or the Monarch model, "we are the biggest and best so pay attention," will not work as it once did. Things have changed and Legacy Leaders get it.

Wright

So what I hear you saying is that the leadership model that many have followed is flawed. Is that right?

Craig

It's not so much flawed as incomplete. A single role is always going to be prone to failure. One of our problems is that most of us never figure out what went wrong with leadership. When the Challenger exploded on its launch, or the Columbia fragmented as it returned to earth, NASA reexamined every aspect of those two shuttles to find the hidden flaw that brought about the failures. When an airplane crashes, the FFA looks at every part to see what caused the failure. Where were the weaknesses? What were the problems? But when leaders fail, whether it's in the church or in the corporate world, we simply put it down as an individual mistake. That's wrong. The problem is a failure of leadership and we need to understand why the leadership compass was so off the mark. The weakness, that hidden flaw, ought to have been detected far before the leader crashed.

The whole concept of Legacy Leadership is not that leaders won't get off course. Leaders will make mistakes, but they can and must be corrected. This model implies self-correction, but it also gives boards and directors a means to review a leader's behavior. As we understand the Legendary roles, we also begin to get the picture of where strengths and weaknesses lie. And the paradox here is that a really strong leader admits his or her weaknesses.

Wright

Can you be more specific?

Craig

Recently a friend told me about a leader who is doing an excellent job of building a travel business from scratch. My friend said, "One of Lloyd's strengths is that he knows his weaknesses and he's found others who have the strength he's lacking to make his leadership and the company strong." That's a Legacy Leader—one who can admit limitations and find others whose strengths compensate.

Too frequently leaders will not admit their weaknesses and that makes them even weaker. Legacy Leaders understand their limitations and work to correct them or add someone to the team with the strength they lack. This may mean hiring someone quite unlike themselves. And that is difficult for some. Often leaders mistakenly hire individuals exactly like themselves and that only exacerbates the problem.

Wright

Stan, who are some of the authors who have inspired you to consider these four legendary roles?

Craig

James McGregor Burns wrote a seminal book on leadership decades ago. It is one of the most comprehensive works on leadership in our time. Peter Drucker has written a lot about leadership. Max Dupree and Warren Bennis (who has also contributed to this book) have written discerning and helpful books on leadership. Steven Covey and Tom Peters have given thoughtful and practical insights into leading. But I think what has been missing is a straight-forward systematic way to understand what leaders do and how they do it. James McGregor Burns first suggested that leadership involves role play. While he didn't name roles, he did state the importance of role play in fulfilling the responsibilities of leadership.

John Greenleaf wrote a great book on servant leadership. There are many who write about Warrior leadership, using fictional leaders as well as real examples. Others write about Monarch leadership of kings and queens using biographical and historical examples. All of these are helpful in understanding leadership, but identifying the roles and assigning attributes simplifies the process of distinguishing strengths and weaknesses of the leader.

Wright

So it's the conscious effort to blend the four Legendary roles that makes a Legacy Leader?

Craig

That's precisely it. A chair with only one, two, or even three legs can't support anyone. A leader who's only fulfilling one, two, or three roles is on the road to potential failure. Legacy Leaders acknowledge which of these four roles are the most difficult for them to fulfill, and, instead of ignoring their weaknesses, work to add the strengths necessary to become the leaders they want to be.

Wright

So we're back to the paradox that you become strong by admitting your weaknesses.

Craig

That's really true. A sign of greatness is the willingness to admit mistakes. Just think how easy it would have been for the Catholic Church in Boston to simply apologize for the abuse and get to solving the problem. What a difference that would have made within the church as well as in the public's perception. Look how easy it would have been for Martha Stewart to have simply said, "I made a mistake. I was wrong to sell my stock on the basis of information passed on from the Chairman of the Board." It's always astounding to me that, on occasion, leaders become too big to apologize or to acknowledge mistakes. That weakness could be a fatal flaw. Recently I saw a front page article in the *Wall Street Journal* with the headline, "Doctors Find a New Strategy, Telling the Truth." Isn't it amazing that telling the truth should become a *new* strategy, rather than what we *expect* from leaders?

Wright

It really is, Stan. Would you give me a more detailed example of someone you consider a Legacy Leader—how they fulfill the four legendary roles and what sort of legacy the leader left behind?

Craig

In the business world one of the best known Legacy Leaders and one of my favorite examples is Sam Walton. It is readily apparent how well he fulfilled the visionary role of a Monarch. K-Mart preceded Wal-Mart as a discount department store—many have forgotten that. In fact, Sam visited K-Mart in Michigan to see what they were doing to be so successful. But on the day Wal-Mart became the largest corporation in the world, K-Mart declared bankruptcy. A visionary leader made the difference.

Sam Walton, in the Warrior role, took action to carry out his vision. It took courage to put discount department stores in rural areas, especially when everyone else was putting stores in suburban shopping centers. He acted on his beliefs. Not only that, he was an effective communicator of his ideals and values, fulfilling the Priestly role. On occasion he did it in ways that were quite unexpected—telling Wal-Mart stories, leading corny cheers and sometimes even cornier songs, making his employees feel a sense of togetherness, as well as a sense of purpose. In doing so, he created a new set of traditions.

Many Wall Street analysts who follow Wal-Mart believe that the company's ability to market a wide range of products at low cost is the result of their distribution system. In his autobiography Sam Walton says his distribution idea came from sitting on a loading dock with one of his truck drivers and talking about making deliveries. How many of today's CEOs ever take the time to talk with the bottom of the organizational pyramid except from a podium? Today most CEOs and top business leaders are isolated from those they lead. Their offices are on the top floors, remote, with private bathrooms and private dining rooms. Most of the time they travel in limos or on the corporate aircraft. They never hear the concerns of or relate to customers or the employees. When these leaders see each other in the boardrooms they ask, "Why is our communication so poor?" It's amazing to me that they just don't get the idea of Servant Leadership.

Sam Walton and others like him knew the perks, but they knew the people as well. Sam Walton did not start out to create the richest family in the world or to build the largest corporation in the world. His intention was to provide good quality merchandise at a fair price. What a legacy he created by putting all four Legendary roles to work to accomplish his goal. Not every leader can be a Sam Walton, but he or she can learn the legendary roles and work on developing the skills necessary to be a Legacy Leader.

Wright

Are there any politicians you would call Legacy Leaders?

Craig

That's a good question. There are a number of historic examples as well as some contemporary ones. Lincoln left us a tremendous legacy. Voicing our history, traditions and core values, his speeches touch us even today. His biographers tell us he had great difficulty with his role of Monarch, but he never wavered in his conviction of what he wanted this country to be. His Warrior strength contributed to his drive and conviction that the Union cause was worth any sacrifice. He communicated more effectively than any of his time, with fewer words, and he spoke as a Servant. He was one of the people, not someone who wanted to be served.

Franklin Delano Roosevelt and Harry Truman were Legacy Leaders. Ronald Reagan may go down in history as a Legacy Leader as well. John McCain is one of today's political leaders who shows all the characteristics of a Legacy Leader. He is decisive and has a vision of what our nation can be. As a Warrior he is not afraid to fight for his country or his convictions. He communicates well in the Priestly role, and he always seems to be a man of the people. That "Come, let us..." is in everything he does. In spite of his national reputation and position, there is a sense of humility about him that is unusual for a person of his stature.

There is really an irony here and that is when politicians are in office, they often seem to forget the public they serve. It appears they are unwilling to sacrifice themselves for a cause greater than they are. Once they get elected their primary goal is to be re-elected instead of courageously giving sacrificial service. I believe that's why we see so many failures among politicians.

Wright

So what about more contemporary presidents?

Craig

It may be surprising to some of our readers, but Bill Clinton and George Bush are very similar. They both ran as "a man of the people," someone the voters could identify with—Clinton with his rural Arkansas roots, and Bush with his jeans and pickup truck. Both wanted to change the status quo to fit their visions of the future. But they both seem to have been carried away with the Monarch role. Clinton recently explained that his affair with Monica Lewinski was simply "because I could." George Bush came to his office with the reputation for compassionate conservatism. When was the last time you heard him talk about compassionate conservatism? He ran as a servant of the people who had built bi-partisan support in Texas. However, as president, he rules as a Monarch and acts like a Warrior. His ability to communicate some of the values that we believe in has been complicated by some of his actions. The legendary role of Servant is fading as he identifies with the other roles.

As a nation we have many issues and problems to solve. We have a healthcare system that often prevents those in greatest need from getting care. There are still large pockets of poverty in this country—people still go to bed wondering where their next meal is coming from. There is a lack of education funding even for our poorest citizens. George Bush's legacy will depend upon his identification with the people he wants to serve. I was able to go to college because of the National Defense Education Act that provided loans for my tuition. Where are those helps today for those who want an education? What are we doing to assist our neediest families? A Servant wants to serve—to help our dreams and hopes for the future become a reality. The legacy of a great president is built upon all four roles, including the role of Servant.

Wright

Stan, many people think leadership is charisma or the power of personality and it is something that you are born with. Do you think that's true?

Craig

I've heard that for a long time and I don't believe that's true. Charisma and personality can help put a person into a leadership position, but those qualities do not make a leader. Some of the most charismatic leaders were also great failures. General Douglas MacArthur, a hero to some in WWII, ended his career by being fired by President Truman. Leadership does not require charisma. It does require character. We are all born with certain personality characteristics that some people ascribe to leaders. I believe that each of us has the opportunity to become what we choose. Qualities of leadership can be taught and learned. It's that fact which makes democracy work. Men and women can learn to lead effectively, with or without charisma. Each of these four roles can be understood by anyone in any part of the world, and can be easily implemented. When we talk about a Monarch or Warrior or Priest or Servant, we all understand what we are talking about.

On the ball field or in the boardroom, your local neighborhood committees, the church, synagogue, mosque, or other place of worship, from high school to the Halls of Congress, leadership is always in critical demand. Effective leaders are in short supply. I trust that this introduction to the *Four Legendary Roles of Leadership* can help create better leaders who will leave positive and lasting legacies that benefit everyone.

Wright

Stan, this is the first time I've heard Legendary Leadership discussed. I believe that all of us want to create a rich and positive legacy for our families, our businesses, and our communities. But I have never been told how to do it. If we wanted to learn more about your concept of Legacy Leadership, how would we do that?

Craig

I hope to have my book, *Legacy Leadership,* finished some time this year. I've enjoyed presenting Legacy Leadership in workshops and speeches around the country for the last several years. But right now, David, I think the best way to do it is through this book, *Leadership Defined.*

Wright

Today we've been speaking with Stan Craig about Legacy Leadership. As we have found out today, his experience in business, the church and community contributed to understanding of the qualities necessary to make Legacy Leaders. I hope this will point the spotlight on these four roles so that more people will create a positive legacy, strengthen their own leadership and become more successful in leading their families, communities, churches, and businesses. Thank you so much for being with us today on *Leadership Defined.*

Craig

David, it has been my pleasure.

An academic definition of a leader is "One person who influences others to reach a mutually agreed upon goal that meets both the needs of the leader and the followers." While that definition meets the needs of academics, it falls far short of saying what a leader does. The real question we need answered is, "Just what does a leader do?" That is why Legacy Leadership is so significant. It describes what a leader does by presenting the four legendary roles every leader must fulfill in order to achieve ultimate success as a leader. The four roles and the strengths they require as well the qualities they bring are:

The Monarch Role—The role of vision. This role requires empowering others and making decisions.

The Warrior Role—The role of action. This role requires courage and a willingness to sacrifice for a long-term goal.

The Priestly Role—The role of wisdom. This role requires communication of the history, traditions and values that define the organization.

The Servant Role—The role of participation. This role requires involvement, support and humility.

The real heart of Legacy Leadership is that not one of these roles in itself can meet the demands facing today's leaders. *Only by combining these roles can you grow stronger as a leader and correct the inherent weaknesses in each role.*

Leadership failure is not acceptable; no leader can just give leadership a try. Too much depends on the outcome. Knowing these four roles, the strengths and weaknesses in each, and working to integrate the best in each creates a Legacy Leader.

Legacy Leadership is a guide for every leader who wants to leave a positive and lasting influence.

About The Author

Stan Craig has over 35 years of experience in leadership, investments and civic service. From a decade as a pastor to his 25 Years as an executive with Merrill Lynch he has been an Innovator—developing leaders and leading others. His speaking career has taken him around the world to speak to corporations and Civic Organizations- "Stan is simply the one of the best speakers we have ever had. He is funny, touching and authentic."

Stan Craig

3625 Medinah Ave

Southport, North Carolina 28461

Phone: 910.540.1447

Email: slcraig@ec.rr.com

Chapter 23

GARY MINOR

THE INTERVIEW

David E. Wright (Wright)

Today, we are talking with Gary Minor. Gary Minor, "The Major Persuader," has been building leaders since grade school. At a very early age, he began emulating and modeling leadership skills, encouraging others and providing opportunities for others to grow and develop into the leaders of tomorrow. Little did he know that those skills would one day become his life's work.

Gary has woven his experience into a philosophy and process that has built effective leadership in hundreds of organizations during the last dozen years. That experience came from the Boy Scouts where he achieved the rank of Eagle Scout, church groups, The U.S. Junior Chamber of Commerce where he ultimately served as Chairman of The National Training Task Force and thirteen years representing individuals and corporations as an attorney.

After many years engaged in the practice of trial law, Gary, "The Major Persuader," took a change in direction in his career. In 1992, he founded the 21st Century Leadership Institute, a performance-coaching firm that concentrates on keynote speaking, executive coaching and highly interactive adult learning experiences. A few years later, he walked away from his successful practice as a trial lawyer.

Since then, he has spent his time helping others reach their full potential. He has recently completed two book chapters, one on team based work systems to be published in *Pathways to Team Work,* and a chapter in *Conversations on Success,* published October 2003. He is also the occasional author of columns on the human side of business in various publications including *The Nashville Business Journal.* He has earned the designation of International Training Fellow from the Junior Chamber International Training Institute, the second candidate from the United States to receive the designation. He is a member of the National Speakers Association and President of his local chapter. He is also a past officer of his ASTD chapter.

His clients include well-known organizations such as the Department of Defense, Motorola, Superior Court for the State of California, Verizon of New England, the University of Tennessee, Aventis Pharma of Canada, Ardent Health Services, USDA, State of Tennessee, Trammell Crow Company, O'More College of Design, Peterbilt Motors Company and Kraft Food Ingredients. Gary Minor, welcome to *Leadership Defined.*

Gary Minor (Minor)
Thank you, David.

Wright
Gary, where did the term "The Major Persuader" come from?

Minor
Well, that's an interesting question. I'm in the middle of a re-branding effort and my marketing director spoke with several clients I have worked with recently. One of the things that came out of those conversations about what my difference was with regard to other speakers and presenters they've had in their organizations is the fact that people are persuaded to actually take action. Other speakers, trainers and folks have spent time with their people and they've been mildly entertained and had thought-provoking ideas presented to them, but there doesn't seem to be much action. However, after I'd spent time with them, people were actually moved to take action and do something different.

Wright

You know, I've asked the next question I have for you to many, many people and I get about as many answers as I ask people. But tell me, how do you define leadership?

Minor

Wow, that's a mighty big question. You know Warren Bennis tells us that management is about making sure *it* gets done and leadership is about deciding what *it* is. John Kotter tells us that management is about coping with complexity and leadership, by contrast, is about coping with change.

The thing that I think about leadership that makes so much difference is clarity of vision, knowing where you're going, charting it in a way and communicating it effectively to other people, so that they can actually understand where you are going and figure out where they can plug into that movement. Then leading by example, you show outwardly over a course of months and years that you are actually heading in that direction yourself.

I know so many leaders in the past who have been effective behind the scenes, but for some reason they did not want to be "seen" leading. They did not want to be in the spotlight, did not want to be the center of attention. They wanted the spotlight to shine on their people. You know, David, from an outsider's perspective, I think that is an accurate view of what you want outsiders to see.

You can carry it too far, though. On the inside, your people have to see you leading. It is not enough for it to be happening and for them to see the by-product, because they don't really know what you're doing. As senior leadership goes, so goes the organization. People will follow what you do. If they can't see *you* lead, they won't follow. It is invisible to them, so they don't know what or who to follow.

Wright

Defining leadership, as you've just defined it, how do you see that different from management?

Minor

When I go back to those two world-renowned experts and see what they have to say about it, I see Kotter's definition of coping with complexity that seems to be very similar to what Warren Bennis says about making sure *it* gets done. It's about implementation. It's about follow-through; follow-up and follow-through to make sure that the details are taken care of and that the overall mission is accomplished. That's what management is about to me. Leadership is about charting that direction, charting that vision, making sure that the changes are made and that people are rewarded for taking the risk to actually do something different, to effect those changes so that the new direction is actually fulfilled.

Wright

You know, it's interesting that a few decades ago the apprenticeship way of learning seemed to be working in the United States. The cobbler would hire some young man; he would work in the shoe shop for years and apprentice. The plumbers would do the same thing. Do you find that good managers can effectively make the transition to leadership positions?

Minor

I have found that many can. By my definition, as well as the two authorities I've referred to and your experience as well, I think you will agree, that it's a different skill set. It's a different approach and a different mindset that leads to a different outcome.

I have spent about four years working with a medical clinic in an ongoing program to develop the leadership and management skills of their senior leadership as well as front-line managers; people that manage the people at the check in desk when you go to the doctor's office and the nurses that keep the exam rooms moving, patients seen, etc. They are right there where the work is done. We have discovered that nurses can be extremely effective nurses. When we ask them to manage other nurses, many will not be so effective at that. If you look at the skill set that makes somebody an effective nurse and then look at the skill set that it takes to be a good manager, the skill sets are almost contradictory. It is hard to make that transition. I think that when you look at the transition from implementation from a more short-term focus day to day operational stand-point of getting *it* done, as Bennis says about management, that's a different skill set and a different approach then deciding what *it* is and then taking the steps to make sure that you lead.

It has been said, "leading out loud," leading visibly enough that people can see what you do, is a different thing than managing. It's just a whole different approach. I've worked with some engineers in a manufacturing setting that were great at project management and great at designing solutions to mechanical problems or solutions to manufacturing inefficiencies; then when they were asked to lead engineering organizations from a larger philosophical perspective rather than just the project level, a few of them were extremely effective; most were not. So, it's not everybody that can make the change because it's just a different way of thinking.

Wright

I remember, several years ago, I was going to a 3-day seminar down in Texas, a leadership development seminar. There were a lot of CEOs in there from a lot of pretty major companies. I remember one of the speakers or one of the trainers that day saying 2 percent of the nation gets up every morning and leads the other 98 percent; and then he added very quickly, "Before you guys puff your chests out, remember those 2 percent chose to be leaders and the 98 percent chose to be led." And so, I guess he was talking a lot about the skill set. So, what kind of experiences have you had that led you to that conclusion?

Minor

Just like in the nursing situation, I have watched many people promoted through their organizations; and you know, going back to the Peter Principle of many years ago, it seems that a lot of people that do not choose to lead are asked to do so. They turn out to be fairly effective managers but then when they're asked to chart direction and make more strategic long-term decisions, they just can't see things that way, can't see into the future and imagine what the future can or should look like and then figure out how to make it happen.

Wright

It never ceased to amaze me. I was in the real estate industry for many, many years; one of the most difficult things that we had to deal with is the fact that the real estate companies would accelerate, well, think they're accelerating their sales, by taking the best salesperson they had and "reward" him or her by promoting them to sales manager. Not only did they lose all of their sales, but just because you can sell something does not mean that you can teach and motivate others to do the same thing.

Minor

Oh, I strongly agree. If you take an athletic analogy, does it make sense for a basketball team to take their leading scorer and promote him to head coach; and then inevitably blame him when the scores go down? Blame him or her for that when, in reality, their job was to produce. In that sales mode, I find that to be particularly unique, because what it takes to be a good outside salesperson is different from what it takes to manage others. You must be a self-starter. You must get an emotional charge out of the close of the sale. You must be an extremely effective listener to figure out how to solve your customer's needs, after you find out what those needs are in the first place. The customer's need is *not* to buy your stuff; their need is to solve their problem.

When you take somebody out of the field that is a consistently high producer and put him or her behind a desk and ask them to handle an administrative role, they're no longer a self-starter. Now they must follow somebody else's rules. They are no longer having face-to-face contact with people, which is what you have to do to be an effective salesperson. You're now stuck in the office, where by definition all the salespeople are not, because they're out there in the field selling. And we're going to hold you responsible by somebody else's decision about how you ought to be performing. All of that is completely contrary to what led that person to stand out as a star salesperson in the first place.

We do that all the time, though. We take the best architect and ask him to manage the architectural division of the firm. We take the best engineer and ask her to head up engineering. Well, when you heap all those administrative and team responsibilities on your best performer, you are by definition preventing them from performing. I will tell you a story about when I convinced a manager to take a mediocre performer and give them a management role.

Now, that sounds contrary to the norm; and that's because it is. I was working with a company that had an internal audit team and there was an auditor on the team that wasn't a very good accountant. When I dug deeper into this fellow's past, it turned out that he was an accountant because his father had decided he needed to be one, rather than because he wanted to be one on his own. As a result, he never really developed a high level of competency with the core skills, because he didn't really want to use them in the first place. He just followed this path because it was easy for him to, not because he wanted to. The guy was extremely outgoing, very extroverted, and very good with people—just a natural cheerleader type; but he wasn't performing well as an accountant.

I knew the fellow pretty well and I suggested to his boss that he promote him to a team leader in the auditing department. He said, "Why would I promote him? He's not an effective accountant." "You're missing the point," I said, as many seem to do quite often and that is that the team leader does not necessarily need to be a star at the core business. Leading and "doing" are two different things. They need to be a good team leader. They need to be able to line up the hotel rooms, because these people leave on Monday and come home on Friday and they do that as often as 16 weeks out of every 20. It's an extremely demanding job; and they're away from home all of the time. What you need is somebody that can line up all the logistics to make that team effective—the transportation, plane tickets, hotel rooms, and all that kind of stuff—and do it in such a way that people feel like they are well taken care of and that they are appreciated. You know, you've got to be able to keep people motivated and upbeat and focused on what they're doing and not homesick. You have to be able to take those people out on Thursday night before they go home on Friday and thank them for a great job if it was done, feed them a good meal and let them have a little bit of fun before you fly home on Friday. With that, I asked, "What does that have to do with accounting?" After a bit of reflection, the manager said, "Nothing." I said, "That's exactly the point."

My suggestion was to put him in a role where he can use his natural talents and skills and minimize his weakness, which is actually the technical skill of accounting. You're going to have a stronger team. You're going to have a fellow flourish where he was previously floundering. He agreed with me that he would at least try it.

The fellow turned out to be a thriving team leader. He was very effective at keeping his team engaged. Turn over went down; productivity went up. This guy was happier and much more productive than he was when he was a member of the team. Their internal customers had a better experience with the audit team itself. It turned out to be a good move for the individual, the team and their customers as well.

Wright

Well, in the real estate business at least, I concluded that in most of the cases—not all—but in most of the cases, when the top salesperson was elevated to sales management, the reason for the promotion was the owners' inability to think of a better way to reward them. So many rewards would have satisfied that person much more. It was just a sign of ineffective leadership. Let me ask you, what types of industries have you worked with in the past?

Minor

It's pretty wide. I deal with people issues rather than specific industry issues. I've worked with pharmaceutical companies. I've worked with medical clinics. I've worked with water utilities. I've worked with manufacturing. I've worked with professional service firms, like architects and engineers. I've worked with commercial real estate companies, police departments, fire departments and retailers.

Wright

So, you don't build organizations as much as you build the people who build the organization.

Minor

That's correct. There are many good people out there who work from the organizational perspective. A few of the best are featured in other chapters in this book. My focus is much more on working both individually or with the small leadership team, building their leadership skills and helping them become much more effective at the entire package of leadership skills.

Wright

I think our readers, especially those who like to model, can get a lot out of success stories. Do you have any you can share with us?

Minor

I will relate a couple of senior level stories and then a couple of organization-wide examples.

I work with a COO of a professional service firm. When I started working with him, he was the CFO. Partially because of our monthly conversations, he has been able to expand his capacity to move from a top quality managerial accountant to a position where he has been able to assume the strategic leadership piece of the CFO job. Along the way, he was able to absorb the HR leadership function of a company with over 375 employees, play a major role in shaping the strategic direction of the company and assume the COO role where he is responsible for the day-to-day implementation of that vision. All of that happened in four years. I still spend a few hours with him every other month.

In another instance, I worked with a quality assurance engineer. She knew quality engineering, but was having trouble moving from a union-based command and control organization to a plant where the top six people in the plant ran it together, under the leadership of a very inclusive plant manager that had moved the culture to a team based work system.

Over a period of about 18-months, she learned how to move from a position where she was in complete control of a narrow silo of responsibility, a manager, to a senior leadership position where she fully participated in the setting and implementing of the strategic direction of the plant. It was the first time she had really been a member of a team that was successful. She had to change completely her view of what work meant, and how to be effective in her organization. That was a fun project for me. I had the opportunity to watch the growth and participate in her success in a small way.

This story involves second level managers. I spend some time with them as well as senior leaders. This group is a national retail chain that I have worked with for about three years. As with most retail companies, they had a very high-rate of turnover with their inside sales people: over 150% per year. Their store managers hire their own sales staff. They sent me their 25 store managers that had the highest turnover. I spent two days with these 25 store managers working one on one with them and teaching them an interview process that detailed how to spend more time focusing on the prospective employees' past performance and less time asking them hypothetical questions about how they *would* do things. A typical question in the old interview process for many of these managers would go something like this; "Well, say you work in one of our stores and say you have a customer with "X" kind of problem, how would you handle that?" You are asking people to step into a role they have never had, to be in a sales situation where they've never been, and you are asking them to deal with a customer they've never met. How they would respond to that question is sheer speculation. From an interview perspective, it is really no help at all.

Instead, I asked them to focus more on experience: "Tell me the story about how you've handled you're biggest problem customer." The key to this process is to ask for three, four, or maybe even five stories along the same line. People have access to people that will help them memorize things and coach them on the interview process now. They can easily be coached and ready for a story or two; but they won't go four or five deep. It takes several minutes, but you gain a much deeper insight into (A) what they even think a tough customer situation is and (B) how they have responded to it in the past. If they can only think of one or two stories, what's the message there?

Next, you turn it around and ask them to tell you their greatest success story; tell me the customer that wrote the letter or that asked for your manager so they could compliment you. You go four or five deep in that process. This is a very simple process where you can learn how a prospective employee views the entire sales process and you can determine what they think that matters.

To finish the story, my client told me that about 6 months after I had spent literally 30-minutes each coaching those 25 store managers after they had experienced a three-hour workshop, the turnover at those 25 stores in the floor sales staff went down an average of 92 percent. That is a huge drop. That's an annual figure; they were able to measure that in 6 months and find that kind of success. That dramatic reduction in turnover and the cost savings that goes with it is added directly to the bottom line.

Another success story, I suppose, would be over in the medical clinic that I referred to where some people that weren't perceived as effective managers or leaders were asked to take on some different roles. Those people were able to shine for the organization, improve patient service, and do a better job of staffing and organizing the office. Doctors were happier. Staff was happier. Patients were happier. You know, the whole process became much more effective when these people were given a chance to perform in another role.

Taking the time and working—like I said, I've worked with that organization about four years on an ongoing basis—and being able to take the time with folks long enough to be able to find these individuals and coach them in a different direction is very rewarding for me. But that's not nearly as important as the fact that the organization is much better off because these people have been able to shine in a role where they would have previously never been considered. I get to spend one on one time with those folks every other month now and I get to watch the light bulbs go off. I get to hear the stories; and I get to help them fine-tune their skills and have an even greater impact on the direction of their organization and their community as a whole.

Wright

What about some of the instances where you were not so successful? Why where those efforts not successful?

Minor

Oh, David, in twelve years, I've worked with hundreds of organizations and they've all been wonderful. Do you buy that? No? Well, it's not the truth.

A couple of times things just didn't work very well; and you can probably guess why. I worked with a governmental unit that provided a service. They said they wanted to take their culture in a different direction. They said they wanted to get out of the command and control culture and move to an empowered workforce setting, where people close to the work could make more decisions and provide a high level of customer service. They brought in outside consultants; an engineering firm and four HR/ organizational types, I was one of those four HR/organizational types. After we were brought in, senior leadership walked away. They didn't support us or support our programs. They didn't actively work against us, but what we could do as outsiders with periodic involvement needed to be reinforced on a daily basis by senior leadership and the middle management team as well. It's not so much that they sabotaged and worked against us; they just didn't back it up, because they weren't really clued into what we were doing. That is because they just wouldn't take an active role in learning what we were doing. They were not interested in any briefing from us; they were not interested in the models we were teaching their people. They were not interested in lending the credibility that comes when the CEO is sitting in the room with a guy who is outside wearing the company shirt with his name on it, driving a truck and meeting face to face with customers on a regular basis.

When those two people are sitting at the same table learning the same stuff at the same time, what do you think that guy who's out there on the front line is thinking? This is important, this matters. The CEO has taken his time to be here to learn this. What the CEO learns in that workshop or seminar is going to be referred to in follow up communications and other settings. Well, if the CEO is not there, he can't refer to it. He can't talk about it. He can't say, "Do you remember when we went through that workshop on change management? This is why we did that and this is where we're going."

If he is not there, he can't do that. Without that senior leadership, we were doomed to be ineffective and the program ended prematurely. That is no big surprise, because anybody reading this that has been in an outside role or worked with an outside group knows that without the support of senior leadership you're just not going to be very effective. One of the consultants even delivered a report that cited trust and credibility issues in a department while recommending that certain individuals be transferred out of that department. The level of buy-in was so low he was thanked for his service and dismissed. He predicted that exact result when he told us what he was going to recommend.

Wright

So, what methods or techniques do you use to build leadership skills and effectiveness?

Minor

That is a good question. It depends on the situation. If I'm asked to come in and do a key note speech which I do fairly often, the methods are fairly one-way communication because when you're given an hour and fifteen minutes on the platform, you can't ask people to interact much. The idea is to inspire, to present a logical argument, to speak to people's heads and then to present an emotional setting, an emotional context, to speak to people's hearts, to generate the movement needed to actually have them do something different, to persuade them to want to do something different.

That is where the major persuasion comes in and where the slogan or name of "The Major Persuader" arose. In order to persuade people to see things differently and feel that they have permission to do something different, you need to be able to address both of those different ways people absorb information. If you want people to think, speak to their heads. But if you want people to act, speak to their hearts. You have to give them enough reasons for them to make an emotional decision to do something different; and you must give them something different to do, too. That is what John Kotter referred to as what leaders really do—they cope with change and help others cope with change as well.

To explain this, I use a model I call The Change Cycle© and explain that in a speech I give called "Riding the Change Cycle; Are you Peddling as Fast as You Can?" I follow up with going deeper into the organization through workshops and one on one coaching. Briefly, I believe that every time anyone is faced with a change in any aspect of their life, before they accept and effectively live with the change, they go through The Change Cycle©. The cycle has four major steps:

Denial, when the person refuses to acknowledge that the change is happening to them.
(NOTES)

Defiance, when the individual begins to acknowledge that the change is happening, but they will not have to modify their thinking or behavior in any way to be able to live in peace with the change.
(NOTES)

Discovery, when the individual begins to explore and "discover" that there could actually be an "up" side to the change and it is worth pursuing further and finally,
(NOTES)

Dedication, when the individual decides that the change is not all bad and they are willing to try the new reality, and possibly embrace it later.
(NOTES)

Notice I said, "Before they accept and effectively live with the change." I make this caveat, because sometimes people are not willing to see the cycle through to conclusion. They choose to make other changes on their own; they retire, divorce, change churches, change careers, relocate, etc. Sometimes, they never leave the denial stage. If that is the case, then likely someone else makes a change for them; they are fired, face legal consequences or forced in some way to do something else that was not based on a decision of their own making.

Truly effective leaders will learn to both master The Change Cycle© and learn how to usher others through it. While I don't believe that you can push someone through it at *your* preferred speed to reach *your* desired result at *your* convenience, I do believe that a real leader will decide to deal with the situation. A real leader will pay attention to their people, know their people and their needs and work to set the conditions in place that makes it as easy as possible for their people to accept the change, move through the cycle and come out of it ready to live with, if not embrace the new reality, on the other side.

I have been asked many times, "Why don't they just do it?" or "Why don't' they get it?" The answer to those questions is different for every person. The point is, as a leader, what can you do to help them "get it," rather than complaining that they don't see what you see, know what you know, do what you do? The successful leader will take the time to figure out the answer and do the best they can to deliver what each person needs in their situation to help them "get it." If you don't take the time to do that, do you really have time to train new people to replace those that left because they believed they were not heard when they expressed a concern or believed that their interests were not taken into consideration in some way. Remember, the ones that usually leave first are the ones that can find a new job the easiest. Those, most likely, are your best people.

Wright

Let me ask you to put on your Alvin Toffler hat and be a futurist for a minute. What do you think is next in the world of developing leaders?

Minor

I believe that the beginning of the 21st century for American business began in about 1986, when the chairman of General Motors was replaced. Then, because of the invention of the personal computer, throughout the late 1980s, organizations eliminated tens of thousands of middle management positions. This broke the psychological contract of life-long employment that had stood since the beginning of the industrial revolution. We have left the age of life-long employment and entered the age of life-long employability.

In the elimination of those middle managers positions, one of the unintended consequences was that there was nobody left in the organization to bring along the next generation of leaders. I think if you look at job descriptions for middle managers in most organizations it *didn't* say one of your jobs is to keep your eyes open and identify the "up and comers" and help them along in the process of becoming effective leaders. That was not on the job description, but it was a very important part of the job. When those middle manager positions were eliminated, the removal of all that mentoring led to the situation where there was no one there to bring along the next generation. I think out of that condition, the concept of business coaches and leadership coaches arose.

Consequently, the outsourcing of leadership development became much more prevalent over the last 15 or so years and I see more of that happening as we move ahead. One piece of data I rely on is the fact that ten years ago, I had one client that asked me to spend one on one time with their managers over a period of many months. Now, I have six. I see companies returning to their core business and not trying to do everything in-house. If you have a hundred employees, you cannot justify the time and expense necessary to have a top-notch HR department. I think you're going to be outsourcing that, in essence, renting that talent when you need it, rather than having it in house and investing in a full time employee to do that.

I think that the number of people who are working outside of the corporate setting will increase as the need for these specialist increases. Obviously that really hit the big time when the PC became an item in everybody's house, pretty much like a telephone or a TV. Now, I see us relying on those experts more. Even manufacturing outfits will be specializing more on the making of their product and outsourcing other functions—their engineering, payroll, maintenance staff will all be outsourced to a specialist in that business.

I also see much administrative routine "white collar" work being done by computers In essence, robots that took over many jobs 10 years ago in the manufacturing sector will be moving to the office building.

This news is going to scare many people, but the marketplace is changing. The psychological contract was broken years ago. The idea that you could go to work for a company and if you did a pretty good job and avoided a felony conviction, you'd be there for life is just about dead. I read a statistic that stated there are 24 million people working from home now. Is the "home office free agent" the largest employer in the country now? If so, how does that position you as a player in the global market place? Even the concept of retiring is changing. You know, people don't retire as they once did, let alone at a specific age. People don't really seem to retire; they just start working less. So, we keep that expertise; we just don't keep them on as full time employees. To answer your question, more outsourcing, more specialization, more free agents performing project work.

Wright

Very interesting. I totally agree with you. This has been a great conversation. I've learned a lot. I really appreciate you taking this much time with me today.

Minor

I appreciate the invitation to join you. This is an interesting project for me; working with the nationally known experts who are a part of it is quite a privilege.

Wright

Today, we've been talking to Gary Minor, "The Major Persuader." If you have been in a state of confusion or denial about changes that are happening in your position as a leader, then you might want to read this chapter again. This is a great interview. Gary, thanks so much for being with us in *Leadership Defined*.

Minor

Thank you for the call, David. Good to speak with you.

About The Author

Gary Minor, known as "The Major Persuader," works with organizations that want to significantly improve the effectiveness of their senior leadership teams. He delivers keynote speeches primarily on Leadership and Change.

He can follow up those speeches with workshops to implement the ideas presented in those speeches and spend time working one on one with members of leadership teams.

He is an Eagle Scout, an International Training Fellow by the Junior Chamber International Training Institute, past officer of his ASTD chapter and an officer of National Speaker's Association, Tennessee Chapter.

His clients include Motorola, Department of Defense, Verizon of New England, Kraft Foods, Books a Million, Aventis Pharmaceutical of Canada, The Superior Court of the State of California and the State of Tennessee.

Gary B. Minor, JD

Executive Director,

21st Century Leadership Institute

2236 Oakleaf Drive

Franklin, Tennessee 37064

Phone: 615.790.3296

Email: gary@garyminor.com

www.garyminor.com

Chapter 24

PAULA K. SWITZER, M.A.

THE INTERVIEW

David E. Wright (Wright)

Today we are talking to Paula Switzer. Paula is a well-known speaker and consultant and owner of Switzer Resource Group, Inc. Her company works with leaders who want to turn employees into partners committed to the growth and success of their organization. Paula speaks on the importance of developing our relational leadership expertise. In addition to owning her company for over 12 years, Paula has held numerous leadership positions in her personal and professional life for over 25 years. Paula has her master's degree in human resources and mentors a team of 25 independent consultants across the country. Paula Switzer, welcome to *Leadership Defined*!

Paula Switzer (Switzer)

Thank you very much, David.

Wright

So right off the bat, what do you mean by relational leadership?

Switzer

Well, it's a term that's been used over the years, David, but here we are referring to the *Seven Elements of Relational Leadership™.* We are defining it as the relationships that we keep with ourselves and others. In reference to the relationship we keep with self, it involves self-awareness and self-discipline. I once heard someone say in the context of facilitating a group that you can't take a group any further than you are. That statement had an impact on me. I think the same applies for leaders. For example, if I have issues of control or trust issues, these will affect my ability to lead. We must start by forming a healthy relationship with oneself. We must truly believe we are worthy and accept ourselves entirely, warts and all. I think this is sometimes extremely challenging to do in our current environment today when any admittance of vulnerability is often seen as a weakness.

Wright

So, let me see if I get this correctly. If I'm trying to lead a group, then they're limited by my limitations or my weaknesses?

Switzer

Absolutely! I have to assess my own strengths and limitations, so I can take the group further.

Wright

So what are some of the other elements of relational leadership?

Switzer

In addition to the relationship with self, we look at the relationship with our fellow leaders, with our followers, with our vision, with our stakeholders, with our support network, and with our source.

Wright

Okay, tell me more.

Switzer

Each of the seven elements also has two sub-elements. For example, the relationship with our followers includes the sub-elements of honesty & trust, as well as adaptability. A good leader must possess the ability to create an environment where people tell the truth, as well as being adaptable in dealing with the differences in others.

Wright

What do you mean by our relationship with our source?

Switzer

This is what gives us strength beyond ourselves. For many of us, it might be our relationship with God, or a sense of a higher power. In this element, the two sub-elements are those of humility and the ability to keep the bigger picture in perspective.

Wright

I guess I understand all of the elements except who are the stakeholders?

Switzer

We are referring here to people who have a vested interest in our success. It could be shareholders, customers, board of directors, and our employees.

Wright

Oh, okay. So which aspects of the seven relational leadership components do you think leaders are currently focusing on today?

Switzer

Well, David, I think one of the challenges we face here in the United States is the emphasis on short-term measurements. As organizations, we're constantly being measured by what we've accomplished in the last quarter. That leaves us with an extremely short-term scorecard. In fact, I recently heard about a company that publicly stated they put their values and their people ahead of profits. Their attorneys advised them to warn their stockholders with a written statement regarding that policy. I found that rather sad. Most leaders believe that they are doing a good job focusing on the relationship with their vision as well as the relationship with their stakeholders. I believe the majority of leaders today are sincere in their efforts to move their organizations forward, and to provide a good return to their stockholders. Most senior level managers know this is a key part of their accountabilities and believe they're doing a good job in these areas.

Wright

So do you think they've got it covered or should they be focusing on something different?

Switzer

Well, that's a pretty complex issue. Ideally, one's focus needs to be balanced. If we neglect any of the seven areas for very long, the consequences can be severe. We all know people who did not manage the relationship with self or perhaps their support network—family, friends. And when these things are not tended to, health problems can occur, marriages fail, and friendships fade. As leaders we constantly have to assess the seven elements and make sure that they are fairly well balanced. If any one of them gets out of alignment for very long, it makes for a bumpy ride.

Wright

You know, come to think of it, balance is important in almost everything, isn't it?

Switzer

It sure is. It's something we constantly must monitor, and we have to be willing to admit to ourselves when we're out of balance and bring ourselves back into alignment.

Wright

So do you have any methods you can share with our readers about how leaders assess their strengths and weaknesses, and what they can do if they find themselves out of balance?

Switzer

Most definitely. We use several processes and tools in that. We need to start by doing an honest assessment of our own strengths and weaknesses. There are many tools out there for assisting with that. For example, we use a 360-degree instrument with many of our clients. The term "360" refers to the idea of getting feedback from all around us; you can think of it almost as a circle. *The Leadership Development Assessment* measures competencies in several areas of leadership, and provides data from the manager's peers, from their direct reports, from internal customers, their own manager, as well as themselves. It is sometimes painful for us to get this kind of feedback, but it is essential to understanding the impact we are having on those around us. I mentioned earlier the two sub-elements for our relationship with self are self-awareness and self-discipline. Well, I have to know how I'm coming across to others so I can determine what's working and what's not. Then I know where I need to make changes and I have to hold myself accountable to make these changes, just as I hold others accountable for their actions and behavior.

We use another tool David later on in the process, after we've worked with a client for a while and after trust has been built. When participants are ready to learn about themselves in more depth, we use something called the *Life Positions* model. It's somewhat of a variation on the work from the 1970s of "I'm okay, you're okay." What we find, which is really quite interesting, is that often fairly high-level leaders are operating from an "I'm okay, you're not okay" or an "I'm not okay, and you're not okay" life position. That may seem strange, but people are pretty good at masking these life positions in their behavior. Sometimes the manifestation of such behavior from these various life positions takes different forms. Let's say I'm a leader who's operating from the "I'm okay, you're not okay" position. I may have a need to acquire material goods to prove my worth. So I accumulate a lot, but still feel unfulfilled in my life at a deep level. Another manifestation of that might be treating others in a condescending or arrogant manner. We have to understand the life positions from which we operate; then we can learn to respond differently by learning new behaviors.

Wright

In the '70s, I was a real transaction analysis junky.

Switzer

Ah, yes!

Wright

And I still think it's the best psychology around. It's just that people were abusing it so much.

Switzer

That's right, and it's unfortunate, because this is such a wonderful tool to understanding self and our way of relating to others in our lives. We introduce the model, and give participants the option of completing the assessment. If they choose to take it, we provide them with coaching and support in debriefing the instrument. Leaders are often surprised at where they show up in the *Life Positions* model. It is a very powerful tool.

Wright

I'm glad you're putting credibility into it. One of the problems I've had down through the years, is that while most of us who deal in leadership issues talk about honest assessments and self-assessments, I always assess myself first as handsome and second as brilliant! And the truth of the matter is you really do need instruments to do this. It's very tough because what you said in the first place was that you, as the leader could very well be the weakest link in the chain. If I don't see that in myself, I can really in deep trouble, can't I?

Switzer

Yes, you're absolutely right, and I think this happens quite often. For example, people can rise in organizations based on their technical skills, at which they excel. However, their people skills may be dreadful. You may be familiar with some of the work today on emotional intelligence, such as that of Daniel Goleman and others. It has been proven over and over again that truly excellent leaders are those whom have a high level of emotional intelligence as well as technical skills and competencies. They are adept at building strong relationships with others.

Wright

Well, could you help us with this problem of developing stronger relationships? What in your opinion is the best way for a leader to develop stronger relationships?

Switzer

I'm glad you asked that question because we must have a strong relationship with ourselves as well as with others. We believe trustworthiness is the foundation for developing stronger relationships. Building trust takes time. It really happens one relationship at a time. We are always either building trust or diminishing trust in everything we do. We find that most leaders truly do believe they are trustworthy and yet their behavior may not be building trust.

Wright

I'm confused. How can someone be trustworthy but not demonstrate trust behavior?

Wright

Well, actually, it happens all the time. As I mentioned, we use several self-assessment tools, and one of our foundational pieces is the *DiSC®* behavioral model. I'm not sure if you're familiar with that or not, David.

Wright

Yes, I am.

Switzer

Great! As you know, *DiSC* looks at different styles of behavior in the work place. There are four dimensions of the *DiSC* model, and we cannot be strong in all four of these dimensions. What we find is often those who are different from us value other behaviors as well as other trustworthiness factors. Let me clarify that. We use something called the *Elements of Trust*™ model in conjunction with the *DiSC* model, and it really explains why there's often a perception of diminished trust in our relationships with others.

Let me give you an example. Let's say I'm someone who has a lot of high D behavior. Now D stands for "dominance" and these are the folks who are fast-paced. They are quick to take action, and they are motivated by results. They are also very direct in their communication. According to the *Elements of Trust*™ model, what is important to them in building trust is dealing with someone who can be straightforward and honest with them. They don't like excuses, and expect people to walk their talk.

A high D may be working closely with someone who has a lot of high S behavior. Now S stands for "steadiness" or "supportiveness." These are folks that are physically slower-paced than the high D. They're methodical in how they do things, and they like a more cooperative, harmonious working environment. According to the *Elements of Trust*™ model, a high S values the importance of acceptance. They accept others for who they are, and expect to be treated the same way. They value true appreciation and caring when it is given or received. The high S's need for acceptance and sincerity is just as important as that high D's need is for results and straight forwardness.

So let's look at a scenario where trust can be diminished based on someone's *DiSC®* style, and what they value in trust behaviors.

Let's say you're working with someone who has a lot of high S tendencies. We'll call that person Sue. Sue has just come back from some outpatient surgery. Sue spoke with her manager (who's name is Don) and informed him that she would be out of the office for surgery on Friday. She would return to work the following Monday, so she would only miss one day of work.

On Monday morning, Don (the high D manager) rushes into Sue's office, and immediately asks Sue about the status of a report he needs finished. Has she completed it yet? When will it be ready? Don does not take the time to ask Sue how the surgery went, and how she is feeling. Trust is diminished with the high S because Sue believes Don is unfeeling and uncaring. On the other hand, trust is diminished with Don because he still does not have a completed report, and in his opinion, Sue has had ample time to finish it. This situation is a lot about style, but it also has to do with what each person values in terms of the trust model. We find the *DiSC* model and the *Elements of Trust™* model intertwined, and a major cause of communication and trust breakdowns in the workplace.

Wright

This appears to be a conundrum. It seems like a leader's rise within an organization is often due to their focus on results. Is the drive for results a double-edged sword?

Switzer

Well, yes, it can be. First of all, let me clarify that leaders come in all shapes and styles. And yes, you're right, many leaders do rise within organizations due to that focus on results; however, any strength overused can become a weakness for us. The important point is that a leader needs to know themselves well enough to know what their strengths are; whether their strength lies in their focus on results, or on attention to detail and quality, or on their ability to influence people through relationships. Whatever their strength is, a good leader will surround him or herself with people who have different perspectives and different styles. What we also find, David, is that as trust grows within relationships, we open up more of what we call our "public area" or our "open area." Are you familiar with the JoHari Window by any chance?

Wright

Yes.

Switzer

Well, we find as trust grows between individuals, the part of the Johari Window called the "open area" or the "public area" also grows and expands. This area describes what I know about myself and why you know about me. So as trust starts to build, I share more with you about who I am. I become open to disclosing things about myself and am open to receiving feedback from those around me. As trust grows, people start to focus on more than just themselves and they can be more open to what the other person is focused on. This can result in the development of new products and services, enhanced teamwork and improved customer service. In this case, everyone benefits.

Wright

You mentioned the focus on shareholders expectations of quick results. How can a leader balance their accountability to their shareholders while working on the important issue of building trust you mentioned in relational leadership?

Switzer

This is where developing partnerships with all of our stakeholders is so important. Many of the seven elements of relational leadership come into play here. For example, with our followers, the aspects of honesty and trust and adaptability are key. With respect to our vision, we must constantly articulate and communicate where we want to take the organization. We must be able to deal with conflicts, both internally and externally, and be able to fine-tune our intuition when we're off course with any of our constituencies. With our employees and fellow leaders, we have to make sure we get everyone onboard with our vision. Those who do not share the same values may need to go. However, as leaders, we have an awesome responsibility to all of our stakeholders. It seems there are many organizations where senior leadership becomes somewhat of a revolving door. Each time someone new at the top comes in, he or she works hard to leave his or her own mark on the organization. Often there are casualties along the path. In my opinion I think we have to stop this trend if we want to build trust and deliver positive long-term results for our shareholders. Without this, we end up having is what I call the "veneer of leadership." It may cover the surface, but it doesn't last over the long haul.

It may appear to cost less on the front end, but we end up paying for it more heavily down the road. We must realize, as organizations and as a country, there are no quick fixes. The answers lie in hard work, honesty, and the development of solid relationships based on trust. When these elements are present, we can deliver the results to our shareholders, while creating a place where people are proud to work. In Jim Collins' book, *Good to Great*, he mentions what he calls Level 5 leaders. These are the leaders that have shown consistency over a number of years and have led their organization to achieve results that have lasted over time. Two of the key qualities mentioned in a Level 5 leader are extreme personal humility and an intense personal will. These leaders are more focused on the organizations success than their own. They are caring leaders. And caring leaders are relational leaders.

Wright

It reminds me of our political situation. It's almost a definition of it. Not only do you change every, sometimes every four and not more than every eight years, but to completely different ideologies.

Switzer

Oh, absolutely! And think of the upheaval it causes for those within the organization, within the government in this case. The same thing happens in organizations everywhere. People never have a chance to settle down and truly commit to the vision, to where the senior team wants to take them, because there are too many changes occurring. The clarity is just not there.

Wright

So what can an organization do to steer clear of the "veneer of leadership?"

Switzer

Well, as Jim Collins says, "You need to get the right people on the bus and the wrong people off the bus." I'm an associate with *Integro Leadership Institute*, which is an organization near Philadelphia, with offices in Australia. Many of the models I've mentioned, such as the *Elements of Trust*™ and the *Life Positions* model are key components of *Integro's* process. The founders of Integro Leadership Institute, Keith Ayers, and his team have developed a process called the *Senior Team Alignment Process*™. The *Senior Team Alignment*

Process™ brings the senior team members together to operate as a true high performing team. In many organizations, the senior leaders are so busy running their own functional areas they really don't spend a lot of time assessing how they are functioning as a team, and what they could do to improve that. And believe me, there's often quite a bit of room for improvement among senior teams. We take them through a lengthy exploration and discovery process. It's hard work but the end result is you have the right people on the bus. Having the right people on board and pointed in the same direction expedites the senior team in fulfilling their vision for the organization. It also provides leaders with the tools to know themselves better and lead from a place of authenticity.

Wright

What can we do to deepen the relationship with ourselves as leaders?

Switzer

Well, first David, we must summons the courage and make the commitment to begin the journey, because it is hard work. It's hard work to know ourselves, truly know ourselves, and to risk moving out of our comfort zone to grow and to develop. However, unlike the "veneer of leadership," a leader has to be solid internally in order to lead their followers in a healthy way. So we use many tools in our process such as providing coaching for the leaders. We believe leaders must have a coach in order to help them know *how* to change their behavior. When someone can admit their mistakes as a human being, they can make great strides in deepening their relationship with self and those around them. It requires accepting oneself as he or she is, and allowing others to do the same. When a person does the work, it pays off in so many areas of their lives, and not just at work. It carries over into their relationship with their spouse or significant other, their children, and other people who are important to them in their lives.

Wright

Well, you may have some instruments to help me. I had a wedding anniversary two days ago and I forgot it!

Switzer

Oh, dear. Did you really, David? When was your anniversary?

Wright

The 27th. I went in this morning and told my office manager about forgetting it and she said, "Well, what did your wife say? How does she feel about it?" I said, "I have no idea. She's not speaking to me."

Switzer

Well, see, she's giving you some feedback. Feedback comes in both verbal and non-verbal forms! We look at positive feedback, and feedback for improvement. I believe her feedback was the latter, David.

Wright

Sometimes leaders just forget, you know. This thing of leadership is really, really a tough subject.

Switzer

Yes, it really is. There have been a lot of fads when it comes to the topic of leadership, but I think it comes down to the relationships we keep with ourselves and others, and building a workplace that's based on trust. This may seem simple, but it is certainly not easy.

Wright

So you've convinced me that relational leadership is the way to go. What concrete steps can be taken at an organizational level to get there?

Switzer

Well, first of all I'd like to say congratulations. As we have all heard many times, "awareness is the first step to change." Secondly, let me say this process is not for the weak-hearted. A CEO once asked Ralph Colby, the original co-founder of *Integro*, "How much is this going to cost us?" Ralph replied without missing a beat, "it's going to cost you plenty." He went on to say this is going to cost a lot whether you use Integro's process or not. Although doing something to build a strong culture based on trust may seem expensive, the cost of not building a strong culture based on trust is much, much more expensive.

At *Integro Leadership Institute*, we use *The Four Cornerstones* model to explain our overall process, which includes four main building blocks, or cornerstones. It's based on a "foundation" of trustworthiness, underneath a "roof" of shared values.

If you can picture a house with four rooms in it, two on the first level, and two on the second level, it maps out the four main components of our process.

Wright

And what are those four cornerstones, Paula?

Switzer

They are self-awareness, building trust, distributive learning, and personal responsibility. In the upper left-hand corner, we have the cornerstone for self-awareness. This is where we start with our participants, whether it is the senior team member, or a mid-level leader/manager. We spend time throughout the entire process on self-awareness. The upper right-hand corner deals with building trust. Through using the *DiSC®* model, the *Elements of Trust™* model and various interventions, we work with leaders to develop behaviors that build trust. Again, there is a difference between being trustworthy, and the ability to build trust.

One of the truly unique parts to our process, and one that provides a great payoff in building trust, is the cornerstone in the lower left-hand corner, Distributive Learning. We require leaders attending the *Leadership Development Process* to complete certain assignments between each session. The *Leadership Development Process* typically takes anywhere from 18-24 months to complete. Part of their "homework" involves taking some of the key learnings back to their direct reports. As an example, they would go back to their direct reports, and have one-on-one discussions with each of them to determine the work expectations each employee has, and to discuss how those expectations might be either met or adjusted. Many of these discussions help with issues such as retention, and helping people stay truly engaged in their jobs.

The bottom right cornerstone is called Personal Responsibility. We find many leaders frustrated by the lack of responsibility employees take for their work. As leaders create an environment where people enjoy coming to work, where employees are engaged, and where trust is the norm, it is a natural progression for employees to take more personal responsibility for their jobs. In this cornerstone, we introduce the concept of the *Self-Directed/Other-Directed* model. It is a very powerful model, and one that I believe could change society dramatically if only more people were on the self-directed path rather than the other-directed path in life.

I remember reading an article years ago about a group of inmates in a California prison. The inmates were asked why they were in prison. Their answers were very telling. Several of them said it was their "girlfriend's (or ex-girlfriend's or wife's) fault. Many others said they had a bad lawyer. Others blamed it on the failure of their "buddy" or the "get away car." Less than 15% said they were in prison because they committed a crime! This is what being other-directed is about. It involves blaming others and not accepting responsibility for the choices we make. It often results in acting like a victim and/or getting revenge.

In the self-directed model, individuals develop a belief of "I choose to" rather than "I have to." It results in better decisions and a sense of personal responsibility in life. As leaders, we want to create a culture where employees become self-directed, not other-directed. We need self-starters, risk-takers, creative people who are willing to do what is right for our customers and each other, and to be accountable. However, there is often finger-pointing and disengagement within departments and throughout organizations. This disengagement costs organizations millions of dollars each year. In fact, some of the recent research from the Gallup Organization and others is staggering when you look at the large percentage of employees who are not fully engaged in their jobs. Many are just putting in their time.

Ask any leader if they have employees spending company time surfing the net or using company resources for personal use, taking long lunches and breaks, or making personal phone calls during work. We all know this happens. And it costs us all. Our process helps leaders develop the necessary skills to create a workplace where this type of behavior is greatly diminished. It helps people move from an "other-directed" way of behaving, to a "self-directed" way of living one's life.

We also use an assessment tool called the *Strategic Alignment Survey*™, which measures the level of employee engagement and the current level of trust within the organization. It assesses the clarity and agreement of areas such as vision, values, purpose, roles, and procedures. The survey breaks the data down by department, division, and numerous other formats to view what is going on within the organization. It is a great tool to use as a benchmark at the beginning and then later on in the process. It can provide the CEO and the senior team with a sense of where they are starting from, and where they want to be. You must be able to measure where you are, and the progress you make.

Our first step is to sit down with the CEO and other senior leaders to dialogue with them about their vision for their organization. We can then discuss the kinds of people they need to achieve their vision. Although this is usually fairly clear to them, the rest of the organization doesn't always understand or share that same vision. Through our conversations with the CEO and the senior team, we then put together an action plan based on the processes we have in place to move the organization forward.

Wright

Well, it was very helpful. I learned a lot in the last few minutes. This has been an exciting conversation. I really appreciate all the time that you took with me today, Paula, just to enlighten us.

Switzer

Well, thank you very much, David. It's been a real pleasure for me to be here, and to share some of what is happening with our clients. It's so exciting to see what a difference it can make when leaders create a workplace built on trust, where relational leadership happens, and when employees become committed and accountable.

Wright

Today we've been talking to Paula Switzer. Her company works with leaders who want achieve their vision more quickly, by turning employees into partners committed to the growth and success of the organization. And as we have found out this afternoon, I think she knows what she's talking about. Thank you so much, Paula.

Switzer

Thank you, David.

Relational Leadership is about the relationships we form—with ourselves and with those around us. It is about being accountable and responsible, and at the same time, vulnerable and real. It is about being a visionary as well as paying attention to the small things that really matter.

Exceptional leaders may differ greatly in their approach and style, but what I believe they share is their passion and their commitment to something greater than themselves. Watching my husband with our son, I am reminded of the constant job of being "on" as a good mentor/leader. He is quietly teaching our son, with everything he says and does. And our son is watching. Through his relational leadership approach, he speaks volumes about what is important in life, and how to approach self and others.

I worked for a CEO in an earlier career, who talked about what he called the "newspaper test." In making decisions about one's actions, he challenged us to consider what we did, and whether we would be proud of it showing up in the morning newspaper. Integrity is about doing what's right when no one is watching.

We must start with ourselves. We have to build a healthy relationship with our self, in order to maintain healthy relationships with others. Only then can we practice relational leadership, and build an organization where employees want to come to work and are fully engaged. Only then can we make a significant difference in the lives of others as well as a positive impact to the bottom-line. The cost of doing one without the other is typically quite high. And remember, someone is almost always watching... Never doubt the impact you have as a leader. Continually look for ways to enhance each person's self-esteem as you come into contact with them. Build strong relationships *and* solid results. Practice Relational Leadership.

About The Author

Paula Switzer believes in building leaders at every level. According to Paula, everyone has the capacity to become a leader. The challenge is creating the right environment to help each person flourish and use his/her special talents.

Throughout her personal and professional life, Paula has held numerous leadership positions, both formal and informal. She was a high school teacher, an insurance salesperson, and a marketing representative for IBM for several years, achieving top sales awards consistently. She received the Golden Circle Award for IBM, the first year she was eligible. This is given to the top 2% of account executives worldwide. She built and managed a customer support center, and served as general manager for a software development company in the long-term care industry.

Paula is a sought after national speaker, consultant and seminar leader, bringing over 20 years of experience in working with groups and organizations. A former faculty member for Fred Pryor Seminars, and a successful business owner for the last 12 years, Paula has spoken to well over 30,000 people in her career.

Paula is an associate with Integro Leadership Institute, which utilizes many of the models mentioned in her interview. In addition, she represents major publishers such Inscape Publishing, out of Minneapolis, MN and Vital Learning out of Omaha, NE. In a spirit of collaboration, Paula mentors a group of 25 consultants across the country, sharing expertise as well as marketing and product knowledge.

Paula has a Master's Degree in Human Resources and speaks fluent Spanish. She is also a member of the National Speakers Association and the International Speakers Network.

Paula K. Switzer, M.A.

Switzer Resource Group, Inc.

Bright Ideas for Brilliant Results!

Toll-Free 888-439-6070

FAX: 913.268.6070

Email: paula@trainingresources.com

Email: paula@relationaleadership.com

www.trainingresources.com

www.relationaleadership.com

The information on behavioral styles is adapted from the widely used DiSC® Model and DiSC Classic. DiSC Classic is copyrighted © 2001 by Inscape Publishing, Inc., Minneapolis, Minnesota. "DiSC" and "Inscape Publishing" are registered trademarks of Inscape Publishing, Inc. Used by permission.

Chapter 25

PAT MAYFIELD

THE INTERVIEW

David E. Wright (Wright)

Today, we welcome Pat Mayfield, the president of Pat Mayfield Consulting, LLC. Pat is a successful business consultant, professional trainer, and accomplished speaker. Pat's company, which specializes in leadership, negotiating, customer service, and business protocol, works with small companies to multi-billion dollar corporations in numerous industries. Pat credits her success as a consultant to her first-hand management experience.

Her career includes being a national award-winning sales manager in several multi-million dollar businesses. She was named one of the *"Top 25 Who Made It Happen"* in the furniture industry by *High Points* magazine, and also received the National President's Award from the Accessory Resource Team for developing a national retail training program.

Pat is the author of three books: *Giving and Getting: Tips on Negotiating, Business Tips and Techniques,* and *Manners for Success*™. In addition to consulting and training, she is the facilitator and trainer for Leadership Fremont, writes numerous business and leadership articles, and is a frequent radio and television guest.

Pat serves on the Board of Directors for Jr. Achievement, for which she was awarded the 2002 Bronze Award for Board members, and is classified as a Professional Speaker in the National Speakers Association. Pat holds an M.A. from Columbia University and an M.B.A. from St. Mary's College in Moraga, CA. Pat, welcome to *Leadership Defined!*

Pat Mayfield (Mayfield)
Thank you, David.

Wright
Pat, how do you define effective leadership?

Mayfield
To me, effective or true leadership is the ability to create change in the thought process and actions of others, and most importantly, to get results. We all know leaders who have the title or position of leadership, but accomplish little during their tenure. Although they are technically classified as a leader, they are not what I consider an *effective leader.* I believe individuals with true leadership skills know where they want the organization to go, have the ability to motivate others to take action, and have the necessary skills to make things happen and get things done.

Our image of a successful leader is not always accurate. When working with groups of leaders in training, I ask them to define and describe an effective leader. Typically, their image of a leader is a high-ranked position, a great talker, and a charismatic extrovert. True, being an excellent communicator is a definite advantage, but many effective leaders are not extroverts. More than 40% of the population of our country consider themselves to be shy. Many are surprised to learn that some of the greatest leaders may also be uncomfortable in certain social or business situations. Shy or introverted people are greatly encouraged to know they are not alone and that being shy is not a deterrent to great leadership.

Also, I believe true leadership is not limited to a high-ranked position, age, or title. Effective leadership can exist at any level or at any age. Generally, effective leaders are skillful in communicating, negotiating, persuading, and problem solving to name a few. Yet, with all these skills, a leader also must have the spirit, passion, and tenacity to motivate others.

I believe one of the highest levels of effective leadership is the successful leader who can transfer his or her skills to a new role in a new industry or organization and continue to be successful. The effective leader is always able to create growth and change, regardless of the organizations' location, hierarchy, goals, or objectives.

A good example of leadership skills transference is Millicent Wasell, who served as CEO of the Labor Relations Board for New Jersey for many years. She built a successful team even though she had little experience in labor relations. However, she came to that position as an experienced high-level leader with finely tuned skills that work with any organization. Millicent shared her formula of: 1) setting clear objectives, 2) delegating and providing support to team leaders, and 3) acknowledging and rewarding each person's successful results. She also shared that a leader should hire the smartest people she can find and give credit to those people when they deliver. Millicent has strong leadership skills plus incredible people skills that enable her to create change and motivate action, anytime, anywhere.

Wright

You've been involved in leadership activities and programs since you were in junior high school. Do you believe that leadership is developed early in life?

Mayfield

Although many of my leadership experiences were early in life, I think leadership can begin at any age. Some leaders will be leaders throughout their lifetime while others serve only one term. Some are intermittent, in-and-out leaders. Some start later in life such as those who wait until their children leave the nest.

An example of later-in-life leadership is my friend, Paul English, an award-winning journalist from Oklahoma City. Although he had not been involved in any leadership roles early in life, Paul became the President of the Oklahoma City School Board. He found himself so personally involved with the issues facing the Oklahoma City schools that he began to speak up and take a stand. This initial speaking up led to two terms of successful leadership during a controversial and difficult time.

Misty Tyree is a good example of in-and-out leadership. She was extremely active in high school as a leader in many organizations. Misty won numerous leadership awards in high school, yet opted to back off extracurricular activities in college. After college she became active in organizations again, further developing her leadership skills. She recently completed two terms on the National Board of Directors for her sorority. Misty is now a sought-after motivational speaker and serves on several boards of directors in the San Francisco area.

The main advantage of starting early is that you have more opportunities and experiences on which to build. The earlier you start the more chances you have to: 1) develop your leadership style, 2) build and practice leadership skills, and 3) understand the common threads of the leadership process.

Also, the more experiences one has, the more he or she understands both the glory *and* the frustrations of leadership. It is not unusual for new leaders to have an unrealistic perception of their upcoming term or tenure, and unrealistic expectations of the members or employees. The reality is that one's term or tenure is not totally predictable or controllable, nor is the membership. An experience leader understands, expects, plans and prepares for the unexpected, while a new leader may be surprised by both the good and the bad.

New leaders are often surprised, regardless of their training and preparation because they incorrectly think that things will be different for them. The key is not to be crushed by the surprises and challenges, but to learn and to grow from them. Early success is important to ensure the new leader does not become discouraged and leave the leadership arena prematurely.

Wright

So where did you find leadership opportunities when you were young?

Mayfield

Most of my early leadership opportunities were in the 4-H program, which offers the experience of competing, club leadership roles, and numerous opportunities to present and perform in public. I have no doubt the early leadership opportunities in 4-H made me more comfortable in participating in leadership roles later in life.

My family didn't live on a farm, so I participated in non-rural activities such as the speech contest, the dress review, and the method demonstration in food preparation, and numerous other events. Since these events were held every year, we had many opportunities to practice and to compete. Fortunately, most of the competitions required some form of public presentation, which provided valuable practice in speech and presentation skills.

These early competitions really taught me that I gained just as much, if not more, from losing than I did from winning. When I lost a competition, I was motivated to look more closely at what I could do to improve. If I were to win the next time I had to improve—simple as that.

I vividly remember one state competition. Now don't laugh, but while competing in the biscuit contest, I looked in the oven and was horrified my biscuits had not risen. When I took them out, I discovered the biscuits were hard as rocks! I couldn't believe I had left out the baking powder! I knew I would not win, so I dropped the biscuits into the trashcan and left. That was the second mistake. The biscuits made a loud thud when they hit the bottom of the metal can, and everybody turned and looked at me. Today, on the rare occasion I make biscuits from scratch, I always include the baking powder! This is a simple example, but it illustrates that we learn from mistakes...especially our own.

In 4-H, I competed at the county, state, and national levels. The national trips I won were extremely meaningful in forming my perceptions of the importance and value of effective leadership. I have vivid memories of staying at the Conrad B. Hilton hotel in Chicago, while competing in the National Dress Review, and staying at the National 4-H Center in Washington, D.C. while representing Arkansas at the National Leadership Conference.

Wright

Where are the opportunities for young people today?

Mayfield

It is amazing how many youth organizations and programs are available for young people today. 4-H, Junior Achievement, The Boys and Girls Clubs of America, YMCA, YWCA, Boy Scouts, Girl Scouts, and church- and school-sponsored programs and organizations. Also, today's sports programs are available for both boys and girls and offer excellent leadership training and team-building experiences.

Recently, I came across an article in *Time* magazine about a young leader from Arkansas. A senior in high school, Jonathan Wichman, had just completed his one-year term as national president of FCCLA (Family, Career and Community Leaders of America), a youth leadership organization. (More information is available on the associations' website www.fccla.com.)

Thanks to the Internet, I located and talked to Jonathan about his term as National President. He shared he was not a particularly motivated 12-year old until the horrible school shootings at Jonesboro's Westside Middle School, in March 1998. Although Jonathan was not a student at Westside, he lived only 15 miles from the school. Jonathan was greatly affected by this defining event and became interested in joining the FCCLA because of this organization's STOP the Violence program.

Being originally from Arkansas, I was especially touched by his story. To go from being disinterested at age 12 to being a national president is truly impressive. When I asked Jonathan what he thought it took to be an effective leader, he said he believes that it is the leader's passion and positive energy that makes the difference between being a leader and being an effective leader.

Wright

So how important is it to have a leadership mentor?

Mayfield

Working with a leadership mentor can be a tremendous benefit to a new or experienced leader. One of the most successful CEOs in California once told me that having a mentor—the right mentor—could make the difference in reaching the top and staying on top.

The *right mentor* can speed the process to the top, increase the quality of leadership performance, and help the budding leader better understand the realities of leadership. Mentors are informative guides to share first-hand experiences, political savvy, and what works and what doesn't. A great mentor also plays the role of devil's advocate and serves as a sounding board. By providing trusted advice and insights, mentors help the new leader develop skills faster, reduce the number of mistakes, and decrease the alone-at-the-top syndrome.

The best mentors have the experience, wisdom, success, and the willingness and availability to share, and can create an environment of trust. Because it is almost impossible to find the perfect mentor match, the protégé needs to determine his or her needs first and then seek mentors with those skills. Some leaders may have great organization skills, while others may be strong in strategy and tactics or in networking and social skills.

The mentoring relationship is only as good as the preparation and participation of the protégé and the mentor. Time availability is a major issue in a mentoring relationship. Protégés need to make it as easy as possible for the mentor to help. Knowing the protégé's specific goals and needs will speed up the process, reduce mentoring time, and increase the quality of the mentoring relationship.

Working with more than one mentor can be an asset to both the mentor and the protégé. Multiple mentors provide a wider scope of information and experience to the protégé. Some advantages of having multiple mentors are: less time needed from each mentor, diversity of expertise, variety of leadership styles, personalities, and agendas.

The mentoring experience can occur not only through personal meetings, but through written communications, and observations as well. In fact, one of my key mentors is someone I've never met. Bill Walsh, former coach of the San Francisco 49ers, has no idea his style of management set the standard for me. Coach Walsh exhibited the style of leadership I wanted to emulate as a new corporate manager. He thoroughly knew the game, worked with a strategy and system, treated his players with dignity and respect and as professionals. His leadership performance was not only an inspiration...it worked!

Wright

Pat, as a consultant, you work with a lot of organizations. So how do organizations find and develop their leaders?

Mayfield

That's a fascinating question because there are so many different ways to discover leaders. Leaders may be found within the company or even in a competing organization. The selection process is rarely limited to established leaders. Newcomers often emerge to the short list of consideration because an executive has observed the leadership potential in an entry-level employee or a new hire.

The process of the selection of leaders is generally planned, but chance meetings and being at the right place at the right time is not unusual. Companies and organizations may even select potential leaders because of the impressions made during the initial meeting. The first three to seven seconds of an observation can truly make an important and lasting first impression.

On one assignment in the corporate world, I had the opportunity to create a new national sales force for a new business, in new channels of distribution, in a new industry. I had no contacts or connections in this industry. It was not until this assignment that I fully understood and believed in the power of first impressions. After interviewing potential salespeople in two major cities, the individuals whom I listed at the top of the "Strong Potential to Hire" list, were the ones who had impressed me from the start.

For the remainder of the nation-wide interviews, I noted how many seconds it took to form an opinion of each applicant. After the sales force was organized, I went back to the rating list of first impressions and discovered all of the individuals I hired made a positive impression within the first three to seven seconds.

Although the sales force I hired was a credentialed and experienced group, I developed and used the Three-E Theory as criteria in the selection process. Most of the sales, product, and company training I could provide myself, but I wanted to hire individuals who exhibited energy, empathy, and enthusiasm...characteristics I do not believe are trainable. When I left that position ten years later, 75 percent of the sales force at that time was original hires. I believe the power of the first impression combined with the Three-E Theory helped in selecting the right individuals for the job.

Many companies develop their leaders through training and grooming based on individual need. Emerging leaders may also be placed on a fast track program, which provides a wide base of experience and exposure in different departments. While many companies sponsor company-based training and internal mentoring programs, many companies are utilizing outside consultants and trainers. The use of outside consultants is increasing tremendously today, as companies do not have the manpower and time to provide internal training. Companies are also finding great value in the diversity of information from outside consultants.

Wright

Pat, many say that great leaders are born and not trained. What's your position on this view?

Mayfield

I believe effective leaders can be either a born, natural leader, or a trained leader. Generally, born leaders have a natural charisma that draws others to them. Because stepping up to the plate is natural for them, they are comfortable in accepting leadership roles early in life. Once they have proven themselves, he or she is often considered the most logical person for the next leadership assignment. Multiple roles of leadership are offered and success breeds success.

However, many wonderful leaders have learned how to be an effective leader through training. Many leadership abilities such as communicating, negotiating, evaluating, and problem solving are trainable stills. Continual preparation and practice will increase one's abilities, while the actual experience in leadership roles will increase one's confidence and self esteem.

Motivation may be the single most important determining factor to those who do not have the natural gift of leadership to become a leader. We have a nation of extraordinary leaders who overcame many difficulties and challenges to be leaders. A great example is Eleanor Roosevelt. She had a difficult childhood; her mother died when Eleanor was only eight and her alcoholic father passed away when she was ten. Eleanor had an enormous fear of public speaking; yet, she became one of our nation's greatest speakers and leaders.

Wright

What do you think motivates one to become a leader?

Mayfield

People want to become leaders for many different reasons, some good and some not so good. We prefer to think leaders have the highest level of intentions, from the good of the cause or the good of the organization, but sometimes the motivations are as simple as greed and personal power.

The motivations for leadership are as varied as the personalities of the leaders. Some of the more positive, idealistic motivations are: helping out in a crisis, being discontent with the status quo, wanting to promote a worthy cause, and helping others who cannot help themselves. Some motivations are not so admirable: greed, jealousy, or preventing the other person from getting the assignment. Other motivations include title, respected position, security, safety, money (or more money), better connections, perks, and ego.

Ego, I believe, is one of the most significant and controversial of the motivations. Some think ego is a negative, but I think ego creates and fuels the passion, responsibility, drive, and hopefully, the accountability of a leader. Even if someone is considered egotistical, this may be what it takes to get things accomplished. Ego can produce many positive results.

Also, the basic resources of time, money, and people are important determining factors in motivating a leader. A leader must have these basic resources to focus and devote themselves fully to a leadership role. Leadership can be an incredible challenge without the needed time, funding, or support. Wise leaders understand the cost of leadership and consider these factors in their decision to lead.

Wright

Your passion for leadership is obvious. What is it that you find so exciting about leadership training?

Mayfield

I believe effective leadership is about growth and change. I most enjoy working with new and experienced leaders who are willing to improve, take risks, and try new skills. The growth cycle of leadership is continuous as effective leaders stay abreast of the changes in systems, demographics, techniques, and technology.

Effective leadership requires consistency and leaders can find performing constantly at a high level to be an incredible challenge. Being an effective leader is hard work and takes a great deal of time.

Not only is leadership not easy, it can be difficult at times. New and experienced leaders will find it valuable to understand that challenges, surprises, and disappointment are part of the leadership formula. Here are four of the twenty leadership observations I use to prepare new organization leaders in the beginning of their terms: 1) you will not be able to fix all the problems or issues in your tenure, 2) people will both surprise and disappoint you, 3) relationships will change, 4) your perspective of your role and people will be different at the end of your tenure than in the beginning.

The majority of the new leaders I train express that they believe it will be different (and easier) during their term. However, it doesn't take long for the new leader to report that his or her perceptions are changing. This awareness is part of the leadership learning curve.

It is this level of change and growth, and especially the willingness of the leader to accept the difficulties along with the pleasures and to keep on going, that I find exciting!

The greatest experience for me is to witness the personal and professional achievements of the leaders I train.

Wright

We hear a lot about successful leaders being visionaries. In you opinion, is that a talent, a gift, or a developed skill?

Mayfield

I believe that being a successful visionary is a combination of all three. One of my favorite quotes is from Jonathan Swift, who said, "Vision is the art of seeing things invisible." Anyone can try to predict and envision the future, but it is difficult to be accurate or even close to being accurate. One great leader in the health industry, who is known for her successful visionary approach, said in addition to her futuristic thinking mindset, she reads numerous newspapers, magazines, and books to help her recognize current trends that can lead to future change.

The organization that has a visionary leader is fortunate, indeed. Howard Schultz, Chairman and CEO of Starbucks envisioned retail stores that sold individual cups of coffee, not just coffee beans, in hundreds of locations when there were only five Starbucks stores.

Wright

In your book, *Giving and Getting: Tips on Negotiating,* you emphasize the mutually beneficial approach to negotiating. How did you develop this philosophy?

Mayfield

One of my consulting clients who was able to reach her negotiation goals, encouraged me to share my negotiating system with others, and thus, the genesis for book, *Giving and Getting: Tips on Negotiating.* This book is based on my experiences negotiating multi-million dollar deals in the corporate world.

Fortunately, I had the opportunity to negotiate with a variety of personality types, negotiating styles and approaches. The other parties often had their own personal agendas along with their professional goals. The ability to determine the real agendas and especially the hidden agendas of the other party became a real asset to successful negotiating. Because I negotiated frequently, I was able to try a lot of different techniques and a variety of approaches.

The years of negotiating experience provided a tremendous training ground to develop negotiating tools that worked. Negotiating with individuals from the aggressive and ruthless to the fair and highly ethical provided a wide range of invaluable experiences. Effective leaders and negotiators have much in common; they must be able to ask for what they want and need, and to be able to get it.

The greatest lesson I learned was when both parties receive something of value, both are more willing to return to the negotiating table prepared to give. As much as I prefer the mutually beneficial approach to negotiating, it is important for one to know how to negotiate with those who use the zero sum game approach. In the zero-sum game, the winner takes all—one party wins; the other loses.

It is not unusual for a mutually beneficial negotiation to turn into a zero-sum game. At this point, the mutually beneficial negotiator must be able to protect and defend himself and his company. Also, some of the other parties just want to win and take all, so you have to be prepared to hold your own.

During all those years of negotiating, I had no idea there was a complex mathematical formula for cooperative negotiating. John F. Nash, Jr. won the Nobel Prize for Economic Sciences for developing the equilibrium theory, which is the mutually beneficial and cooperative approach to negotiating. Dr. Nash's fascinating story was told in the award-winning movie, *A Beautiful Mind*.

Wright

I understand you give presentations on business protocol. Because our country has become so casual I have to ask, is it really that important any more?

Mayfield

I think because we have become so casual, protocol and etiquette training have become extremely important. I've noticed a definite trend for protocol training for all levels of leaders. In addition to an increased interest in the protocol for our culture, I'm experiencing increased requests for protocol training on other cultures and countries.

Protocol is invaluable to leadership success. Most corporate leaders or other highly visible community and political leaders have extremely good manners and are comfortable in a multitude of situations. The ultimate goal in protocol is for one to know the rules and to be comfortable in any situation. The leader who is comfortable is the leader with the competitive edge. The leader who is comfortable can focus on the business at hand, not which fork to use.

When I started my consulting company, one of my first assignments was to provide protocol training for the new hires of a large corporation. For this assignment I developed a handout on protocol, which eventually became my first book, *Manners for Success™*. Because of customer requests, I'm currently working on a new version, which will include protocol of other countries and cultures. That's how important the business of protocol has become.

Wright

When you were named one of the Top 25 Who Made It Happen in the Furniture Industry, you were quoted in *High Points* magazine that your favorite saying is *"Keep the Faith."* Why is that an important slogan for you?

Mayfield

The slogan "Keep the Faith" has meant a lot to me throughout my life because it is a wonderful reminder that I do have faith and that faith will keep me strong. We don't know what the future holds, but knowing that no matter what happens, we'll get through it, is incredibly reassuring. I have had a lot of changes in my life, some good, some not so good, moved 19 times all over this country, have had several careers and positions, and yet it's the faith that doesn't change.

"Keep the faith" is not just about getting through difficult times, it is a wonderful reminder to simplify, to live in the moment, to value our fiends and our family and most of all, to focus on others. And lastly, I do have a great deal of faith, which reminds me that I always want to have His grace and never lose it.

Wright

Well, what an interesting conversation. I certainly appreciate you taking this time with me today. I think this is going to add significantly to our book, *Leadership Defined*.

Mayfield

David, thank you so much. It is an honor to be a part of this program.

THE CALL TO LEADERSHIP
HELP WANTED: LEADERS — ANY AGE, ANYWHERE, ANYTIME

The position of leadership may require the following attributes:

DECISION MAKING: The leader must be able to make a decision; make, take, and maintain a stand; create change; build strategies and tactics that work; hire or select the right people; and resolve problems.

PEOPLE SKILLS: The ideal candidate will have the ability to lead others to take action, pacify the naysayer, deflect undue and unfair criticism, explain and justify due criticism, deal with difficult people, defuse conflicts, and be graceful under attack.

THE "ATE"S: The leader will need the ability to delegate, motivate, evaluate, participate, negotiate, articulate, calculate, and never be late.

MONEY: The leader should be able to understand the financials of the organization, create rationale short- and long-term budgets, obtain necessary funding, and be willing to accept equitable or inequitable pay and benefits...if any are available.

SPEAKING: The leader may need the ability to work with the media, be interviewed by the press, appear on radio and television, give interesting speeches, speak extemporaneously, give informative reports, introduce others with ease, and give an appropriate toast.

THE EXTRAS: The ideal candidate will be able to devote the necessary hours to the role, have an understanding family or support group, be creative, be a good writer, be organized, and most importantly, be a visionary.

PERSONAL: The best candidate will be able to handle close scrutiny, inconvenience to family, and the pressures that accompany the job. Also, the ideal candidate will dress appropriately, know proper protocol, have good manners, have a proper hand shake, like a variety of foods, not chew gum in public, remember names, have good grooming habits, avoid scandalous activities, will be a fair player, smile when appropriate, and lastly, will be modest.

Leadership positions are found in the following areas: your neighborhood, community, county, state, and nation. Numerous positions are available through schools, local non-profit organizations, small and medium businesses, large corporations, public sector positions (appointed and elected), and local and national associations.

Please Apply! Great Rewards Ahead!

About The Author

Pat Mayfield, the president of Pat Mayfield Consulting, LLC, is an accomplished speaker, professional trainer, and successful business consultant. Pat's first-hand expertise is based on two decades as a national award-winning sales manager. Audiences give high marks to her practical, use-right-now ideas delivered with humor and enthusiasm. "Top of the Tree Leadership," "Negotiating Tool Box," and "The Business of Protocol" are three of her most popular presentation topics. Pat also offers organization leadership facilitating. She holds MA and MBA degrees and has authored three books.

Pat Mayfield

Pat Mayfield Consulting, LLC

P. O. Box 10095

Pleasanton, California 94588

Phone: 925.600.0584

Email: pat@patmayfield.com

www.patmayfield.com

Chapter 26

RICHARD TYLER

THE INTERVIEW

David E. Wright (Wright)

Today we are talking to Richard Tyler. Richard is the CEO of Richard Tyler International, Inc., an organization that is one of the top training and consulting firms in the world. Mr. Tyler's success in sales, management, customer service, and quality improvement, and his reputation for powerful educational methods and motivational techniques have made him one of the most sought after consultants, lecturers, and teachers. Mr. Tyler shares his philosophies with millions of individuals each year through keynote speaking, syndicated writing, radio, television, seminars, books, tapes, and CDs. Mr. Tyler's book, *Smart Business Strategies, the Guide to Small Business Marketing Excellence*, has been hailed as one of the best books ever written for small business marketing. His *Power Learning Series* of business books and his *Conversations On* books are a great success. His philosophies have been featured in *Entrepreneur Magazine* and *Sales and Marketing Management Magazine* as well as in hundreds of articles and interviews. Mr. Tyler is the founder of Leadership for Tomorrow™, an organization dedicated to educating young adults to the importance of self esteem, goal setting, and lifelong success. Mr. Tyler is a member of the *National Speakers Association*, the *Interna-*

tional Platform Association, the *American Society for Training and Development,* and the *Society for Human Resource Management.* Mr. Tyler has served on the *Houston National Speakers Association* Board of Directors. For 14 consecutive years Mr. Tyler has been listed in *Who's Who in Professional Speaking.* Mr. Tyler is an Advisory Board Member and past Chairman of the *"Be An Angel Fund, Inc."* which helps multiply handicapped and profoundly deaf children to have a better life.

Richard Tyler, welcome to *Leadership Defined!*

Richard Tyler (Tyler)

Thank you, David. I am delighted to be here!

Wright

Richard, your firm conducts extensive sales performance training as well as leadership excellence training. Do you see a connection between leadership and successful selling?

Tyler

Absolutely; many of the principles we teach in our Sales-Excellence courses are also taught in our Leadership-Excellence programs. That's not to say that the two are the same, but many of the principles that make a person successful as a leader are the same principles that make a person successful as a sales professional. As an example, take communication. The foundation of all masterful selling is excellent communication skills. Not surprisingly, the foundation of great leadership is also excellent communication skills.

When you're talking about such principles as excellent communication, commitment, valuing others, integrity and sincerity, there is no distinction between whether you're teaching "leadership skills" or "selling skills." If you wandered into one of our sales excellence programs and then visited one of our leadership excellence programs you would overhear some similar discussions. That's because we believe that *character* is what drives success and it is why these components are key elements of our education programs.

We believe that changes on the surface are short-lived. If you want real, lasting change, it has to occur at a deep level. So our programs are designed to address change at this level and, yes, there is a strong connection between leadership and successful selling.

Wright

So where do you see leadership playing a key role in the sales process?

Tyler

A good leader will manage the entire sales process using sound leadership principles. But if I had to identify one area specifically where sound leadership is most critical, it would be in what we call the "Wants and Needs Analysis™" phase. This is where the salesperson must take on a leadership role to ensure that the right information is gathered to determine exactly what the customer's wants and needs are. This is the part of the process that many try to "manage" as opposed to "lead," and the whole sales process suffers.

Let me provide an example. Imagine that Jim, a software sales professional is meeting with a new client. In the initial discussions, Jim asks the client what products interest her. She mentions a specific piece of contact-management software. The sales professional asks how soon she would need the software and then how many licenses her company needs. Jim is diligent in following through with processing the software order and in making sure everything is delivered timely. He feels good that he has met his customer's needs.

One month later, Jim calls his new client to ask how the new software is working out. He quickly discovers that she is not very happy. He then learns that what she really needed was a much more comprehensive customer relationship management product—a product that Jim sold. Jim *managed* the sale of the software—he made sure she had the correct number of licenses and that she got it on time. In this case, Jim should have spent a lot more time probing to truly understand the client's real needs and not just react to the customer's first response. By probing and leading the customer through a discussion of how she would be using the software, Jim would have been able to discuss the CRM software and ultimately had a very satisfied customer—not to mention a bigger sale. Effectively resolving a customer's concerns that may arise is critical to leading the customer to a positive investment decision. Leading in this environment also includes creating balance in acquiring what information is necessary to move forward and what keeps the customer psychologically comfortable. Yes, that's sales, but it is also leadership.

This is a simple example, but it's reality—leadership matters in the sales process yet it is often not practiced.

Wright

A lot is made of natural leadership. Do you believe that leaders are "made" or are they "born?"

Tyler

I believe that leadership skills come more naturally to some than others; however, everyone can become a more effective leader and every great leader that I know works to develop their leadership skills. In fact, many of them would never have been mistaken as leaders earlier in their lives. There is a common misconception that good leaders are all alike, that there is one mold, which forms all successful leaders. People mistakenly believe that if they can just fit themselves into that form, they'll become successful leaders. That is simply not true.

The image of the smooth, wise, outgoing, yet poised person who can instantly create order from chaos with one line of perfect, quotable wisdom is what we are often led to believe is the model image of the "effective leader." That style may be effective for some, but I've known just as many effective leaders who are reserved and introverted as those who are outgoing extroverts.

My point is this: leadership skills, like most other skills, must be developed, regardless of the personality a person is born with and develops through childhood. And it doesn't really matter who you are or what your role is in life. Whether you are a CEO, a parent, a manager, a nurse, a sales professional, or whatever, there are components of your role that make you a leader—you may not be a good one, but you *are* a leader.

When people recognize this and take steps to improve their leadership skills they usually improve those skills quickly. And when they see the improvement, it increases their appetite for working harder to improve even more. Before you know it, they are being recognized as successful leaders.

Wright

So exactly what makes good leaders successful?

Tyler

First, we'd have to define "successful." There are many good leaders—even *great* leaders—that many would say experienced a lot more failure than success in their lives. Look at Abraham Lincoln, considered one of the United States' greatest leaders. Before becoming

President, he failed at business, farming and many times in politics. But that didn't mean he wasn't a great leader. What made him successful as a leader were the leadership characteristics he developed throughout his life. For example, he developed an astute ability to observe and listen to other people; great leaders get to know those they lead. He focused energy on those things he could influence; great leaders understand how to prioritize. Lincoln handled conflict by finding common ground; great leaders understand how to cultivate teamwork. He drew upon his own experiences to communicate his messages; great leaders know how to create a common language to communicate and reach agreement. These characteristics are the types of skills that can be taught and cultivated to enhance a person's success as a leader.

I am convinced that the deepest human desire is to feel loved, wanted, needed and important. When a person understands this and develops the characteristics that support helping others satisfy this desire, then leadership is the result. A person leading a team is successful if she is able to clearly demonstrate that every member of the team is needed and that the goals of the team are important. This seems so simple and obvious, but the problem is that it isn't easy to accomplish. Just consider your own experience with teams. Chances are you have had more negative experiences than positive ones. And yet every team you served had a leader—maybe it was even you. Isn't it the leader's responsibility to make sure every member of the team understands his or her responsibility? Shouldn't each member of the team feel valued? Few people would disagree; so why are so many teams ineffective? It goes back to what makes leaders successful. Unless certain fundamental characteristics are in place and practiced, leaders are not likely going to inspire great results and the team and the team objectives suffer.

Wright

Are these the kinds of fundamental characteristics that require a significant change for some people?

Tyler

Yes. And as we all know, change is rarely easy—particularly when we're talking about changing what might be for some, basic personality traits. For many of us, change is an ever-evolving process—it's not a one-time thing. But I also believe that it doesn't have to be dramatic to be effective. Often, regular, incremental change is the most powerful because it has the greatest likelihood of being sustainable. It's like a person who decides to lose 50 pounds in a short period of time by going on a crash diet. It almost never succeeds because the proposed change is so dramatic and so difficult that it is too easy to give up.

The critical first step on the road to improvement is the commitment to make change—even if it's a commitment to start with some small changes. We teach that such a commitment must be a **Commitment to *Excellence*™**; a mental determination to accept only excellence no matter how difficult, no matter how uncomfortable and no matter how stressful. Sometimes a student will recoil a bit when they hear us talk about this commitment. They hear the words, "difficult," "uncomfortable" and "stressful" and think, "Wait a minute, I don't think I'm ready for that." But the reality is, significant, meaningful change will never happen without this kind of commitment. If a person is interested in improving leadership skills, or any other skills for that matter, this initial commitment is absolutely necessary. When the decision is made to commit to the process of improving, yes, significant change *is* often required. And the whole process of making positive changes permanent is a hallmark of all our education programs. In fact, we have a process called the **"Tyler Learning 6"™** that is a foundational element to all our education. This six-step process provides a system that our students can use to help make change easier and permanent.

Committing to change is the important first step. But it is just the beginning of course. Often the biggest challenge for all of us wanting to significantly improve our leadership skills is to know *what* to change.

Wright

Okay, so how does a person who wants to change figure out exactly what needs to be changed?

Tyler

Good question. Once you have identified the things you know you need to change, there are some things you can do to identify those things you may not be aware of. Many people identify with a particular role model. Whether it is a colleague, a public figure, an author, a speaker, a friend, whoever it is, spend some time writing down the characteristics that you admire about that person. Is it how they talk, how they carry themselves, how well they can command attention, tell a story or conduct a presentation? Is it how they treat those around them? Whatever those things are—and you should pull positive characteristics from several sources—assess your own level of skill against your role model regarding these skills. If there are big differences anywhere, you know you've hit upon some areas to improve.

You can also find someone you trust—I recommend not using your significant other for this exercise—and tell them that you are serious about improving your leadership skills. Tell them that you are coming to them because you have always been able to count on them for candid feedback and that you value their opinion. Ask them to identify at least one or two areas that could be improved. I always tell people that if they decide to engage in this process, <u>be prepared</u>. The first reaction we all have in the face of constructive feedback is to get defensive. After all, you're asking for information that you don't have. When you hear it for the first time, it may not be easy to take. So prepare yourself by committing to listen carefully, write down everything that is said and suppress the urge to get defensive. Just make sure you get the feedback written down as it is presented. You'll have time later to review it, consider it and respond to it. If you don't write it down as it is being presented, you'll miss a lot of it because you will be subconsciously defending yourself and you may start thinking *"What? I don't do that! Who thinks that I'm that way? Hey you're one to talk!"* and so on. You should also understand that the feedback may not be reality, but it will be the perception from someone you trust.

Great leaders are very aware that perception is reality and there are reasons that perception exists. Remember too, that the person providing the feedback is really going out on a limb. It's probably going to be someone who has a good relationship with you and that person wants to help, but doesn't want to damage the relationship. Acknowledge that; thank this person for the candid feedback and discuss what changes he or she thinks would help improve your leadership skills. Most people will not go through this process, and it's really too bad. This can be one of the most valuable tools to understanding what needs to be changed and how it can be changed to improve your leadership.

A third way to identify what needs to be developed to improve your skills as a leader is professional training. This is often the best way to get lasting results quickly. A good leadership training organization can help you quickly identify what skills should be developed and then how to develop them. Again, I go back to the ranks of successful leaders. Many will tell you that they never stop learning, that they never stop formal training. They understand the importance of continuously sharpening the saw—always improving what's in their leadership tool kit. Some of the most successful people I know return to our training programs year after year. Most people would say these professionals are so successful that they no longer need formal leadership training. That's a misconception because if you are not improving, your skills are deteriorating and that's why the best keep returning.

Wright

In your professional leadership training programs, what are some of the techniques you use to help leaders improve their skills?

Tyler

We use a variety of techniques because we know that people learn in different ways. We help our leadership students diagnose their own leadership style and what areas need the most development. We use visual aids, active participation, small group exercises and real-world scenarios. We also use a lot of specific examples to help develop the concept and improve retention.

We help make the process of learning key techniques easier and recalling them automatic by using a series of memory devices called *Mental Anchors*™. As the name implies the techniques anchor the process into the mind for quick responses. In our programs, we teach that there are four levels of learning—four stages that take a person from being completely unaware of what needs to be changed to practicing new, well-developed skills without even thinking about it. The process is not unlike learning to drive a car with a manual transmission. The first time out feels completely alien to you. You've got this third pedal and you have to advance the shifter in proper sequence to get the car moving—it seems very confusing and very unnatural. Over time, with lots of practice, you begin to understand what is supposed to happen and why. Then, with more practice you begin to see progress toward making the car do what you want. After even more practice, you start to operate the car without thinking too much about the proper sequence, and eventually, it becomes as automatic as, well, an automatic. If you have a good teacher, you will learn quickly and get to that "automatic" stage relatively quickly. If you don't have a good teacher, you can become very frustrated and may even give up without *ever* learning.

There are some very good programs out there for leaders today, but the one thing I would always suggest to look for in a professional training organization is practical application. Far too much money is wasted on programs that pack hundreds or thousands of people into an auditorium or conference center to simply lecture for hours or days. Although there is nothing inherently wrong with a seminar series, it shouldn't be mistaken for a program that will foster positive, long-term change. There is nothing like real world practice to help develop skills, so in our programs, we give our leadership students the opportunity to practice their skills and get objective, action oriented feedback.

The most important technique that we teach is that leadership development is an ongoing process that doesn't stop once a leadership program ends.

Wright

We seem to know good leadership when we see it, but we seem to have a hard time finding it in ourselves. Why is that?

Tyler

Like anything, those who are very good at it make it look easy. But I have found that many people also overlook traits that others see as valuable. In fact, many people *are* leaders yet they don't think of themselves as leaders. In this circumstance, the challenge is that since people don't see themselves as leaders, they don't put forth an effort to improve their skills as leaders. Eventually, their performance suffers and they don't even know why.

For most people, identity as a leader comes from their employer. If the people who *are* leaders don't see themselves as leaders, then the organization is missing some big opportunities. When I'm invited into an organization to help determine ways we can help improve overall performance, one of the first questions I ask is, "Who are your leaders?" This gives me a good indication up front how the senior management team views leadership. If I get a short list of the people who are the most highly compensated and who have the most impressive titles, I know right away that "leadership" is more than likely confused with position. Identifying the real leaders and empowering them with tools to assess and develop their skills is one of the fastest ways to accelerate corporate performance.

We have a large number of clients that see the benefits of ongoing leadership development. They are successful as an organization because they realize the importance of identifying leadership skills and cultivating them in their people on a regular and ongoing basis. Oftentimes, companies ask us to customize our training programs to fit their industry and integrate the techniques into their overall corporate culture. We may conduct dozens of programs and train hundreds of people for one organization. These companies have seen the impact of getting the entire organization focused on improving their leadership competence.

Those companies that confuse leadership with position, and reserve leadership training only for those with the biggest titles miss the incredible benefits that come with building and empowering leaders throughout the organization. And by the way, great leaders also make great followers. In any given situation, a person who is a leader in one scenario might be a follower in another. The more leaders there are in an organization, the better and more successful the organization. Many times we are working with a company and we're in a meeting with a number of people around the table. Most of the time, it only takes a couple of minutes to figure out who the leaders are in the meeting and who the followers are. And lest there be any doubt, the "leader" makes it clear who is in charge. On the other hand, I love working with those companies where you can't tell where people fit on the organization chart. These meetings are the ones that are pulling in input from all participants and there are no artificial barriers to participation. Those are the meetings where there are a lot of good leaders involved.

Wright

You mentioned that you believe that there are different styles of management that are effective. Is a person's leadership style something that is fixed or should it change based on the situation?

Tyler

It is certainly true that an organization's leadership and management style needs change depending on where the organization is in its development. It is important to point out here that management and leadership are different. When educating people at our seminars I like to start with a simple view of the differences. In its purest form to lead people is: *to inspire them to achieve or do things they would not necessarily achieve or do left on their own.*

To manage people and ourselves is: *to direct, encourage, expect and inspect the day-to-day activities that are the action plan of the objectives to be achieved.*

To lead and manage effectively we have to make some determination about ourselves. Time and again we see examples of leaders at the helm of corporations being replaced by someone who is said to represent some change that the corporation needs in order to move forward.

However, it is very rare that an individual leader's style can change very significantly even if required by organizational evolution. This certainly shouldn't come as a surprise to anyone. It's hard enough to change anything; imagine becoming successful and then having to admit that what made you successful is no longer adequate. Most will never make the transition. We've all heard it many times: a new organization needs an entrepreneurial spirit; a maturing organization that is out of the start-up phase needs operations management spirit to establish effective processes and a large, mature corporation needs a seasoned corporate veteran to guide the ship. This is true to some degree; however, excellent leaders will recognize their shortcomings and find people that have the skills necessary. Remember, every organization can benefit from all three skill sets.

Generally speaking, every great leader has a unique style that takes advantage of the leader's character strengths. There are many different styles of leadership although I do not believe there is one right leadership style; I do believe that great leaders are adaptive. They know how to modify and adapt their style to handle diverse situations. Their underlying preferred style may not change, but the way it manifests itself can. One leader of an organization that is facing a very difficult crisis may choose to meet one-on-one with employees to discuss their concerns and encourage them. Another day, the same leader might prefer to charge up the troops with a big pep rally. In the end the result might very well be exactly the same. The leader simply adapted his style to get results based on the organization's needs. It takes a great deal of skill to be able to effectively adapt a leadership style to various situations, but it can be done. The more comfortable a person becomes at understanding his or her leadership style and how to effectively develop and use the leadership skills already possessed, the better that person will be at being able to adapt his or her leadership style.

Wright

Why do so many of us struggle when it comes to knowing how to be a better leader?

Tyler

When you consider that we spend most of our lives being taught how to be followers, it's really not too surprising that we struggle a bit to become better leaders. All through school we're taught rules of following: stay quiet, walk in a single-file line, raise your hand before speaking, wait your turn, follow instructions, complete this assignment this way, and on and on. Then, when we begin our careers, we are in entry-level positions where we focus on learning the rules of the road. We believe—and rightly so—that what gets rewarded is being an obedient follower. We all understand that every organization has a very well developed unwritten rulebook that guides the savvy employee through the rules of being a good follower. Then one day, we're handed a management title and we often don't know where to begin. The rulebook didn't cover that. We never learned how to be a leader as kids—we were too busy trying to figure out how to be a follower. We never had "leadership 101" in college—in fact, no one ever offered it. So, we say "Now what?"

The process of shifting gears and finding role models and sources to help is not easy. Many people scour the business section of the bookstore to find that perfect "Leadership How To" book. What people often tell me is that they find entertaining and inspiring reading about very successful people. But they are left with very little if any practical guidance for the leaders in the trenches needing concrete guidance.

A friend of mine told me that when he went to business school, he was really looking forward to the university's speaker series because the list of speakers was the "A-list" from American business. But he said time and time again, he was disappointed with the presentations because although they were often interesting, he found very little practical insight.

We hear these stories over and over, and have been hearing them for years. That's why we focus so much attention on providing practical guidance and tangible tools to help leaders develop their skills.

Wright

Does this suggest that just because someone is successful as a leader, he or she may not be able to teach successful leadership?

Tyler

Absolutely! Again, we go back to the point that leadership isn't a curriculum people are accustomed to. It's not something we were ever taught in school. The fact that some leaders are successful certainly doesn't mean they are great teachers of leadership—or that they would ever claim to be. Doing something well and teaching others how to do something well are two very different things. Many professional athletes are incredibly successful in their sport, but would fail miserably teaching that sport to others. There are plenty of historical examples of this in all fields.

I have found that many companies have a mentoring program. These are programs that match employees who have demonstrated success in the organization with new or inexperienced employees. This is a great idea, but it is one that usually falls short of the companies' expectations. Here's the reason why: The person being mentored goes into the relationship looking for concrete, specific information to help them improve their skills and move up in the organization. The person who is the mentor is rarely prepared to give this kind of information and instead assumes that general guidance or some anecdotal wisdom is what is required. The "mentee" is disappointed in not getting much specific assistance that can be used to get ahead quickly and the mentor is disappointed in the mentee's enthusiasm so the relationship falls apart or just continues without being as effective as it could be.

The problem is that a mentor program is not a replacement for formal training. Employees chosen to be a mentor may be successful, but that doesn't qualify them to teach others exactly how to be successful. Put in the proper context, mentor programs are very valuable; they just need to be used appropriately. A person who has the opportunity to work with a mentor should jump at the chance. Just remember that this relationship will provide one input. A person committed to developing leadership success will take input from multiple sources: from mentors and colleagues, from the examples of prominent leaders, from their staff and family. Even historical figures whose thought processes are well documented are excellent sources. Leaders in training should always remember to engage in a regular formal training and development process from an organization with demonstrated success in building outstanding leaders.

Wright

Richard, I always enjoy conversations with you and this is no exception. I've thoroughly enjoyed our discussion today. Do you have a final thought that you would like to share with our readers?

Tyler

Yes I do, but first I want to thank you for asking me to contribute to *Leadership Defined*. It is an honor to share my thoughts along with so many distinguished individuals. The concept I want to leave the readers with is that leadership is not some lofty idea or set of skills designated for a select few who run companies or organizations. Nor is leadership just for a few athletes on the field. Throughout our lives we will all be called upon to lead at one time or another. For some it will be more frequent and on a grander scale, but nonetheless we will *all* be called upon. It may be as simple as leading a small group discussion or as complex as leading a department, a division or a company. It may be in planning an event or taking charge of a ministry at our place of worship. It may take the form of a project at work or it may be the all important guiding of our children toward the morals, values and ethics that will be their foundation for strength and faith throughout their lives. In each of the instances I mentioned being the best leader possible for the situation we find ourselves in is vitally important to the over all outcome. As an example, Chief Petty Officers leadership in their role on a naval vessel is just as important to the successful operation of that vessel as is the Commanders leadership in his or her role. Each relies upon and enhances the other. None of us can escape leadership nor should we hide from it; so the best course of action is to embrace it and take pride in doing the best we can each time it is our turn to step up. When we commit ourselves to lifelong learning with leadership principles as part of our education we guarantee a happier, more prosperous and more rewarding life for all the people we come in contact with.

Wright

Today we've been talking to Richard Tyler whose firm conducts extensive sales performance training as well as leadership excellence training. And as I have found out today and I'm sure that our readers have just found out, this man knows exactly what he is talking about. Thank you so much, Richard, for being with us today on *Leadership Defined*.

Some Final Thoughts

Richard Tyler's Key Leadership Observations

Effective leaders *know* those they are leading. This requires excellent communication skills--one of the most important ingredients to effective leadership. Outstanding leaders understand that these skills must be developed and continually improved.

Some believe that becoming an excellent communicator means becoming "popular" with those they lead. But being popular and being an effective leader are two very different things. They are not mutually exclusive—just different. The other common misconception is that leaders must be hard charging and demanding. The reality is that neither style is an inherently effective leadership style. Develop fundamental leadership skills and discover your own leadership style.

Throughout our lives we will all be called upon to lead at one time or another. For some it will be more frequent and on a grander scale but nonetheless we will *all* be called upon. Those who decide to focus on developing their leadership skills will make the greatest progress by first focusing directly on others, then on themselves.

One of the best ways to accelerate leadership effectiveness is to complement formal training with a positive mentor relationship. But in order for the mentor relationship to be effective, both the mentor and the person being mentored must openly and regularly discuss their expectations.

Effective leaders focus on the things they can influence and they know how to prioritize. One key priority for effective leaders is skills development. Building solid leadership skills takes time, commitment and hard work. We can all appreciate the value of regular training for professional athletes. Unfortunately, we tend to forget that the same commitment to leadership skills development is necessary for the professional leader.

So make the commitment today to develop your leadership skills. The reward will be more success tomorrow.

About The Author

Richard Tyler is the CEO of **Richard Tyler International, Inc.™** an organization named one of the top training and consulting firms in the world. Mr. Tyler's success in sales, management, leadership, quality improvement and customer service and his reputation for powerful educational methods and motivational techniques, has made him one of the most sought after consultants, lecturers, teachers and success coaches. Mr. Tyler shares his philosophies with millions of individuals each year through keynote speaking, syndicated writing, radio, television, seminars, books, compact discs and tapes.

Mr. Tyler's book, *SMART BUSINESS STRATEGIES™, The Guide to Small Business Marketing EXCELLENCE* has been hailed as one of the best books ever written for small-business marketing. His successful books include; *Leadership Defined, Real World Customer Service Strategies That Work, Real World Human Resource Strategies That Work, Real World Teambuilding Strategies That Work, Conversations on Success, Conversations on Customer Service & Sales, Conversations on Health & Wellness, Conversations on Faith*, and *Marketing Magic*. His philosophies have been featured in Entrepreneur Magazine® as well as in hundreds of articles and interviews.

Mr. Tyler is the founder of the Leadership for Tomorrow™ an organization dedicated to educating young adults in the importance of self-esteem, goal setting and life-long success. He serves on the Advisory Board and is past Board Chairperson to Be An Angel Fund, a non-profit organization helping multiply handicapped children and profoundly deaf children to have a better life.

Richard Tyler
Richard Tyler International, Inc.™
P.O. BOX 630249
Houston, Texas 77263-0249
Phone: 713.974.7214
Email: RichardTyler@RichardTyler.com

WEBSITES

www.RichardTylerInternational.com
www.RichardTyler.com
www.SalesImmersion.biz
www.TylerTraining.com
www.ExcellenceEdge.com
www.DiscEducation.com

BOOK WEBSITES

www.LeadershipDefined.biz
www.ConversationsOn.biz
www.RealWorldStrategies.biz
www.MarketingMagicBook.biz

Leadership Defined